Speaking FROM THE Heart

Thoughts on
the Bible and about
being a Christian
believer today

LIVINGSTONE THOMPSON

BALBOA
PRESS

A DIVISION OF HAY HOUSE

Author Credits:
Supervisor of Postgraduate Research, All Hallows College, Dublin City University, Ireland; Former President of the the Moravian Church in Jamaica

Balboa Press books may be ordered through booksellers or by contacting:

Balboa Press
A Division of Hay House
1663 Liberty Drive
Bloomington, IN 47403
www.balboapress.com
1 (877) 407-4847

Printed in the United States of America.

ISBN: 978-1-4525-1812-1 (sc)
ISBN: 978-1-4525-1813-8 (e)

Library of Congress Control Number: 2014912165

Balboa Press rev. date: 9/29/2014

Dedication

To my siblings
Cecil, Tyrel, Vincent, Paul, Canute, Judith and Petal

Contents

Acknowledgements

This book was published with the kind support of the Centre for Moravian Studies, Moravian Seminary, Bethlehem, PA, USA. In particular I would like to thank Dr Craig Atwood and the Dean, Frank Crouch, for their personal interest in the publication.

A special word of thanks must go to friends and family members who not only supported me but also gave feedback about the manuscript. In particular, I thank my wife Jean-Marie for her helpful insights and attention to details.

Thankful mention should be made of the many Moravian churches in Jamaica and Northern Ireland and other churches in the Republic of Ireland, particularly St Mary's Church of Ireland, Navan, Calvary Community Church, Navan and Living Hope, Trim, where I've had the privilege to share in worship.

Naturally, as author, I take full responsibility for all the views expressed in the book.

Foreword

Reflections that grow out of the disciple of rigorous research and processed intimate experiences effectively advance the discussion of any topic in dramatic ways. This book embraces that deep, personal, spiritual journey and as such will be of tremendous benefit to readers.

The realization of the depth and relevance of the book is immediately on display as you read through the material contained in these pages. The author is telling a story built on a solid foundation of years of research as a world-renown scholar. At the same time, the author provides a refreshingly new and creative interpretation of scripture and the Christian tradition. This interpretation is influenced by his real-life experiences in the cross-cultural and theological contexts, with which he is so familiar.

There are historical references and contemporary expositions that help to make them both relevant and life-giving for the mission and ministry of the church in the twenty-first century. More importantly, the book points towards the future and may serve as a source of comfort, or maybe even discomfort, depending on your perspective. There are no denominational limitations to the application of the basic principles underlying the hermeneutic of this publication. It is another excellent literary presentation by Dr Livingstone Thompson and I look forward to the positive impact it will have on the ecumenical world.

Bishop C. Hopeton Clennon
Senior Pastor
Central Moravian Church
73 W Church St, Bethlehem PA 18018

Introduction

Why this Book?

Speaking from the Heart is a book about the Christian faith. It is a series of reflections designed for daily use by those who contemplate difficult questions about faith and the Bible. It is not meant to be a theological book or a biography, although aspects of both might gleam through the pages. These thoughts and ideas that I share arose from my own need to face what living as a Christian means today. The book also represents moments when I paused for thought and serious reflection. This is not to say I'm not been thinking all the time, although some of the decisions I've made might suggest otherwise. However, they were the moments when I was seized with a sense of urgency to re-focus on life's purpose. I hope to live for many more years but I've lived long enough to see many of life's contradictions, which make me wonder about purpose, or what seems to be the absence of it, in the way that many live and in the way that many have also died. What you are about to read is the outcome of a number of influences. It is an attempt to speak honestly and with conviction about faith in God. Other titles could have been chosen but when I shared the possibilities with family and close friends, this title received the greatest number of first preferences. I'm grateful for the support from family and friends but I take full responsibility for the content, which is somewhat a spiritual journey.

A few years ago some close friends from the church communities were invited to share in my birthday celebrations at the Dunderry Lodge restaurant in Meath, Ireland. I was quite pleased to receive, among my birthday gifts, a lovely touch-screen I-pod from my family. They know that I'm a fan of new gadgets and technology, all those things that will become relics of the age. I thought that the dinner was the end of the celebrations. However, the next day being Sunday, to my great surprise another group of friends, mostly from the Africa Caribbean Forum that I helped to form, arrived together at the house for another birthday celebration. It was during that pleasant afternoon, snow being still on the ground, that one of my friends from Nigeria challenged me to think more deeply about my age. In his words, when one gets to this age in Africa he is considered to be a senior in the community and therefore all respect was due to me. I actually never thought of it in those terms but suddenly I was beginning to feel like a senior – being the oldest one in the group that gathered. This was all new because there were not many times before when I was the oldest at a function for adults. I'm trying to come to terms with this idea of a being a senior in the community and these reflections are part of that, as they come genuinely from the heart.

Writing a religious book, in the midst of upheavals in religious thought and questions about the meaning of the Christian faith, might be seen by some people to be very pretentious. In the wake of questions raised recently in the media, the credibility of church leaders and Christian thinkers has taken a precipitous fall. People have become more suspicious of the church and of religion. The plummeting of credibility has not only encouraged those with tenuous links to drift away but has also alienated those with strong commitment and years of service. The moral or ethical stance of the church is no longer taken for granted. The pronouncements of church leaders, rather than being given particular weight, are more often treated with contempt. Some people are genuinely sad at these developments but for others they couldn't have come sooner. These, then, are difficult and uncertain times for the person of faith. In this context religious speech should be in moderation, if any at all. It is bad enough that religious pronouncements are treated with contempt but it is worse when they are not even heard. This is the risk that *Speaking from the Heart* faces. It could be that people do not even bother to read it because it is not expected to be saying anything new or worth hearing. The author who puts a book of this nature in print at this time must, therefore, be prepared to be called foolish. At the same time, religious speaking in these times might indicate prophetic courage – speaking "whether they hear or whether they forbear".

In this task, however, I am inspired by publications of Christian authors who have shown great courage in facing the difficult questions that an affirmation of the Christian faith puts to them. Among them is Hans Kung who wrote the book *On Being a Christian,* 1974. This little book came to be regarded as a "mini Summa" on the Christian faith. Kung's aim was to discover what remained permanent about the Christian faith in the midst of upheavals in Christian doctrine, morality and discipline. Another inspirational author is David Jenkins who wrote the book, *The Contradiction of Christianity,* 1976. The book arose out of the Edward Cadbury series of lectures that Bishop Jenkins gave at Birmingham University in the same year that Kung's book was published. Jenkins was prepared to face the consequences of possible contradictions between his vision and hope for being human and his vision and hope of being Christian. Those publications typify some of the issues that people in the decade of the 1970's faced. Coincidentally, it was during the second half of that same decade that I came, for the first time, to seriously face the question of what it means for me to be a Christian. The answer to that question is part of what is reflected in this book, the purpose of which is to ponder the implications of affirming the Christian faith and, as the line from my ordination liturgy puts it, to consider what "my acceptance of the Christian call pledges me."

You are probably reading *Speaking from the Heart* because you are a person of faith. If so, then I hope that neither this book nor your faith will disappoint you. It is written in a way to allow you to read a portion each day and then to take time for reflection. At the end of a series of chapters I have added *Something More,* which is given as a break between the chapters.

If you do not make the claim to have a Christian or religious faith, it is also my hope that you will find something of benefit in these pages because you are a person with a purpose. If you have no surety about your purpose in life then I hope that these reflections will support your discovery.

These thoughts are shared in faith and hope, with thanks to the many people who, in one way or the other, have contributed to them. These include family and friends, as well as people with faith and without a claim to faith, whom I have met along my journey.

L. A. Thompson, PhD
August 13, 2014
287ᵗʰ Year of the Renewed Moravian Church[1]

CHAPTER 1

A Journey in Faith

Bethabara and Before

*M*y thoughts about things spiritual, which were formed in the Christian community and expressed primarily through the Moravian Church, have their foundation in my parents and at Bethabara, where I had my religious upbringing. My father, Luther, practised what could be called a spirituality of engagement because his Christian faith propelled him into active community involvement. He grew up in the Anglican Communion but also came under the influence of the Moravian Church. His parents, like all rural people of their time, while being members of the Moravian church, would also have come under the influences on the Poco-mania movement. Poco-mania, which literally means "little madness," refers to the ecstatic utterances and dances that characterise the group's liturgical practices. The movement is a blend of Africa indigenous religion with Christianity.

Luther was aware of his world and kept abreast of all the social, political and economic issues in a way that put his more literate children and peers to shame. My mother, Isolyn, practised a spirituality of prayer because of her attentiveness to family and communal prayer. She initiated prayer time at home and was seldom absent from the prayer meetings at church or in the district. Isolyn's mother was a leader in the Poco-mania group but Isolyn herself would have had her early formation in a different Pentecostal religious setting.

These two pathways of spirituality, one having active community involvement and the other having overt religious piety, are still visible in the ways my siblings and I approach life. In retrospect, I can now see that these influences have also been part of my walk of faith. I describe life as a walk of faith because of my keen awareness of how vulnerable human life is. I consider life as a walk of faith also because of my belief that life finds its ultimate purpose in God, the Ultimate Being of the universe.[2] I think of life also as a walk in hope because of my awareness of the tentativeness and limitations of human thought and action. My hope is in Jesus as model, messenger and minister of God's intention for the world. When I say this I mean that the idea and the reality of Jesus, whom Roger Haight calls a symbol of God, is the one in and through whom I've surrendered and wish to live out my purpose as a human being. This is a choice I've made and with which I'm comfortable and contented. I do recognise that other people can make other choices and might still claim fulfilment and contentment in being human. Nevertheless, it would be selfish of me not to share what I have found and how I see this business of life. In a certain sense this book is directed towards that end.

At Bethabara I came to love and regard the church as an instrument of God's will for the wholeness and well-being of the world. From this point of view it is probably quite understandable that I chose to candidate for the ordained ministry of the Moravian church because in that way I was resolving my preoccupation with the purpose of life. Life's ultimate purpose is not in the vulnerability of human existence but in God who for me is source of all existence. The church is an instrument of that purpose and a life of faith and hope is reflective of my conviction about God and God's will. I owe this realization first and foremost to my parents and to the Bethabara Moravian Church.

Faith in Changing Times

In applying the influences of active engagement and prayer, I came also to realize that just as human actions in the name of God are actions in faith and hope, and are in that sense tentative and limited, so too is the church. The tentativeness and limitations of the church are expressed in the fact that the church is forever changing. Indeed, the reason we have a Christian faith that has survived the test of time is because of ongoing change. The Bethabara I knew when I had my early religious formation is different from what it is today. The Moravian Church of the 1960's, happily, is different from the Moravian Church today. This is true for all the churches that have survived. In order to survive they had to change – albeit slowly. This changing character must not be seen as some unmitigated disaster. It is good that change has come. Just as Luther and Isolyn and the forbears died because their bodies could not keep up with the demands of the ever-increasing years, so too will churches and institutions die unless they renew. Those that fail to change will find that they cannot keep up with the demands of the new generation and will therefore become irrelevant. I realize that in time my body will surrender its strength and capacity for life in the face of the ever-increasing years. Notwithstanding the pain of loss and separation that this will quite likely cause my family, it is also good because my continuing existence and my increasingly inflexible body and mind would hinder and inhibit progress and I would become a burden. Change is therefore necessary for survival and relevance. This is not to say that all change is good but it is clear that at least some change is necessary. It remains true that only those institutions that have seized the importance of changing are preparing themselves for tomorrow. This is also true for the individual.

For those who like me sometimes become anxious about growing old and risk becoming irrelevant, consolation might be found in the poem that was my late mother's favourite, by John E Roberts, *I am Not Growing Old.*

They say that I am growing old.
I heard them tell it time untold,
in language plain and bold,
But I am not growing old.[3]

Speaking from the Heart then is about faith in changing times. It reflects the realization that a major characteristic of the present age is the absence of clear and definitive norms in terms of values and beliefs. The age can also be described as post-modern in the sense that nearly all institutions of authority, be they religious, political, medical, financial, legal or educational, have had their authority questioned and they no longer benefit from the trust they once knew. The age may also be called pluralistic and in that sense post-Christian because there is no one set of authority or one set of values driving the forward progress of the nations. In fact, many people are happy to be set free from what they would have perceived as oppressive Christian values and beliefs. It is also an age of vulnerability because in the absence of unquestioned authority a vacuum is created into which all kinds of authority rush to win themselves converts. However, with their disciples' appetite for suspicion, it is not long before the new, self-made authorities find that they too come in for questioning and soon concede their new found status to other emerging authorities. And so the cycle is reinvented in which disciples with longing eyes and hopeful expectations embrace new authorities only to banish them through lack of trust. *Speaking from the heart* is about finding a course and a reliable pathway in a post-modern, pluralistic and post- Christian age.

Friends

A devotional book should be easy read for any person of faith. My most recent publication, *A Protestant Theology of Religious Pluralism*, was a book for specialist theologians. It retrieved an impressive body of theological material from the writings of John Amos Comenius and Nicholas Ludwig von Zinzendorf, both outstanding personalities in 17th and 18th century Protestantism. The decision to publish *Speaking from the Heart* came after several hints being dropped by my wife about the dense nature of the previous books. That point of view was reinforced during my attempts to explain what my second book was about. One of the friends in the Bible study group, which sometimes met in our house, asked whether I would not write a book that would guarantee more sales, since only those particularly interested in deep theological matters would bother to read *A Protestant Theology of Religious Pluralism*. The same challenge came from other friends with whom I often discussed matters of faith. I know that they are not as concerned about the need to increase sales as they are about having a book that would be more readable. An earlier book, *A Formula for Conversation: Christians and Muslims in Dialogue*, published in 2007, which to date has sold only a few hundred copies, was subjected to similar comments by friends. One friend said, "It is not exactly bedtime reading". Against that background I hope that *Speaking from the Heart* responds to those concerned for something accessible, as well as those who want a little more than bedtime reading. My aim then is to share some thoughts that have been central to my understanding and practice of the Christian faith. If only one person were to find in these pages a reason to hope in God, an opportunity to strengthen faith, then the effort would not have been in vain.

Wanderings

Speaking from the Heart has come at a time of wandering. Our family arrived in Ireland in August 1999 but it was only a year or two later that we realized that we were at the forefront of a period of rapid inward migration. I had up to then been nearly twenty years in the pastoral ministry. By 2009 that flow of people into Ireland accounted for 10% of the 4.5m population. The increased immigration and a housing boom went hand in hand but both suffered the same fate when the crisis came in 2009. It was in the crucible of these changes that many of the reflections took shape. One might say, therefore, that it was born in the economic crisis of 2009 but that it had been in gestation since 1982, when I began pastoral ministry in Lititz, St Elizabeth, Jamaica.

In 2009 I was already ten years away from full-time pastoral ministry, having taken time out to do postgraduate studies in Ireland. My plan was to return to full time ministry when I completed research at the

Irish school of Ecumenics/Trinity College. If fact I was back in Jamaica for two years, 2003-2005, during which time I served as President of the executive board of the Moravian Church and warden/ lecturer at United Theological College of the West Indies, as well as chaplain at the chapel of the University of the West Indies. The family stayed on in Ireland while I returned to Jamaica. However, the family separation was too much to bear and impacted heavily on my decision not to seek a second term as President of the Moravian Church. So, in May 2005 I was back in Ireland, this time for an indefinite stay. When we arrived in 1999 we worshipped primarily with the Church of Ireland in Navan but after a few years the need for companionship for the girls led us to establish close links also with the Calvary Community Church, which had a more robust youth programme and more children the same ages as our girls. Thereafter, and especially after returning in 2005, our worship time was shared between the two churches. Only occasionally did we worship with the Moravian Church in Northern Ireland, although we seldom missed the quarterly services of the Dublin Moravian Diaspora. That changed later as we formalised our membership with the University Road Moravian Church in 2012.

Living in Ireland has been a sort of exilic experience because although our third daughter is Irish-born and even though we acquired property and established business in Ireland, we always had the sense of just passing through. For me the exilic sensation intensified after 2005 and it took several months for me to settle mentally. Even though I preached more frequently in that period than I did between 1999 and 2005, there was always a yearning after God and for a greater sense of spiritual fulfilment. It was probably not surprising then that in 2009 I began to sense a call to return to ministry, though I was not sure what form that would take. There is a sense in which these reflections are a response to that sense of being called again. I began to think about the congregations and fellowships in Jamaica that I had served, supervised or preached in: Lititz, Ballards Valley, Bethlehem, Scholefield, Springfield, (Tatewood), (May Bowl), Claremont, Gracefield, New Fulneck, New Irwin, Trinity, Covenant. There were also fellowships in Mona, Spanish Town and Hellshire. In fact, as I looked over the congregations and fellowships that are currently in the Jamaica Province of the Moravian Church, the only one in which I did not preach is Fairmount in Manchester. I realize that a full picture of a part of my life and ministry could not be constructed without reflection on these years. Therefore, *Speaking from the Heart* reflects the experiences of the years of wandering.

Faith and Crisis

There is a sense in which the coming together of these reflections was influenced by the travails of my brother, Paul, whose legal impasse with the leadership of the church has gone on for many years. He and I were in college together and I was ordained a year before he was in 1984, so our ministerial years have basically developed together. When he was studying in Germany I supervised the New Irwin congregation in his absence. When I left for Ireland he succeeded me as supervising minister for Trinity. In turn I succeeded him as Moravian warden at the United Theological College of the West Indies, when he took up the post as principal at Bethlehem College, St Elizabeth, Jamaica. The crisis was unnecessary and his subsequent disillusioned drift to the outskirts of the Moravian ministerial circle was painful to see. It was not the first time that a close ministerial colleague had unresolved conflicts with the church and most certainly may not be the last. However, the impasse has forced me to think of the meaning of ministry, the meaning of the gospel; what it means to be a witness to the gospel and what kind of witnessing community is the Moravian Church. To say the least, it is truly sad that the colleagues, who were his friends, seemed to have lost a run of themselves and missed an opportunity to show fraternity and true generosity of spirit.

Most critically, however, the whole affair made me think again about my own ministry and what is was that qualified me even to refer to myself as a minister of the gospel. It made me think of the travails and challenges of my walk with God; the high and low points of my journey in faith; the peaks and the troughs of ministry; the times when I felt close to the Lord and the times when I felt at a great distance.

The travails, ups and downs of walking by faith are prisms through which the thoughts expressed here must be seen. They were developed through the highs and the lows, the peaks and troughs and at times from different perceptions of the state of my faith. It is important then that you, the reader, will not presume that I exemplify any ideal that is written here. As it probably is for you, sometimes I too struggle with walking the narrow path.

The truth is that these thoughts were developed through much agony and with fear and trepidation. For example, whenever I came within an hour or two of the time for a sermon to be delivered I would descend into silence and withdrew as if in depression. This would be followed by a great feeling of anxiety that took the form of heavy perspiration and sometimes a deep sense of agony. On a few occasions I've had to make the confession that I was neither worthy nor ready to deliver the message and it was a wonderful feeling of relief when it was over. This is really ironic because many people take it for granted that preachers love to talk – and I'm sure some do. For me, however, there is something presumptuous about preaching and religious speech and even more so about saying, "Thus says the Lord." It is a very weighty matter because issues of purpose, faith and hope can be positively or negatively affected by what we say. Therefore "fools rush in where angels fear to tread".

CHAPTER 2

In the Beginning, God

"In the Beginning, God..." [Genesis 1:1]

Introduction

*L*et us talk about God. In a literal sense this is what theology means; talk about God. Understandably, this might create embarrassment for some people who imagine that it is not "cool" to do so. For those who choose to do so then it can be an expression of courage. At the same time, a topic like this runs the risk of being very speculative because of the different ideas about God and the divine life that people have. Christians express their beliefs about God in ways that are different from Muslims, who are themselves quite different from Hindus, and so on. It means also that talk about God can be divisive because people will want to assert that what they believe about God cannot be surrendered to other beliefs. In brief, theology is risky business but the risk should not render us speechless. Rather, it must inspire us to be mindful of the context in which we speak and of the need not to be arrogant in our expressions because we are really speaking about our own convictions and not necessarily empirically, verifiable facts. This does not mean that empirical verification is to be trusted about convictions. Rather, it means that there are some things that are beyond empirical verification that can only be believed. One example of this is the issue of how the world was created. Whether or not you are a person of faith, there is no way of being able to verify how the world came into being. Scientists and people of faith alike must simply be convinced of a certain view. There have been many theories but its beginning can only be an idea we believe or a theory we accept. It is beyond verification, which brings me to the idea of God in the beginning.

The background for this reflection is a conversation that I had with a medical practitioner. He asked me how I was doing and in the manner in which I usually answered, I said to him I was keeping body and soul together. As I think of it now I realise how presumptuous my response was because in truth and in fact, I believe that it is God who keeps my body and soul together. This is another way of saying that I believe that my daily sustenance is not simply my own efforts but that in a way that I cannot explain I'm being sustained. So if you hear me say that I am keeping body and soul together, please remind me that it is God who is doing that keeping – as the chorus goes, "Jesus in my body and he's keeping me alive, Jesus is keeping me alive"!

However, you must not be distracted by my response because that was not the thing that inspired my thought. Rather it is something the medical practitioner said almost *ad lib* in the conversation. He said, "in the beginning God." When I pause to consider what he had to say about a task on which he was working, I cannot remember anything else except this saying, "in the beginning God..." I have since reflected on the simplicity and yet profundity of the expression. I decided that this statement was too filled with meaning for me not to spend some time exploring what it could mean for me and, consequently, what it could mean for you. What I believe the practitioner was saying to me was that he is in the hand of God and that from the beginning it has been God.

God in Casual Conversation

In light of the practitioner's comment I realised again the value of biblical awareness. Not only did I recognise the comment as a quotation from the Bible, which told me something about him, but I also immediately began to raise questions about what meaning he placed on the quotation. We were actually involved in what the scholars called biblical hermeneutics: discerning the meaning of scripture for everyday life. The Bible was featuring in his casual conversation to influence thought. He did not know that I would be writing about the witness he gave without realising it. He would not know how many people you will speak with after reading this to further spread the influence of speaking about God. However, that is the miracle of the seed growing secretly; we know its beginning but we cannot tell the extent of its growth. Stored in the pages of my mind was this expression that I read in the Bible so many times before. The words of my friend led my mind to do a search to realise that I knew the saying very well but now I needed to reflect on it in a new way. I realised again also the value of conversing with those who speak of things to do with the Lord. I realised again the meaning of the saying, "iron sharpeneth iron." We cannot predict the extensive influence the word about God will have when we speak about God in our casual conversation.

As I considered the idea of God and reviewed the first chapter of Genesis, I saw again how the writer was preoccupied with the work of God. He presents God as an active God: God said, God saw, God called, God made, God set, God created, God blessed. God worked and God is working. We can then affirm in faith that God is active and working. However, the statement, *in the beginning God*, goes even deeper in its incompleteness. If you look at the text in Gen 1:1, you will see that the saying is incomplete. In the Authorised King James Version, the verse in fact says, "in the beginning God created the heaven and the earth." However, it was the incompleteness of the statement that caught my attention. Therefore, I would like to stay with it in that incomplete way for a moment because what it says in its incompleteness is different from what it says when it is completed.

This is of great (theological) significance for with the incompleteness we emphasise the future completion. The pause and incompleteness give the feel that more will be said or needs to be said. The strength of the incompleteness is to attest that God is still at work because, in truth, we have not yet seen the completeness of God's work. We cannot tell all that

God is going to do. God is still working. No only is God working but God is still working on me. God is still working on my children. God is still working in my church. God is working with my neighbour. God is still working in my community. God is still working in my country. God is at work in his world. God has not finished yet. So, when we leave the statement with its incompleteness it has meaning. We do not have to say something about God for the words to have meaning. Just say, "God" or say "God is", or "God will" or "in the beginning God." The meaning of the word is not limited to what we have to say. God fills the universe but God may also habituate himself to the smallness of the words we use. Our God is an awesome God. So, when the peoples of the nation despair in the face of crime, and rage against the witness of the church, let us remind them that God is still at work. Tell them not to write God off as yet for God is still working. When the peoples of the nation despair in the face of economic hardships and when your children fail their exams and feel it is the end, remind them that God is still at work. In this sense we can speak about the incompleteness of God's work. The point I am making then, is that the incompleteness of the statement reminds us that God is still working. God is not finished yet. God is still active.

God before Creation

Beyond that, however, when we say, "in the beginning God..." it is an assertion about the **pre-existence** of God – or more accurately, the being of God before the created order. This is an area of ongoing controversy between two passionate groups of people. On one hand we have those who have an orientation to faith and hence believe that it is God's creative will and power that brought creation into being. We can say that this is age-old wisdom because this point of view seems to have existed from the beginning of human civilization. On the other hand, however, we have those who see no justification in postulating the existence of a creator, since for them the processes of the world are sufficient to explain our existence. The commonality between these two orientations is that they must be held as conviction, as belief, since there is no way of placing ourselves outside the world to demonstrate what we believe, or to objectively verify our point of view. The discussion between these two positions may be interesting but will not lead us further than what we already accept.

Consequently, the pre-existence of God is something that is believed. It is not a verifiable fact but rather a foundational principle, upon which other convictions are built. What we mean by pre-existence is that we believe that prior to the coming into being of things that have gone or can go out of existence God had already been in existence. The existence of God, I believe (and this is operative), is not dependent on the existence of the world, although the converse is true. God does not need the world to be God but the world needs God to be the world. So, when the world came into being it was God who was bringing things into existence. About this we speculate but cannot speak in concrete terms. However, the idea that God pre-existed the world gives us consolation and hope. God is before our existence so our experiences are not news to God.

From this belief in God's pre-existence we can say that the dynamics of things in the world are not unfamiliar to God. So what does this mean for a life of faith in God? If God existed at the beginning of the world, then we can confidently affirm that God is at the beginning of our troubles. We can confidently affirm God at the beginning of our joys. When the barrel of meal runs dry we can say, "in the beginning God…" and when the barrel of meal is full, we can say, "in the beginning God…" When we marry we say, "in the beginning God…" and when we celebrate many years in marriage we say, "in the beginning God…" When our children are born we say, "in the beginning God… and when they leave school to become active in the adult world we say, "in the beginning God…" When we plant, we say, "in the beginning God… and when we reap we say, "in the beginning God…" At the start of our day we say, "in the beginning God…" and when we come to the end of our day we say, in the beginning God…" God is there before anything else. In this sense we can also speak of God's pre-existence.

God in the Now

When we say, "in the beginning God…" it is also a statement that affirms the **presence** of God. This is a truth that we derive from John 1:1, which also speaks about the beginning. The accent of John's statement is on the presence of the Word with God. John in his discourse wanted to show that the Word, which was present with God at the beginning, is present with us in the world in the person of the Son. In John's view, we ought not to speak about the pre-existent One without speaking of the One who is also present. In other words, we cannot speak of pre-existence without meaning also presence because if there was no presence the idea of pre-existence would be foolishness. In God, then, pre-existence and presence come together. The glory and consolation of this affirmation is not hard to see. The Psalmist (139) speaks eloquently of the presence of God. God is present and I cannot but be found in God's presence. God knows when I sit down and when I get up. "If I ascend to heaven, God is there. If I make my bed in hell, behold, God is there. If I take the wings of the morning and fly to the uttermost parts of the sea, even there shall God's hand lead me and God's right hand shall hold me". Wherever I go I encounter God. I go to my field, God. I go to school, God. I go to see my girlfriend, God. I go to see my boyfriend, God. I go to the shop, God. I go to Church, God. God on the bus; God in the car; God in the aeroplane; God in America; God in England. God in Kingston; God in Russia, God in Saudi Arabia, Iraq and Afghanistan. God in the desert; God in the city; God in the slums and God in the suburban areas. God in my home. God at the end and in the beginning, God.

The truth of God's omnipresence some of us forget and others of us miss. It is the failure to recognise that we are on holy ground in this world that leads us into temptation; that leads us into sin. We who are presumptuous in our sin are either forgetful, ignorant or arrogant concerning what the Psalmist says, that "the hills melt like wax at the presence of the Lord (97:5). We forget that the word says that the one who will stand in the presence of the Lord is the one who has clean hands and a pure heart. In God's presence, the Psalmist says, there is fullness of joy, at God's right hand there are pleasures for evermore (16:11). We therefore say with the song writer, "You are awesome in this place mighty God." So, when we say, "in the beginning God…" we are not only referring to the pre-existence of God, we mean also the presence of God.

Mind you, this affirmation is hugely problematic because there are too many places in which people of faith have been subjected to the worse kind of atrocities and we're left asking ourselves whether they were abandoned by God. The problem of suffering, especially of those who have the expectation of God's protection, is something we must think about. What I would say is that people who experience, witness or know of extreme atrocity must judge for themselves whether it is worth believing in God after that. I will not be so presumptuous and suggest to them that they must or that they must not because the whole business of faith is too mysterious. If you can live without faith all power to you because the thought of it for me is a very frightening thing.

God of Promise

If the statement "in the beginning God…" is a statement about the pre-existence and the presence of God, it can also be taken to mean a statement of **promise.** The same God who was in existence at the creation of the world is the very God who is present with us in the world today. And the God who is present is the God who will be with us in the future. Indeed, the Hebrew name, YaHWeH, which was revealed to Moses when he was called to lead Israel out of Egypt, may also mean I will be. So, I call the statement a word of promise. Jesus gave this assurance to his disciples: "I will be with you to the close of the age." The consolation of the statement "in the beginning God…" is not only that we are not alone but also implies that we will never be alone. "In the beginning God…" This is a promise. The word promise does not appear frequently in the OT but who could forget the testimony of Solomon who said that not one word failed, of the good promises that the Lord made (1Kings 5:56). In other words, the present is the fulfilment of the past promises. In the NT, the idea of promise is found in several places associated with the Holy Spirit. John 16 speaks of the promised gift of the Spirit. Acts (2:33) speaks of the promise of the Holy Ghost. We are therefore on sound biblical grounds then, when we speak of God as pre-existent, God as presence and God as promise. God has been, God is and God will be. In God we live and to God we move because we have come from God. Or, to put it as the late Bishop Neville Neil would often say, "God is the beginning and God is the end. God is the end for God was in the beginning."

Conclusion

When I am faced with the uncertainties and the difficult questions of creation or when I am confronted with the trials and troubles of this present life; when I am tormented about the future and what will become of me, my family, my church, my country and my world, I will say, in the beginning God. When I am at my end, or when I must face a new beginning, I will say, "in the beginning God…"

CHAPTER 3

The Plumbline

*And the Lord said to me, 'Amos, what do you see?' And I
said, 'A plumbline.' Then the Lord said, 'See, I am setting
a plumbline in the midst of the people. [Amos 7:8]*

Introduction

*A*fter the down turn in the construction sector in Ireland,
a number of amazing features relating to building began
to emerge. Over and over again there was evidence of
poor application of building standards. A whole building complex
in Dublin had to be evacuated, so that corrective measures could be
applied because the building was a serious threat to health and safety.
When I came upon the reading from Amos, I started to look for other
allusions we have to building, and building construction in the Bible. I
thought that it would make for an interesting study. There are a host of
references to builders and to roofs, walls, doors, floors, and rooms and
to foundations. We also hear of the Cornerstone in Isaiah, which the
epistle of 1Peter picks up and uses in a new and exciting way in reference
to Christ. However, we do not hear as much about the plumbline –
probably because we do not see any reference to it in the NT. It is a
simple piece of engineering which, with all the advances in technology,
has not been surpassed as the most accurate way to ensure that a wall is
at right-angle to the ground or, as the builders say, plumb. I want then

to explore the use of the plumbline which, according to Amos, the Lord would set in the midst of his people.

Need for Building Standards

To take the building analogy a little further, what I'm inviting us to see is this: we can think of the building process as an analogy for our lives. Even children can appreciate this analogy and many do. There are those who come to this realization when they are well into their building project, bad habits are formed, they are inflexible and not willing to change. However, when we come to that awareness, like any builder, we have to do a number of checks and ask a number of questions: how secure is the foundation? Where are the weak points? What are the health and safety threats? In the Gospel of Luke Jesus extols the wisdom of the builder who digs deep and lays the foundation on a rock (6:46-49). Job also realized the inherent weakness in our building: we live in houses of clay he says and our foundation is in the dust (4:19). And when the foundation is laid we must then consider how we build: What material will I use? Again we are cautioned by Paul in the letter to 1Corinthians that the material we use, gold, silver, precious stone, wood, hay or stubble, will be subjected to quality test; they will be tested by fire and the builder will suffer loss if the material is burnt up (3:12-13).

So when Amos in his vision saw the Lord standing by the wall, with a plumbline in his hand, the message was clear; it was a quality check for rectitude or straightness; a quality check would be performed. If the wall were found not to be plumb, as the Psalmist in 62 implies, it would have to be battered, as one does with a tottering fence; a wall that is not plumb can be a serious threat to health and safety. We can appreciate this kind of language about quality standards and best practice because they are a regular part of the diet of everyday conversation. Mind you, there is a certain irony and difficulty about the whole question of standards. On one hand there is consciousness about the need for standards of performance in the public service: proper banking standards, proper standards for the health services and health professionals; proper environmental standards; well-regulated buildings, etc. On the other hand we are in a minefield where it comes to the question of quality moral and ethical standards at the individual level because people do not want their lives to be programmed. In fact, if we are to go by a recent bill to legalize civil partnerships of all genders, space is being created for all kinds of standards for the family to be recognized. Now that is only half the problem. The other half of the problem, is there is no plumbline that can be accepted by all as the standard to guide how individuals might build their lives. Consider then the potential for disaster: the absence of an accepted plumbline at the individual level compounds the necessity for the dazzling array of standards in the public space. So what are we going to find when the Lord stands against the wall of this society with the plumbline in his hand? What are we going to see when the quality check for our society is performed? This is the message of the plumbline.

Applying the Plumbline

Even though it might be difficult to find an agreed standard and even though there are negative attitudes to the idea of moral and ethical standards for other than public officials, we have in Amos a plumbline that is applicable to everyone in our society. Contrary to opposition to the application of norms, our lives are like buildings and there are standards that are needed to avoid destruction. Moreover, the Lord by his word asserts that he himself stands as the one performing the quality check and his people will not have an option. They may not claim that it has no application to them. It is not a situation as when nations chose what international protocols they wish to sign. One of the difficulties with agreeing international protocols for greenhouse gas emission, for example, is that some important greenhouse gas producing nations did not sign up to the protocols. This means the requirements could not be applied to them. In the case we consider here, however, it seems there are no such options. Amos in his prophecy asserted that even if one did not accept the authority of the word, they would still be subjected to its principles. We have examples of this in national and international courts. The plumbline standard of the word is what the Lord chose. He did not choose an approach in which he would destroy his people, as the locust would destroy the tender shoot. He would destroy as the forest fire would the tender grass. Rather, he has applied a plumbline because he wanted his people to rectify their lives. He wanted the house of Jeroboam to come in line.

And how will the plumbline be applied? Four ways are detailed in the text (7:8-9). The first way was that the plumbline will be applied in the midst of the people. In other words, in a way that would ensure that everyone would be subjected to it: for the whole crowd; for the benefit of everyone. No one will be passed over. Each builder is checked; each person is assessed. For societies that have different standards for different classes this is an important observation. This should not be seen to refer only to the law, where justice tends to depend on the competence of the legal representatives more than on the standards of the law. It must also be seen to refer to the accountability. It is not unusual for those who work in the "so-called" public sector to be subjected to a different set of demands from those in the "so-called" private sector, as if they belong to different societies; as if it is a different public that purchases or benefits from their goods and services.

An ironic thing we sometimes see is that often leaders tend to have a different standard for themselves and subject others to a more onerous set of expectations. This is certainly true for the political class, which want privileges for themselves that they deny to others. The crises that we have seen in the banking sectors in recent times and the turmoil we see in many Eastern communities have to do with the selective application of the standards. The principle Amos espouses here is one based on justice and equality. In the event that the root and branch application was not clear, there is the naming of the high places, in a language to describe where the leaders of the society would gather. In ancient Israel the high places were associated with religious rites and ceremonies which, more often than not, were copied from the nations who did not honour the Lord. In the high places there could be the performances that were believed to advance the prosperity of the nation.

So when we speak of the high places we might see in it the allusion to the leadership of the society. The plumbline is not a standard only for the rank and file; by the same standard or rectitude the leaders as well as the masses will be quality-checked.

It is not unusual that some religious people think that they are so close to God that they needn't bother about accountability. They are saved, so clearly they have already met the standards and what we are talking about does not apply to them. In the event that this kind of consideration did arise, religious leaders and those who gather in the places of worship are singled out for mention in this reference to the sanctuaries. The religious leaders and the people who gather for the religious services are to be held accountable as well. We should not imagine that there is a different standard for those attending worship services. It is in this vein that the New Testament speaks about judgement beginning at the house of God.

The house of Jeroboam is really another name for the nation of Israel because it was during the reign of Jeroboam that Amos had this vision. The whole nation would be set under the quality-check of the plumbline of God's expectation for holiness and righteousness, for justice, peace, fidelity to truth and to the protection of the poor. The question then is this: how plumb is the building, which is your life?

CHAPTER 4

People with an Attitude

*"Rejoice in the Lord always; again I will
say, Rejoice." Philippians 4:4*

Introduction

Generally, we dislike people who are arrogant, self-centred and
nasty but it is hard to dislike someone who we find to be
pleasant and respectful. For this reason some Christian efforts
at evangelism have floundered because those leading the charge have
been anything but pleasant. Let's then talk about evangelism. Can
it be an attitude? Can it be an attitude of joy and rejoicing? In the
period leading up to the 250th anniversary celebrations of the Moravian
Church in Jamaica, there was a rising tide of expectation that the
moment would give rise to a fresh impulse to the growth of the church.
Today's generation of Christians have been awakened from slumber to
realise that unless we undertake bold, new evangelistic initiatives at this
time, the Church will be left behind in the society's forward surge.[4]
Although parts of the Christian community are growing numerically,
overall it is experiencing decline. At the same time, other religious
communities, for example Muslims, are seeing meaningful growth. No
one is going to be waiting for the Church to play catch-up. The society
does not have a particular sympathy for the Church that we can rely on
for survival. Churches like the Moravian Church, with numbers of less

than one million members worldwide, must make the case that at this time they have a witness to bear that is both relevant and vibrant. One complaint we often hear from members of the older churches is that they do not know how to evangelise; that there are critical skills evident in other religious groups that are missing or underdeveloped in the older churches. The confusion, of course, is that churches often do not distinguish between church growth and evangelism. In 2004, Woolever and Bruce published a book entitled, *Beyond the Ordinary: Ten Strengths of US Congregations.* It was based on a study of over 300,000 members in over 2, 000 churches in America. The study found out that one of the most important predictors of church growth is a congregation with a welcoming attitude. This is indeed amazing. It has reinforced my own conviction that evangelism is not just a set of skills to be honed but rather that it is an attitude to develop - a mindset.

Philippians is often referred to as one of the prison letters of Paul because he seemed to have written it from prison or soon after his release (Phil 1:12-13). In any case, his imprisonment forms an important part of the background. Prison today, as it was in Paul's time, is not a nice place. Prisoners often develop sad and broken spirits because of the length of incarceration, the conditions and not to mention the food. The main thing that is critical to the wellbeing and emotional survival of prisoners is the visit of family and friends and the knowledge of their continuing love and care. So if you have family and friends in prison, please visit with them as often as you can, especially at times of the year when families gather and reminisce. Given the harshness of prison conditions, then, we might be surprised at the attitude of rejoicing that is evident in this letter (see 1:4; 1:18; 2:17-18; 3:1; 4:4). How could Paul be so joyful under those conditions? What is the meaning of this joyfulness? It would be good to discover the source because one thing that is clear is that the attitude started to have a positive impact on those around him. It is this fever of joyfulness I am suggesting that we need to catch because it has evangelistic potential.

People who are joyful have reasons to be. In an economically depressing context, where complaining about hardships is the order of the day, being joyful is a counter-culture response. People who insist on being joyful in this situation may seem silly but they challenge the complaining and the depressed. If that spirit of joyfulness can be nurtured in our midst, people must ask, what is it that they know that we don't know? Or, what is it that they have that we do not? Paul challenged the Philippians to show this joy at all times. We get the idea that the sense of excitement had to do with the good news, but what specifically? There were some concrete reasons we can explore, so that the joy he showed can become to us an attitude.

Partnership in the Gospel (1:5)

The first reason given for his joy was the partnership in the gospel that the Philippians shared. The word for partnership here is (*koinonia*), the Greek word from which we get the words communion, fellowship or partnership. The joy of which he spoke here arose out of a deep experience of support and care which others showed. To show joyfulness as an evangelistic attitude, it must be clear to us who are the partners in the gospel. A common error in today's evangelistic efforts is that those who should be partners often perceive each other as competitors. Christians use the ethic of market capitalism to overwrite the ethic of the kingdom of God and the witness of the gospel becomes strategies to undersell our competitors. Rural communities, in particular those that have seen net outward migration over the last few decades, can become a serious trap for gospel practitioners. Perceiving that there are only limited possibilities for growth, the temptation can be to make highlighting the weaknesses of others the priority. How else would one justify the polemic talk between leaders; how else could we justify feelings of jealousy and the ongoing tension between the faithful of the different communions? By confusing membership in the church for discipleship of Christ, a mockery is made of the gospel witness. For this reason Paul's talk about partnership/communion in the gospel and his joy is timely.

There are two levels on which we can expect to see communion among Christians: there is the longitudinal plane with the saints of

God through the ages, those who have overcome the world to become that great cloud of witness by whom we are encompassed; "who in every age served God and continued faithful unto death." We can call the saints of bygone years by name and say that we are in communion with them for the sake of the gospel. They have laboured and we have entered into their labours. "The lines have fallen to us; we have a goodly heritage." Soon we will join the ranks of those who have passed and we hand over the heritage to our children. Respecting that communion with the saints, whose heritage we occupy, we make every effort to honour their input by not allowing the baton to fall from our grasp. We maintain partnership and connection with them through the liturgies and institutions we received from them. Since like them we want to be faithful in our time, we renew the liturgies and rebuild institutions to make them even more responsive to the needs of our time. Sadly, because of our selfishness and self-centredness we often dishonour the communion with the saints and undermine our Christian heritage.

We might say that the other plain of our communion is with the witnesses of the gospel in our time - the latitudinal plane. Communion on this plane justifies the ideals of the ecumenical movement and cooperation between churches. Although for many Christians this is a "no-brainer", there are many for whom it is still problematic. In fact, by the time we came to the end of the 20th century, we saw many set-backs in the achievements in ecumenical cooperation that were quite visible in the earlier part of the century. It was not only that ecumenical programmes were discontinued because of falling financial support but also that the conversation about the need for cooperation and collaboration was overtaken by talk about denominational survival and doctrinal purity. In many churches the fear about being corrupted by ecumenism is still very real. In this atmosphere of suspicion, rejoicing in the partnership of the gospel seems very far-fetched. And yet this is precisely the challenge that the text from the Letter to the Philippians puts to us. It implies that the fellowship among Christians both within and between the churches is necessary for our rejoicing. More than that, it suggests that meaningful and sustainable evangelistic efforts will depend on that real partnership. Only in partnerships can we fulfil the words of Jesus in John's Gospel, "that you may be one that the world may believe." This is why we say evangelism has to do with our attitude – our attitude to our received heritage and our attitude to people in our time.

Proclamation

Another reason for the writer's rejoicing was the knowledge that the gospel was being proclaimed (1:18), even though not all the time out of pure motive. His readiness to rejoice, even though selfish and impure motivations may be driving the witness of the gospel, really focuses the mind because we are led to ask what kind of motive for preaching the gospel would be considered impure. We must certainly exclude the sad situation of individuals with different kinds of dysfunction and addictions using their involvement in the witness of the gospel as a cloak for their weaknesses, deviant and, at times, illegal activities. Probably in every generation since Christ there have been those who broke the trust invested in them by virtue of their position of moral authority or abused their positions of power and brought unnecessary scandal to the witness of Christ. In many parts of the body of Christ today the witness of the gospel has been impaired by men and women who, with corrupted motive, remain part of the witness. One consequence of this is that many people have become cynical about the gospel and religion. Your own church might have had its share of abuse of power and positions, as the ethic of dirty, cover-up politics have been applied to pastoral and administrative problems, all in the name of the witness of the gospel.

The author of the letter to the Philippians observed that God was able to use all kinds of situations to make the gospel known and that the eventual proclamation of the gospel filled him with joy. This comes as a surprise because it would seem that the writer is saying that the end justifies the means; that we are never to mind how they do what they do as long as the gospel is proclaimed. However, a closer reading of the text does not allow us to be so liberal in our interpretation. He became aware of the fact that the actions of others who were involved in the same ministry were making things difficult for him, "increasing my suffering in my imprisonment" [1:17]. Were they circulating untrue stories about him? Did they paint a bad picture of him to the authorities? Were they making a case for his continuing imprisonment? Whatever it was the effect was to make life more difficult for him. Yet the author did not make his sense of security and comfort the basis on which to judge the witness of the gospel. He learnt what many of us today need to learn, namely that we do not preach ourselves but Christ. So, rather than making a case about the negative impact that their strategies were having on him, instead of bemoaning his personal dissatisfaction and discomforts, instead of seeking the glory, he rejoiced that the gospel was being proclaimed.

Now let us fast-forward to the situation today: can we rejoice that down the road people are turning to Christ, even though their conversion does not result in the numerical growth of our congregation? Can we rejoice in the proclamation of the gospel even though we are not comfortable with the gimmicks and communication strategies others are using? My suspicion is that we will not. Rejoicing in the proclamation of the gospel is an expression of confidence in God, who is committed to the salvation of all people in all circumstances. "I know not how the Spirit moves, convicting people of sin, or how believing in his word, brings peace and joy within; but I know whom I have believed and I'm persuaded that he is able to keep what I have committed to him against that day." I do not like how you do what you do but it is not about me. Let Jesus Christ be praised.

Lest you are upset and mystified about this you might want to consider for a moment that it is your attitude, your gimmicks and your strategies that people find offensive. What if people are unimpressed by the way you worship? What if people want you to go from house to house and talk to people about Jesus? What if people expect you to talk to people on the bus about Jesus? How would you feel if a stranger engages you in a conversation about a personal relationship with Jesus, would you welcome this? Some people do not like this assertive, in your face attitude. They find it offensive and filled with sales tactics.

Others believe that it is a sign of confidence and conviction. The point is that we are not the fount of all wisdom and even our best efforts and intentions could prove offensive to others. We may have to put up with others and trust that despite their strategies and motives people might yet come to praise God.

Pre-empting the Return of Jesus

A third thing that shines through is the author's joy about the Lord's coming. (4:5). Consciousness about the Lord's presence is critical to our evangelistic witness because it drives us to a sense of urgency and gives us an increased sense of accountability. This is the foreground of Paul's joy and this is the main point of the text. Evangelism is the attitude of rejoicing that arises from the consciousness of the nearness of God to execute justice and judgement. It is an attitude of trust in God's promises – not only that he will be with us to the end of the age but also that he will come again. This was the assurance that Jesus gave to his disciples in John. His leaving would cause them pain but their pain would turn to joy. Those who truly believe that will have an attitude of joyful expectation. The attitude of rejoicing makes people do all kinds of unexpected things but most of all it makes them share the reasons for their joy.

Yet we must admit that some people simply cannot get their heads around the idea of the return of the Lord and there are differing views about this within the Christian community. It might help first to realize that the different views about whether the Lord will come and how he would return, if he does, have always existed in the Christian community. In fact, the Letter of 1 Thessalonians was motivated by a somewhat similar issue. People wanted to understand what would happen at the coming of the Lord to those who were already dead (I Thessalonians 4:13ff). In responding to the concern, Paul alludes to the coming of the Lord. Similarly, in the Letter of I Corinthians, Paul tried to respond to the question about the character and timing of those who would be raised from the dead (I Cor 15:12-58). In both cases he alludes to a time in the future when those who are alive will be called together with those who have died. In both cases he refers to the sounding of a trumpet to call attention to the momentous occasion.

The conviction that the present order of things in the world is not the final is the basis for that hope and expectation. People who are convinced that all there is to life is that we are born, live and then die, cannot experience any joy at the thought that the Lord will return at the time of a trumpet sound. However, there are those who refuse to accept this dismissive, pessimistic view of life and choose to live with hope. We hope that the God, in whom we trust, the one whose purpose is expressed in the creation of the world and the one whose purpose was also expressed in the life of the Jesus of Nazareth, is not finished with us and so we say, he will come again.

The coming of the Lord is not an empirical fact to be proved. It is a conviction to hold in hope. It is not as futile as we think because in every generation we see efforts geared towards improvement in the human community. We seek an improved quality of life. We seek better remedies for diseases that are now terminal. Being conscious of the inter-connections with the world, we seek ways to make life on the planet more sustainable. The efforts are not all successful but they are getting better. All these actions, projects, research and programmes aimed at an improved quality of life are also undertaken in hope. So we live and work in hope that we can show that life is not just about being born, living and dying. We want sustainability. We want good quality. We are also conscious that these ideals will depend on people in each generation making sound and appropriate moral and ethical judgements. The conviction that things will be better, that this is not all there is, fills us with hope and joyful sense of purpose. It was this sense of future betterment that the apostle was expressing when he spoke of the coming to the Lord. It was a way to say that our future is bright and that conviction about the future fills the present with joy. This bright future, which we call his coming, is a reason to cultivate now an attitude of joy.

The partnership in the gospel, the proclamation of Jesus and the apostle's pre-empting of the Lord's coming were not only the reasons for his joy but they were also part of his evangelistic strategy. In an effort to model the joyfulness of the kingdom of God, he spoke to the Philippians about his fullness of joy that springs from the gospel. There's something to say for this joyful attitude.

CHAPTER 5

Justice without Prejudice

*"His delight shall be in the fear of the Lord. He shall not
judge by what his eyes see, or decide by what his ears hear;
but with righteousness he shall judge the poor and decide
with equity for the meek of the earth."* Isaiah 11:3-4

Introduction

The issue of justice and access to justice, especially for the poor, is something of concern in several countries today. Take for example the situation in Jamaica. In a recent report the Chief Justice noted that there were some 400,000 cases waiting to be heard. This backlog means that there are many people for whom justice is being delayed and therefore for them justice is being denied. It should not surprise us that the poor are the worst affected.

The prophet Isaiah (11:4) has something to say about judging and deciding, which I believe is relevant for the pursuit of justice today. It is relevant because it challenges us to find a different way of judging and deciding, one that seeks to minimise the impact of prejudice on justice. Speaking of the one that would come from the stock of Jesse, Isaiah says: *"His delight shall be in the fear of the Lord. He shall not judge by what his eyes see or decide by what his ears hear."* In other words, in making judgement he would be mindful of his prejudices against the poor and seek to do justice on their behalf. In an effort to establish some sure basis for making judgements, the 17th century philosopher and mathematician, Descartes, suggested that we should start by doubting everything that can be doubted. He was not even prepared to believe that what he saw with his eyes was beyond doubt because he knew from experience that his eyes could deceive him. This is the idea behind the movie sequel, the Matrix, a simulated reality in which things are in truth not what they seem. It is critical, then, that we do not simply rely on what things appear to be, in order to make our judgements. When it comes to a court scene this is ironic because although we know that people's eyes often fool them, we speak of eyewitness account. I believe a witness can say, I heard someone say something but I do not recall hearing about an ear-witness account. Of course one of the ironies of appearance is that the well-dressed person is more often given the benefit of doubt. Not so for the poor and ragged!

One of the reasons we trust the radar gun used to detect speed is that there is something empirical about it. The officer does not rely on his or her own visual judgement to determine whether or not a motorist is speeding. In one of the exercises that I use in cultural competence training, I illustrate that we all have prejudices. I show participants some familiar sayings set in triangles that appear to them for two seconds. To ensure that they have time to read again each saying, the series of triangles is repeated and they write down what they see. In over 90% of the times participants overlook that an extra word had been placed in the familiar phrases. They depended on what they were accustomed to seeing and hearing to determine what was shown. They exercised their prejudice, which means making judgements based on what was seen and heard before.

According to the prophet Isaiah, the one that would come from the stock of Jesse, upon whom the spirit of wisdom, understanding, counsel, might, knowledge and the fear of God would rest, would not rely on appearances or hearsay. He would try to minimise the impact of his prejudice in the justice he exercises. The point to be made is that in order to do justice, especially to the poor, it will be necessary to find a way to minimise the impact of our prejudices. The prophet Isaiah suggests a way in which this could be done, a way which was also central to the message of Jesus

Doing the Right Thing

The first is to give priority to righteousness – doing the right thing. In the words of Isaiah, "with righteousness he shall judge the poor." This is all well and good but the words of the prophet leave us with two difficulties. We must clarify what "doing the right thing" means and we must be clear about what we mean when we say "the poor". On the first issue, it is not easy at times to determine what the right thing is. In a recent discussion in Ireland a former member of the parliament (Dáil) who became a Member of the European Parliament (MEP) was urged to do the right thing because she was in receipt of her Dáil pension, as well as her MEP salary, effectively two salaries. Although under the law it was her right to keep both, there were those who felt that exercising this right was at odds with the general situation in the country, where many had to take cuts in salary and where others lost their jobs in the wake of the downturn in the economy. She needed to demonstrate empathy with the rest of the society and forego a part of her large income. In this case the provisions of the law were out of sync with the mood of the moment, thus creating an ethical dilemma for the MEP. The discussion on the matter was divided between two conflicting ethical positions. On one hand we had those who felt that she ought to give up a part of the salary because in the context of the economy it was the right thing. On the other hand there were those who felt that this was not to be demanded of her because she was simply in receipt of those things for which the law provided. The first advanced their case using the way it appears to the society as a whole, as the basis of the judgement, while the second group focused on the individual. The one from the stock of Jessie, Isaiah says, will do the right thing with respect to its impact on the poor, which brings us to the second difficulty, who are the poor?

Often in our society the poor are the ones who bear the brunt of an unequal legal system. They are the ones we arrest for both petty and major crimes. They are often killed in shoot-outs; they form the inner city gangs. For these reasons, our jails and prisons are filled with young men from the lower income strata of society. These poor men are financially weak and powerless. The poor are the ones least able to stand their ground and resist the trampling of their rights. The poor are among the least educated. They are the most vulnerable in the society, the ones most susceptible to the downturn in the economy, to diseases and to premature death.

The challenge, then, is for us to follow Jesus, the one coming from the stock of Jesse, who makes justice for the poor the hallmark of his ethical actions. At all levels of society, we must face the question of the impact our actions and decisions will have on the lot of the poor. The prophet Isaiah seems to be putting forward a proposition, which Jesus later developed, that the righteousness of a nation is judged by the situation of the poor. Jesus asserts that the poor are blessed because the Kingdom of God belongs to them. This is not a promise of something to be received after the poor dies. Rather, it is to say that the reign of God, which Jesus comes to inaugurate on earth, finds its evidence in justice for the poor. It is also the case that one of the ethical pillars against which to test whether a position is right, is to consider the effect that it will have on the most vulnerable in the society. This is probably the approach the MEP might take in considering her ethical dilemma. Is my action having a direct and immediate negative or positive impact on the lot of the most vulnerable in the society?

Doing the right things can also be described as seeking equity for the meek. The word meek is always taken to mean someone who is mild, who "can't hurt a fly". However, in the Old Testament the meek are the ones who carry the burden of an unjust society; the underclass. In that sense, there is no distinction between the poor and the meek. It is not that the meek allow themselves to be trampled. Rather, it is that things are stacked against them and they fail regularly in their bid to rise above the circumstances of oppression. The idea of justice without prejudice is a challenge for the society to judge itself in terms of the lot of the meek. How are the actions of my division impacting the well-being of the underclass? In the words of the Magnificat, said by Jesus'

34

mother, Mary, we see a vision of a re-ordered society: "the Lord has put down the mighty from their thrones and exalted those of a low degree." There is a vision of using the *equity for the underclass* as the basis of our judging and deciding.

From time to time we hear about the protection of human rights. One of the rights enshrined in the United Nations Charter of Rights is, "the right… to enjoy a healthy and productive environment." For a large section of the underclass this is a dream rather than an imminent reality. What a difference it would make if this aspect of Jesus' message could be heard! The message we hear from Isaiah is that we must do away with the prejudices we have against the poor and vulnerable. The counter-action is to put the experience of the most vulnerable at the centre of the way we seek and exercise justice. Base your actions and decisions on justice for the poor and equity for the underclass, which bears the burden of an unjust society. When this message is taken seriously, much of what we do is turned up-side-down. Jesus comes for one, Jesus comes for all; Jesus stands for justice for the poor, Jesus stands for equity for the underclass.

CHAPTER 6

Angry with Jesus

*Peter felt hurt [angry] because he [Jesus] said to
him the third time, 'Do you love me.'*
John 21:17

Introduction

F am inviting you to look carefully with me at the story of
Jesus and his disciples in John 21 and find your place in the
story. With an eye for symbolism, you might notice that there
are seven persons present. I believe it is significant that we have named
and unnamed disciples. This is the nature of the Kingdom of God and
it is the nature of the Church; some are known and others are unknown.
The conversation we are about to consider takes place in the hearing
of several witnesses, some of whom we know by name but there were
others, yet unnamed. The writer would have assumed that at this point
in the story we would recall what we heard already about those named.
Peter, who denied Jesus, was the one brought by his brother Andrew.
Thomas, called Didymus, who doubted Jesus' resurrection, was the one
who wanted to die with Jesus. Nathaniel, who was brought to Jesus by
Phillip, was the one who wondered whether anything good could come
out of Nazareth. The sons of Zebedee, who the other Gospels name as
John and James, were never named in John's Gospel, but according to
the other three Gospels, they were the ones who wanted to sit on either

side of Jesus when he came into his Kingdom. The Christian tradition has also tended to regard John as the disciple whom Jesus loved, who was next to him at the Last Supper. The point though is that there are named and unnamed witnesses.

When I read the Greek text of the conversation between Jesus and Peter in John 21:17, I was struck by the reaction of Peter to the question Jesus put to him. The reaction stood out because it was not immediately evident what the reason for the reaction was. So my first task was to see why Peter was so grieved. [I should point out that although I normally use the New Revised Standard Version (NRSV) I am using at this point the King James Version's (KJV) rendering of the text. Those of you who have the NRSV will notice that in the place of "grieved" it has, "felt hurt". I decided that the older rendering is more accurate at this point because the word for grieved, from which we get the word *lupus,* is the same root word that is used in Mark 14:34. Here Jesus is in Gethsemane and said that his soul was truly sorrowful, to the point of death. So Peter was not just upset, he was under great distress. It could be that Peter was grieved, in the sense of being upset because all the questions were being put to him and not to the others. This consideration is quite plausible because later on in the story Peter was rebuked for asking Jesus about the fate of another disciple. We ourselves are inclined to question why the Lord does not seem to make the same demands of others that he seems to make of us. Am I the only one that can feed sheep? What about the others? Or put it another way, we are often more able to see the grace and favour that the Lord shows others than we see the grace and favour we receive. We sometimes think that the Lord is singling us out to make an example for discipline and not for blessing. It would make a difference to see the Lord's dealing with us as a privilege.

It could also be that Peter was grieved because it appeared that Jesus was asking him the same question three times. If that were the case, it means Peter was being impatient with Jesus. His reaction could imply that he was thinking to himself, as if to say, "But he just asked that question and I answered him!" However, there is a third possibility that I want to explore with you. I believe Peter was grieved not because it was the third time the same question was asked or because he was the focus of the questioning. I believe the sorrow, the sadness and the heaviness were related to a shift in the tone of the question. I will explain why I say this.

Miscommunication

The conversation with Peter is not just repetition but it is also a play on words. The first two times that Jesus asked if Peter loved him, he used the word *agape,* which is used with reference to the way God loves. It is this word, *agape* that we find in John 3:16, "for God so loved the world…" It is normally described as sacrificial love. However, when Peter answered, he used the word *fileo*, which is the word usually used in reference to admiration or to like doing something. It is the word used in Luke 20:46, where it says the scribes "love" to be greeted in the market place. It is also used in John 11:3 in reference to Lazarus, the one whom Jesus loved. Clearly, Lazarus was not the only person Jesus loved but that was a reference to a friendship, which Jesus had with the whole family. With the response Peter gave, we must ask whether his answer was on the same plane as the question Jesus asked. This is indeed a critical matter. We are prepared to walk with Jesus but only on our own terms. We are prepared to make sacrifice but only of certain things. We are prepared to give to the Lord, but only to a certain extent. What we see then, is Jesus and Peter conversing but not on the same wavelength. The writing of the Psalmist is relevant here: the Lord's thoughts are higher than our thoughts and his ways are higher than our ways. How will this gap in the conversation be bridged? Will Peter raise the level of his conversation or will Jesus come down to Peter's level?

Appreciating Difference

When Peter responded to Jesus the first two times, Jesus asked him, first to feed the lambs and then to tend, or literally to shepherd, the sheep. At closer observation we see that these requests are not one and the same. A lamb is always a sheep but a sheep is not necessarily a lamb.

This difference calls for a different strategy of care. The outstanding Moravian Bishop Amos Comenius seemed to have grasped the logic of this difference. In his proposal for the reform of the church he said that for the purpose of effective pastoral care, the church should be divided into three levels, as is the case in schools and that each level will need its own minister. We need one kind of minister for the beginners, another kind for the progressors and a third for the masters. The level of beginners is first, where the youth must be taught by stories that contain points of doctrine. At the second level, the progressors must deal with the essential articles of faith, hope and love. The third level is for the masters, the elderly who are expected to reach the topmost heights of understanding. In other words, the care and nurturing in the faith is critical for the children as it is for the adults. We have tended in recent times to think only in terms of feeding the little ones. It is a misconception that Sunday School is for children only. Ministers and leaders are challenged to improve the methods of their teaching, so that the elderly will find a place in the Sunday School. In this age of easy access to information, we cannot justify remaining uninformed and untaught. The seniors must be given new pastures! When it comes to the well-being of the sheep, it is not only a question of their security, which the shepherd must ensure. It is also a question of their diet. This is an important message for parents as it is for the nation as a whole. Our well-being depends also on our diet. A constant diet of certain things will make us sick and deficiency in certain foods will lead to malnourishment. If the lambs must be fed and the sheep must be fed and tended, then you will see that enabling people to come to faith and mature in the faith is a fundamental task of the Church. Those of us who would stand in the heritage of Jesus must revisit the evangelistic and the teaching ministries of Jesus.

At Cross Purposes

When we come to the third question, we arrive at a shift in the story. Bear in mind what happened before this moment. In response to Jesus' question, in which he used the word *agape*, Peter responded using *fileo*. His love was at a level different from that which Jesus raised the question. However, it was Jesus who moved to Peter's level. In a radical and unexpected change of tone Jesus asked the question using the same word for love, with which Peter was responding. This shift in tone has serious implications. No longer could Peter take comfort in the fact that Jesus' way was higher than his way. No longer could he give the excuse that he could reach up to the level of sacrificial love that Jesus was demanding. Jesus reached down in the Holy Spirit. Vouchsafe! (come down). Here Jesus condescended and occupied the ground on which Peter was standing. This is the miracle and grace of the incarnation. Jesus was not speaking from the lofty heights of heaven. He was speaking on the same level of human being! The resurrected Lord was underpinning the reality of the incarnation with language. He was using language to show that the incarnation was a strategic move that God made. This is an important observation to make. It was this shift, this coming down to the human level why Peter was grieved. Peter was always offended when Jesus took a low level. In an earlier incident Peter took Jesus to task at the suggestion that he would meet death when he arrived in Jerusalem. He said Jesus should not speak in those terms but Jesus had news for him. In yet another incident he was offended by Jesus' offer to wash his feet, but Jesus had news for him. The shift in language must have reminded Peter of his assertion that he would die for Jesus if necessary but soon after he denied him. The shift in language threw Peter off course because he now knew that Jesus understood what he was saying. The place in which he was seeking refuge in language was exposed. Jesus saw and was standing in the very place where Peter was.

CHAPTER 7

The Intentionality of Praise

"I will recount the gracious deeds of the Lord, the praiseworthy acts of the Lord, because of what the Lord has done for us." Isaiah 63:7

Introduction

When we come to the end of a year, a usual feature of both print and electronic media is for a series of programmes called the Year in Review. The media houses trawl through their news items and make a selection of stories, which in their view are worthy of recounting. I often find these programmes interesting because many of the items would be news to me because I would be hearing them for the first time. Others I would have been aware of but would have forgotten, partly because of the ever increasing array of new items. In this case also the review is a welcome reminder that for many people life has changed irrevocably. Every now and again the years in review fail to include an item, which in my view was noteworthy but then I quickly remind myself that their list is not designed to tell the whole story of noteworthy things but only their story.

This idea of the year in review gives a good insight into how we can hear the writer in Isaiah 63: 7 when he says, "I will recount the gracious deeds of the Lord, the praiseworthy acts of the Lord because of all that the Lord has done for us." For these reviews, as well as for the prophetic writings, there are a number of things we ought to emphasise about the act of recounting and I will consider these in turn.

As we shall see, when we look at the text in greater detail, the recounting of the prophet had a clear intention of calling to mind those things for which God was due praise. So we are not just talking about noteworthy things; we speak rather of praiseworthy things. In these divine acts God is declared to be worthy of praise. Praise is declared as coming from the individual, which means it is personal. It's a personal story of praise. It's my recounting and it's my testimony. The recounting, though personal is not kept to oneself but made public and we shall see why.

I therefore call this the *intentionality of praise*. By this I mean there must be a deliberate effort to call to mind the praiseworthy things. My intention here then is to call forth praise. So, what can be said about this intentionality of praise?

Praise is Personal

One of the interpretative tasks we face when we read this and other passages in Isaiah is to be clear about who is speaking because there are so many things written in the first person. In the section leading up to our main text we see several indications of what the "I" would do: "It is I announcing vindication; I have trodden the wine press alone; I will trod them in my anger; I looked but there was no helper; I stared but there was none to sustain me; I trampled down the people; I crushed them; I poured out their life blood." These references to personal acts suggest that they are acts of God. They seem to be noteworthy acts but when one considers the sense of anger and allusion to violence in the imagery I'm not sure that there would be consensus that these are praiseworthy. I cannot solve this dilemma but my concern is to know the speaker who, after all that listing of the personal actions, says "I will recount the gracious deeds of the Lord".

The difficulty of being able to call forth praise in the contexts of a series of acts, which are juxtaposed with such gruesome imagery of violence, is what emphasises that praise is personal. It is personal in the sense that it is by a particular individual, in a particular place and time; an individual who is the recipient of the acts of grace. This is my story, this is my testimony; this is my journey. The lesson then is that when you set out to recount your blessings, it is not about getting the agreement of others for what you are recounting and for what you are to give praise. It is your life; it's your story; it's your praise.

When the stiffness and formality of worship life in the Moravian Church in Jamaica was giving way to a more expressive form of worship it gave rise to a story that reflected the tension over the extent to which people could be expressive in church. So as the story goes, there was this brother whose ecstatic outburst of praise during worship was becoming a problem to the more conservative pastor and elders. So the elders during their meeting selected one of their number to visit the brother to let him know that these ecstatic outbursts of praise were disruptive and that he was to desist. The elder found the brother in his field loading a hamper on his donkey and explained to him the concerns, to which the brother responded:

Please tell minister that I must praise the Lord for what has done for me; do you see this field of potatoes, who do you think did this for me? I will praise the Lord! You see all those heads of cows over there; who do you think did this for me? Let me praise my God! You see how my children have progressed through university and are walking with the Lord? Let me praise my Jesus! I am 70 years old and never have I had to spend a day in hospital! Let me praise my God! Look brother, just hold this donkey let me praise God!

The Psalmist says, "I will bless the Lord; his praise shall continually be in my mouth." The song writer also declares, "I will bless the Lord with every breath that I take. And if eternity ends and starts over again, even then I will praise the Lord." So you don't have to agree with me but that is ok because this praise is personal.

Praise is a Principle

I will recount gracious deeds and praiseworthy acts. When I write the story of my life I choose what I include and I decide the character. I'm currently reading Nelson Mandela's biography, A Long Walk to Freedom. I have not gotten very far but there is a sort of confessional theme that runs through the early chapters. Evidently because of his religious upbringing, he comes clean in admitting to lies he told and the trouble they got him into but that is not all; he is also careful to mention the people, who otherwise would have been forgotten or not known, both black and white, who had a positive impression on him. He didn't have to mention them but he chose to do so because it seems he wanted to ensure that his life was not all about him and his efforts; it is principled that mention, praise and thanks would go to whom it's due.

This idea of praise as a principled thing, which the prophetic writer outlines here, is important. As you reflect on your life experiences you can, if you chose, make it a litany of sadness and rejection. You may join the dots of failure to weave a tapestry of sorrow and worthlessness. If you want, you could ensure a spirit of heaviness is worn instead of a garland of praise. The challenge that I find in this text though is that the writer insists that praise is given because it is right. There's an interesting line in the liturgy of the Church of Ireland which says, "It is right to give him thanks and praise." So I want to focus attention for a little on this idea that I praise God because it is right. If I do not praise God where his praise is due it is a really an act of injustice because the praise then is given, or is considered to be given, where it is not due. This is the concern that the writer addresses in the later verses: "It was no messenger or angel but his [the Lord's] presence that saved them. In his love and his pity he redeemed them. He lifted them up and carried them all the days of old." (63:9) These are acts that the servant of the Lord is recounting. But consider now the injustice: (63:10) – "but they rebelled and grieve his holy spirit." In this case, failure to give the praise to God was to undermine the praiseworthiness of God, which is another way to say that they rebelled against God.

Psalm 54:6 and a few other Psalms have this idea of praising the Lord because it is good. This principle of the goodness of praise is itself noteworthy. There are different words translated good in the OT. The one we find in Psalm 54:6 is the same we find in Genesis where after the different moments in creation the word declared that God saw that is was good. What might that mean? It would suggest that the thing created as well as the act of creation itself have an inherent quality called good. Now people might not be ready to credit God for the creation but they cannot deny creation nor can they in all honesty say it is a bad thing. The goodness of creation as a process and the goodness of the products of creation are self-evident. Why would someone go out of their way to try and prove the goodness of creation? They couldn't even if they try. The goodness of creation and the goodness of the products of creation are things we accept. They are first principles; foundational assertions on which we build and by which we live. In this sense we might understand the Psalmist when he says I will praise the Lord for it is good. It is a self-evidently good thing, which is similar to when something is self-evidently right. The protection of children from harm, for example, is right. So self-evident it is that there really is no need to make a case for it.

Similarly, praising God is not simply a matter of religious fanaticism, as some people might think of it; praising God is a matter if intellectual honesty; it is a reasonable and good thing. I do it not because of what I might gain as a result. Far from it! It is analogous to being kind to children, kind to neighbour and protecting the poor and vulnerable in the society. We do not do these things because of what we hope to get. We do them because there is a certain quality and inward capacity to do what is good. I praise God not for blessing, not to boast but because it is a good, reasonable thing; because it is right.

The intentionality of praise then is personal but it is also a thing of principle. It is good to praise God, it is right to give thanks and praise; I praise God because it is for me a principle of honesty.

Praise in Public

The final point about this intentionality of praise is that it's public. Like stories in the year in review, praise is news, especially for those who didn't realise that this is going on. It is not only news to them but it is good news to all. I say it is public because, in line with the text, it is "of what the Lord has done for us... the great favour to the house of Israel that he has shown them" (63:7). It is public in the sense that it is subject to critique and scrutiny. It has to stand in the public gaze; the people must be able to say, "Amen"!

Of course this is where we have a challenge because the public may not agree and may not say amen. More than that, when you make a public recount of what you consider to be God's gracious deeds and praise-worthy acts, you could be ridiculed. However, as we said earlier, the intentionality of praise it is not about finding consensus. It is about what the individual believes to be good and right to ascribe to God.

Confessedly, this is an area in which I find myself wanting. Nevertheless, it is my conviction that bearing a public witness, giving a public account of the acts for which I believe the Lord must be praised, is something I ought to do as a public testimony. When I make it public I declare where I stand and this is in itself a proclamation and a witness. When I declare it publicly I make sure that those who know of the events know that my position is one of praise to God. In this way I not only do justice to God but also to my own conscience, against which I cannot lie.

Let me then end with my incomplete list of praiseworthy acts. I praise God that my health has been sustained and that I have been preserved not by being smart but by the gracious providence of God. I praise God for my family and friends who, despite my own failings that they know, have not withdrawn from me. They give me a reason to make effort. I praise God that despite financial difficulties last year I was able to earn and could share with others. I praise God that even though I'm faced with the uncertainties of the ensuing year, I am yet possessed with a clear mind and strength by which I can act in faith and hope. Finally, I praise God for you my brothers and sisters, with whom I share faith in Jesus Christ our Lord, the faith by which I live. The list is incomplete but like yours it is personal. As I'm sure that you will also do, I recount these before you, as praise to God because it is good and because it is right.

CHAPTER 8

Being in the Spirit

For all who are led by the Spirit of God are children of God.
You did not receive a spirit of slavery to fall back into fear,
but you have received a spirit of adoption. Rom 8:14-17

Introduction

I n the Christian calendar Whit (White) Sunday or Pentecost, which comes fifty days after Easter, reminds us of the event, about which we read in Acts 2, when the Holy Spirit came upon the disciples. However, it was also the name of the Jewish Feast, which was celebrated fifty days after the Feast of Unleavened Bread. The name Whit Sunday may be derived from the fact that from around the 4th century, Pentecost became an occasion for baptism, where candidates would be dressed in white robes. From the account in Acts of the Apostles it is evident that the believers had an unusual experience of the presence and power of the Holy Spirit. According to the story, the Holy Spirit gave the disciples the ability to speak in tongues (languages) other than they were normally able to speak. It is not surprising, then, that to speak in tongues is taken to be one of the indications of the presence of the Holy Spirit. The question of what happens in a life, or in a community, when the Holy Spirit is present remains an important question for Christians to answer. When we try to answer this question, we are in fact discovering something about the nature of the Holy Spirit, which is our aim here. We should not suppose, though, that we are able to completely answer this question – certainly not in a brief chapter.

Chapter 8 of Romans is concerned with the questions of what it means to be in Christ and what it means to be in the Holy Spirit. For those who have already made the decision to walk with Christ, this investigation is a reminder about what it means to have the Spirit of Christ. For those who have not yet made that decision, which happily remains an option, this reflection is an invitation to consider a different kind of life. The life in Christ and the Spirit is not a life of bondage. Rather, it is about a new identity and a new set of relationships; it is about sharing; it is about joys and about privileges. Romans 8 would have us see two main benefits to the community and the individual, when the Holy Spirit is present. The first is a life of liberation (Romans 8: 1-13) and the second is a life of communion with God (Romans 8:14-38).

The Spirit Liberates

One of the emphases in Romans 8 is that the spirit liberates. The period in modern history, which we can call the Pentecostal Re-awakening or the Pentecostal Reformation, has also been concerned with this question of freedom, as given by the spirit. The Pentecostal Reformation started somewhere in the 19th Century when Christians began to describe their experience of faith more in terms of their relationship to the Spirit than in terms of their relationship to Jesus Christ. This reformation succeeds the Lutheran Reformation, in which the experience of faith was described mostly in terms of relationship to the person of Jesus. In the Pentecostal Reformation, the freedom that the spirit gives has been interpreted in terms of speaking in tongues and the free, unplanned participation in the worship experience. That is why some churches will even insist that unless you are speaking in tongues you have not had the endowment of the Holy Spirit. The Pentecostals see the stiff and restrictive forms of worship participation, which we have inherited from Europe, as bondage to a culture, from which we should express our freedom. So today, all the churches are seeking to come to terms with this way of describing the experience of faith. The challenge from the Pentecostal Reformation, then, is that we set ourselves free from the cultural hindrances to our worship forms. So, whereas the Lutheran Reformation was largely a time of debate about the implications of faith in Jesus, the Pentecostal Reformation has been about the meaning of the Holy Spirit, forms of worship and the language of faith. We can see the shift in the worship forms in Churches that bear the image of the Lutheran Reformation, as an attempt to assimilate the benefits of the Pentecostal Reformation. This is how to understand the outbreak of clapping, hand waving and other expressions, which we see in many churches today.

The Bondage of Sin and Death

However the freedom of Romans 8 is more than a freedom to speak and to show free, unplanned participation in worship. It is a freedom from sin and death. With the presence of the Holy Spirit in our lives, we do not have to live in bondage to sin and death (8:2) because we have been set free from the law, that is, by the regulation and operation of the Spirit. We were not given a spirit of bondage (8:15). When we speak of bondage we refer to a system, in which we are held, or believe we are held captive, so that we do not feel free to act outside the dictates of that system. We live in fear of what will happen to us unless we obey the laws of that system. For example, much of the security check to which we are subjected when we travel nowadays is based on the assumption that there could be a terrorist attack. When someone fears that his 'manliness' will be undermined or compromised if he makes a commitment of his life to Christ – that is bondage. It is probably the most popular form of bondage we see today, where people are captured and held hostage by an idea. It is being hostage to an idea that lies behind fear. When a person is fearful, it is because they have constructed a scenario, in which they are in danger or exposed to danger and death. The idea on which the scenario is built is the source of the fear. It is bondage.

We can extend the examples further: bondage is when a young man feels that the only way he can survive is through the trafficking of drugs. It is bondage when, as a society, we believe the way to ensure progress is through the expansion of the gambling opportunities. The difficulty, of course, I have with current political/economic leadership is that they seem unable to see and they even deny any linkage between the work ethic that leads to drug trafficking, about which they are concerned, and the work ethic that thrives on gambling, which they seem keen to promote. It seems to me that the same spirit of bondage is at work in both. It is bondage when as a society we have come to live at ease with an ever-spiralling cycle of violence and murder. It is not only the perpetrators and the victims who have the problem. We aid and abet by our cold indifference and unwillingness to make the development of a culture of peace in communities a priority. It is a form of bondage when young women and young men feel that they cannot restrain themselves from inappropriate sexual acts and activities. When children see violence as the only way to resolve differences, they are in bondage, and so are we, who they mimic. When we are unable to hope beyond the life we see in this world; when we close our ears to the message of the gospel, it is because we are in bondage to the system of the world. The Prince of this world has blinded our eyes and has made our ears heavy so that we cannot hear. However, when the Holy Spirit is present, we have freedom from bondage for the Holy Spirit is not a spirit of slavery to fear. So the liberation of which Romans 8 speaks goes far beyond the form of worship and the language of faith. It has to do more so, with a kind of life; a life that is free from bondage to sin and death.

Communion with God

The spirit given to the church and to the world, of which the celebration of Pentecost reminds us, is a spirit of adoption. This is an important reminder because we live in a world where many people have no sense of family, no sense of home and no point of reference. Many are dislocated and even though they might be in virtual contact with others, they are alone and feel lonely. When we consider the ease with which people can communicate today the reality of loneliness is somewhat ironic. It might come as a surprise to you that the increasing effectiveness and speed of communication is happening at the precise moment there is an increase in the rate of suicide in many countries. Why should this be so? It seems that the ease of communication cannot substitute for a sense of belonging. People yearn for companionship and communion with others and when these are lost so too are the reasons for living. This idea is reinforced in Ephesians 1:13 that we are sealed with the Holy Spirit. I understand this to mean that we are given a clear identity as we are given a clear sense of belonging.

The gift of the Holy Spirit therefore rescues us from the feeling of "nobody-ness" – that sense of having no purpose or value in the world. By reminding us that we have a family and that we have a point of location and a point of reference, the spirit of adoption leads us into communion with God. With this understanding you can see the power of the affirmation we make when we share in the Lord's Supper. It is meant to demonstrate that our lives are lived in communion with God. The Holy Spirit, who frees us from sin and death, is the self-same spirit that leads us into a special kind of relationship with God. The spirit sets us free to be somebody in a world where there are many 'nobodies'.

When we discover something about the nature of the Holy Spirit we also discover something about the Christian life because the Holy Spirit is given to the Church and to the world. This is the story of Pentecost; the outpouring of the Holy Spirit in the world and upon believers. When we understand the work of the Holy Spirit in the world, we also understand what it means to live and walk in the Spirit because we have been called to a life in Christ and in the Spirit. The Spirit <u>leads</u> the children God (8:14) because the Spirit is the spirit of adoption not a spirit of abduction. When the spirit is present we say Abba Father – that is we cry to the father. It is by the spirit we develop a life of prayer because we know in whom we believe; we have someone on whom we can call. In giving us a new identity, the Spirit confirms [συμμαρτυρει = [<u>summarturei</u>] bear witness in us] that we are children; that is, it gives assurance of salvation and our participation in his life. As the spirit of adoption, the Holy Spirit owns our past and secures our future. For us who are ashamed of what we were and are uncertain of what we shall become, being adopted by the spirit comes as a great consolation.

Sharing the Life of Christ as Fellow-heir

Let us be clear. Living in the Spirit is life and peace but it is not just an evening stroll in the park. It is a life lived in confrontation with the systems of bondage in the world. In fact, we might say that when we live a life that confronts the systems of bondage and fear, we are, in fact, sharing the life of Christ, whose death was a consequence of this kind of confrontation. This might come as a surprise to some who would imagine that the life of Christ is a benign one of love and peace. Indeed it is but it is also one of courage and resistance in the face of evil. So the question is whether we have the guts for this kind of life. My suspicion is that many people who speak disparagingly of the Christ-like life really don't have the guts for what that life demands.

An exposition of Romans 8 can show that there are at least three things to consider when sharing the life of Christ. The first is the privilege, on one hand, of being called fellow-heir (8:17). The word in the original Greek text, συγκληρονομοι, [sunklerovomoi] is a very interesting and complex one, comprised of three ideas. In addition to the idea of together, another idea contained in the word means that something has been appointed by the law. The privileges and responsibility of the heir are determined by law and in some cultures by tradition. These are not things that people choose. When applied to the one who comes to share life with Christ the point must be made that as heir there are things that are unavoidable because they follow necessarily from the place of being heir.

This idea of sharing the inheritance of Christ must bring a sense of hope and consolation. At the same time, given the unforgettable suffering that characterized the last days of his life, it might also fill us with a sense of fear and alarm. I confess that it is not easy to say what all of this means. The text (v.32) asks whether the God who freely gave

Jesus for our salvation will not likewise give us everything else. It further states (v.34) that Jesus was raised from the dead [as the first-born of the new creation] and that he is seated at the right hand of God. In other words, the kingdom, the power and glory are his. It is humbling but exciting to think that all these are ours through Jesus. I can only say that with Jesus we have the same destiny. Are we prepared, then, to throw in our lot with Jesus and let the chips fall where they may? You will soon realise that this way of Christ is not a way for cowards but is a way of the courageous. This brings us to the second implication of sharing life with Jesus.

Fellow-sufferer with Christ

We are cautioned to see that the way of Christ is also a way of suffering and that to take up the life of Christ is to become a fellow-sufferer with him (συμπασχομεν [sumpascomen]). This is definitely problematic because it is hard to see the necessity of suffering in God's design. In other religions, for example Buddhism, although suffering is no less an issue, it is accounted for in such a way that the individual is always responsible for the fact that he or she suffers. In that case, because suffering is so fundamental to the unenlightened, the goal of life is how to avoid suffering by one's own effort. For the Christian, however, the matter of suffering is not theorized in such a straightforward way and there is no clear explanation or justification for it. In fact, the suffering of the Christian is complicated by the fact that it happens alongside two unyielding beliefs: one is that the God in whom we trust is omnipotent and the other is that the Saviour was himself subjected to suffering.

Notwithstanding God's omnipotence, suffering comes to the Saviour and the believer as fellow sufferers. How can we appreciate the suffering caused by deadly hurricanes and earthquakes which have caused endless suffering in countries like Haiti? It is hard to imagine some good that makes that suffering necessary. After the genocide in Rwanda, one book that was published was entitled, *The Angels have Left Us*. We struggle to come to terms with the hardships in Africa, the war in the Middle & Far East, the violence in Jamaica, the suffering and death caused by terminal diseases like cancer and HIV/Aids. And yet, the Bible says that we are fellow-sufferers with Jesus. Seen from this point of view the life of Christ is not a privileged position free from the hardships of daily living. It seems that it is a challenge for us to see that life in the Spirit is not a life at ease. It is not a life that is lived in the comfort of wealth and glass houses, where we are detached from the realities of human suffering. Living with Jesus means facing the hunger, the malnutrition, the poverty and the culture of death, knowing that our lives may at best experience severe limitations or at worst is snuffed out because of a commitment to those who experience suffering. "It is not an easy road."[5]

As if to provide a consolation, the text asserts that in this life in Christ we are not only fellow-heirs and fellow-sufferers but also that we will be glorified as Jesus was glorified. In other words, we are fellow-glorified [*συνδοξασθῶμεν [sundoxasthomen]*]. With the use of the expressions fellow-heir *(συγκλρονοοι)*, fellow-sufferer *(συμπασχομν)* and fellow-glorified *(συνδοξασθῶμεν)* there is a play on words, which would be a little more obvious in the original language. However, even without being able to read the language one can notice that all three words begin in the same way. Sharing life in the Spirit means we accept that we are heirs together with Jesus. We know by experience and by the witness of others that walking with Christ does not preclude suffering, which makes us fellow-sufferers with Jesus. However, we are not weary in our doing well because we believe that we will be glorified together with him.

We live in an age in which we want to see the fruits of our labour here and now but we cannot see the outcome of all our toil. Many have died without seeing the things for which they worked but we have entered into their labours. Bob Marley made that criticism of Christian preaching when he said he is looking for his heaven on earth he is not looking for any God to come from the sky.[6] It seems though that we must act in faith, knowing that the things for which we struggle may not come in our lifetime but that God will not overlook our labours and shall glorify us in Christ because God will glorify those who glorify him. According to the book of Philippians, because of his faithfulness, Jesus was given a name above every name. Joint glory with Jesus springs from being faithful even as Jesus himself was faithful. We have been given a Spirit of adoption, not a spirit of abduction and bondage. Life in the spirit is a life free from the bondage of sin and death and a life lived in communion with Jesus. It is a life that ends in glory because it is lived in faithfulness, to the point of suffering.

Something More
Christmas

Introduction

*T*he passage on which I'd like you to focus is John 1:14: ***And the Word became flesh and lived among us and we have seen his glory, the glory as of the Father's only son, full of grace and truth.*** And the word became flesh. This is not something you will necessarily find easy to say but I'll ask you to be bold and bear witness to this and say this to the person next to you: *the word became flesh.* This is an amazing mystery but what does it mean. This text is often read at Christmas, which is observed by millions of people around the world. Christians began this festival from around the mid 4th century, as an annual holy day to commemorate the birth of our Lord Jesus. The nominating of a date for his birth counterbalanced the view that had emerged in which some questioned the reality of Jesus' human life. Jesus was so shrouded in fantasy and imagery that some people, especially a group called the Gnostics, began to deny the realities of his human birth, life and death. Replacing the earlier January 6 date with which Jesus' birth was first associated in Eastern Christianity, December 25 came to symbolise the stanch affirmation by Christians that, the word [God's logos, God's idea, God's intention, God's will] took the form of flesh and dwelt among us. By naming a date for his birth Christians wanted to insist on making the affirmation that our God, who is the creator of the world and the Lord of history, was manifested in the flesh and therefore in history, as a human being.

This action on the part of the early church was a practical witness to the belief that the life of Christ was not imaginary. This is the Christian story and this is the reason why the idea of a birthday for Jesus came into being. Yet we have to admit that this Christian holy day has become a public holiday with multiple meanings. It means different things to different people. For the retail business person, it is the time when sales are best. For the economist, it is the time when most money is in circulation. It is the time when many people think longing of home. For some families it is the time to get together. For some people it is about giving and gifts; some people prefer to talk about Santie. The Christian message of the word becoming a human life must contend with the other meanings that people now pour into the day we call Christmas. It has become a shared space.

However, this struggle for the ownership of Christmas is not new. In fact, the word of scripture from John 1:14 came out of a struggle, not for the day but for the idea of Jesus being the divine in human form. It arose from a context in which the life of Christ was *denied*. In the face of this denial the early Christians declared; the word became flesh. It was a struggle in which some made an argument for the concealment of Christ. In the face of this concealment our forebears of the Christian faith confessed that he lived among us. In the face of misrepresentation they made it their attestation that he was full of grace and truth. The early believers in the Christian faith wanted to say that this Jesus, who we worship as Lord is not a fake, he is not a joke; this Jesus whom we adore, this name that is an offence to some, this name above all names is not a fraud because his birth was a historical fact. He became flesh and lived in the world. His life was real.

Human Communication

Since we are determined to make the affirmation that the word became flesh in the contested space of Christmas today, there are two things, arising from this affirmation that we should bear in mind. The first is that human life, being in the flesh, is God's preferred mode of communication. It is believed that communication technology is the most important revolution that has occurred in the last century. It is hard to imagine the world without mobile phones and the world-wide-web. These have transformed the world of communication in the same way the world was transformed when the printing press was discovered centuries ago. However, in the same way in which the printing press has lost its revolutionary edge, so too will the internet and mobile phones eventually give way to other cutting edge technologies because we yearn for good, lasting, secure and speedy means of communication. I recall, often with a chuckle, when I bought my first computer with all of one gigabyte (1G) of memory capacity. In its day it was able to do fascinating things – at least, so I boasted. However, that mind-boggling 1G of memory has been surpassed even by ordinary hand-held devices for children. The greatest threat to modern technology is that they will become obsolete so there is an ever-increasing array of new attempts to be on the cutting edge.

The idea of divine communication *via* human form must be the mother of all revolution in communication technology. In this revolution, we affirm that God reached across the divide between human and divine life and expressed himself in the life of our Lord Jesus. So when we say happy Christmas, let us bear this communication revolution in mind and be happy. In Jesus Christ, God is speaking to us. Is this cutting edge technology or what? So how does God speak to us in the midst of modern communication technologies? He speaks in a human life for, *the word became flesh.* As much as people might like to avoid it, we affirm that we all must reckon with the life of Jesus because in him God has accomplished a communication revolution for time and eternity. The implication of this is immense and time would fail us to explore it to the fullest extent. Suffice it to say that the divine communication revolution is symbolized in the expression, "through Jesus Christ our Lord", by which we end a session in the human to divine communication we call prayer. We say through Jesus because it is recognised that the word made flesh is the mode of communication that enables us to speak to God and God to us.

If we cannot get our heads around this, I invite you to consider a second point. It is not only that God is speaking to us in the flesh, in human life, in the person of Jesus, but secondly, speaking in the flesh is a durable and reliable mode of communication. Those who still embrace and value the role of human beings in communication are being God-smart. Those who do not allow modern modes of communication to eclipse their own human life take a leaf out of God's book. We hear people extolling the virtues of Skype, which enables families to communicate virtually face-to-face. Yet I cannot imagine someone saying "I do not need to meet up with you because we have Skype. The modern modes of communication must then be treated as instruments not as masters or makers of communication. Indeed we must not allow modern technologies to be a substitute for our fleshly communication. So yes, send the snail mail and the email; yes, send the voice mail and send the text; send the live streaming and use the webcam but remember that none of these can achieve what happens when human beings meet and feel the warmth of the other's embrace. There are some things that only fleshly communication can accomplish. How will you shake my hands, if you have not come close enough to me? What good is our gift if people do not feel from our fleshly communication that we really care?

So this is where the Christian meaning of Christmas parts company from the rest. For the Christian it is primarily about how God chose to communicate. When we say happy Christmas, it is among other things, the joy of God's communication in the flesh, for the *Word became flesh*.

CHAPTER 9

Living in Scarcity – The 3rd World Teacher

Then the word of the LORD came to him "Arise, go to Zar'ephath, which belongs to Sidon, and dwell there. Behold, I have commanded a widow there to feed you." So he arose and went to Zar'ephath; and when he came to the gate of the city, behold, a widow was there gathering sticks; and he called to her and said, "Bring me a little water in a vessel, that I may drink." And as she was going to bring it, he called to her and said, "Bring me a morsel of bread in your hand." And she said, "As the LORD your God lives, I have nothing baked, only a handful of meal in a jar, and a little oil in Aa cruse; and now, I am gathering a couple of sticks, that I may go in and prepare it for myself and my son, that we may eat it, and die." And Elijah said to her, "Fear not; go and do as you have said; but first make me a little cake of it and bring it to me, and afterward make for yourself and your son. For thus says the LORD the God of Israel, `The jar of meal shall not be spent, and the cruse of oil shall not fail, until the day that the LORD sends rain upon the earth.'" And she went and did as Elijah said; and she, and he, and her household ate for many days. The jar of meal was not spent; neither did the cruse of oil fail, according to the word of the LORD which he spoke by Elijah. [1Kings 17:8-16]

Introduction

O
ne might naturally wonder about the relevance of a text like this for teachers. One should not take for granted that this internal questioning is because it is the beginning of the process of interpretation. To wonder about the relevance is to discern what to say and sometimes it is not easy. In order to appreciate the point of this story, it may be helpful to focus for a moment on what it meant to be a widow in ancient Israel. In a society where the emotional and financial security of the household depended on the man's ability to provide for his wife and children, a household without a man would be vulnerable. Naturally this is not the case today but that is how it was in Far Eastern societies. It was for this reason that the marriage practices required a man to marry his brother's wife, if his brother were to die without bearing children. The widow in ancient Israel then, was used as the symbol of insecurity, risk and poverty. The way the tribes treated their widows was the acid test of justice and mercy in the society. According to Joshua 22:9, it was the wicked that would send a widow away empty. The book of Job (24:3) and Deuteronomy (24:17) also issue a caution against using the widow's property as security against her indebtedness. The prophets in Israel, for example Amos and Isaiah, in several places warn the lawmakers that it will be terrible for them to prey on widows and dispossess them. The imagery of the widow was also used in the New Testament to drive home important lessons about righteousness, justice and mercy. According to Mark 12:42, it was a widow who gave the two mites, which was all her possession. Jesus said of her that her gift was received. According to Luke 7:12, the woman from Nain, whose son had died, and who appealed to Jesus was a widow. Luckily for her, Jesus intervened in her dilemma, brought her son back to life and restored her hope in the future. Luke 18:3 tells that the woman who did not stop bugging the king for justice in the case against her adversary was a widow. In James 1:27 the writer says that true religious piety is shown in giving attention to the needs of the widows. And finally, it was the need to give attention to widows in the

early church, according to Acts of the Apostles, why it became necessary to organize the ministry by appointing deacons. [Acts 6:1-5]

In the story of the widow of Zarephath, then, the writer would want us to bear in mind all that it meant to be a widow. The literal meaning of the word Zarephath is "melting houses". This is an allusion to the furnace used in making glass, which we are told was practised in ancient Phoenicia. By the time we get to our widow in the story, though, those days of economic prosperity were over. We don't need to stretch our imagination too far to appreciate the hardship this woman was facing, unless of course we do not know what it is to experience economic hardship. In the best case scenario, even with a man in the house, these times of hardship would be a challenge. So the difficulties of a widow are multiplied because as we are told the woman's husband was dead and she was left alone with her only son. The hardship was further intensified by the drought, in much the same way as it does in places like Sudan and Ethiopia today. From images we have seen or stories we have read we know that this is not a joke – the possibility of dying from starvation is a real and present danger. That is the context of the story.

So how is this related to life in the rural areas, especially for poor families and for those who must deliver services like education? How does it relate to the delivery of health and other social services in a debt-ridden country that does not have a social welfare system? The relevance of this story is that families and service providers that operate in areas of economic hardship face similar choices to those faced by this poor widow with her last morsel of bread. The story, which is charged with the dilemma of making ethical choices, is about how the widow went about using her last morsel of bread. Let us look at the ethical challenges that this widow faced and I suggest that they resemble the kinds of challenges that poor families and service administrators face today.

*Making a **Difference** in a Desperate Situation*

There is hardly any need to make the case that the woman was in a desperate situation. According to the story, she was gathering sticks to make her last meal. There is something ceremonial about it because she knew their appointment with death was certain; it was just a matter of time. Imagine her going through the woods, picking up a piece here and a piece there and another piece over there and another. It was a dance of death. However, before it arrived, she was making one last bold effort to delay something that was inevitable. In this action of gathering sticks she was seeking to make a difference. She wanted to do something that would keep the hungry beast of death away as long as she could. The rural and urban poor gather sticks every day. We see them rooting through the garbage heap to unearth a morsel to save life. We see them at the side of the road selling a few harassed items with which they have been walking around all week. We see them at the traffic light offering to wipe windshields. We see them on the hillside in the rural areas putting in a grain of corn, putting in a head of yam or a sprig of sweet potato. The land is not theirs because for generations they have had a dispossessed existence. They lease the land like their parents and did the same as their parents before them. This is subsistence farming for subsistence living. Like the widow of Zarephath they are gathering sticks – seeking to make a difference in a desperate situation. The ethical choice is clear because the alternative to this is malnutrition and starvation, which are always standing at the door like a hawk waiting for the dying animal to make its last kick.

Teachers and other service providers in third world countries, like Jamaica, gather sticks every day. In many cases this happens literally because they may have to resort to wood fire in order to ensure that some food is provided for the children. There is no money to afford the utilities. In fact, in many cases the utilities have been cut off because they were not able to pay the bills. If the school has no running water to support the operation of proper sanitary facilities then that is like gathering sticks. This is nothing more than doing the death dance because the outbreak of sanitation related diseases looms large around the corner. When teachers have to do the fundraising to fix the leaking classrooms or to buy cartridge paper, chalk and markers, it is because they want to make a difference in a desperate situation. When teachers have to come early each morning and clean the classroom because the door cannot be locked and the windows are broken and disreputable vandals use the classroom as both bedroom and even as toilet, this is like gathering sticks.

It is not hard then to illustrate the desperate nature of the situations in which teachers have to perform. They continue doing what they are asked to do because they want to make a difference. It amazes me that given such a reality, the impression could be given by those who like to talk, that when a child leaves school being unable to read and write we must first blame the teacher – the very ones who gather sticks in parched land because they want to make a difference. I do not want you to lose sight of the point though. Like the widow gathering sticks are the schools in the 3rd world. They face a desperate situation and are seeking to make a difference and in most cases without complaint. The ethical choice is clear because the alternative to this is death - blighted lives, ruination of community and untapped potential.

Considering **Demands** of the Neighbours

The second challenge that the widow of Zarephath faced was to respond to the demands of Elijah. This became an ethical issue because the scarcity of the resources meant that she had to prioritise: whose needs would come first here? Would her family's needs or that of her neighbour, the prophet? For some people in a situation like this it is a "no-brainer". Of course the needs of the family ought to take precedence over that of the neighbour prophet. However for this widow the decision was not as clear-cut. As a woman in need she was able to empathize quickly with a needy passer-by. She had been there and was familiar with the expectation that help might be found, however small. Her experience of want sharpened the images in her ethical lenses.

This brings up an issue that we might digress to consider. Often times those who have responsibility to consider the demands and requests of the poor have never experienced poverty. As a result of the lack of experience there is no empathy and no appreciation of what it is to be told "No"! Many of the people who work in funding agencies providing development aid have no idea at the experiential level what they are dealing with. This is often reflected in the criteria they set for qualification, the questions they ask and their suspicion. There's no empathy, no sensitivity and judgements are made on irrelevant and unrealistic grounds. Journalists writing and speaking from the security of their own jobs and home berate the ethical actions that people in situations of crisis take. They do not know what it means to gather sticks and they have never been faced with the challenge of having to decide between meeting the needs of their family and that of the neighbour.

However, the situation was for the widow an ethical dilemma. The need of the neighbour was so real to her that she could not dismiss it. Moreover, a number of things combined to impose an ethical burden on the widow. These included her understanding of hospitality, the social expectation of deference and respect for an old man and the society's expectation that a woman must serve a man. No sooner than the poor woman left to get him the water – remember it was a drought - Elijah called for her to bring something in her other hand. He not only wanted something to drink but also something to eat. To her consternation, the man was demanding her last morsel of bread. It was this demand for the last morsel that revealed that she was in fact doing the death dance in the gathering of sticks. In a real sense, if she were able to respond to the demands of the prophet, it would have to be a miracle, which brings us to the next point – doing an act in faith.

Doing an Act in Faith

Like the widow of Zar'ephath, the third challenge was that of having to decide how to prioritise resources. The demand for the last morsel created an ethical dilemma for the widow. Whose need should take pre-eminence? What was to be her priority? The expectation of the prophet, together with the social pressure of deference to the aged suggested that she should take care of his need first. Her instinct as a mother told her that the need of her child couldn't be sidestepped. What was she going to do? The ethical challenge that the widow faced was to do something in faith. She could not spend the whole time deciding and assessing the situation. She did not have the luxury of setting up a task force to study the situation. It was not the moment to do a feasibility study. The urgency of the situation was that she had to do something now. The moment required an action in faith. We say acting in faith because she did not know where the resources would come from to do what she wanted to do. She hoped in the promise and the assurance from the man of God. It was a judgement call. She chose to act in faith and gave out her last morsel to the one who made the more passionate plea.

We thank God for those who have acted in faith with very limited resources at their disposal. We thank God for those teachers who believed in the potential of certain students and gave them the extra help, even when they were tired at the end of the day. We thank God for those teachers who hoped for a day when the community and the support of parents would make a real difference in the life of the school and spent their energies in faith, even when their families demanded their time and attention. There are those teachers who sacrificed to improve their own competence, from very little resources, not expecting to be rewarded with any significant pay increase but because they wanted to be in a better position to help their students. That is what we call acting in faith.

As it was for the widow of Zarephath so it is with schools in situations of scarcity. The challenge is to make a difference in the face of death and desperation; to rise to the demands and the expectations of her social context; to decide about how the limited resources would be apportioned and to do something in faith and hope for a miracle.

CHAPTER 10

A Happy Life –
For School Leavers

*Happy are those who do not follow the advice of
the wicked, or take the path that sinners tread,
or sit in the seat of scoffers;* [Psalm 1:1]

Introduction

There are a number of developmental tasks that we have to perform in growing up. Our happiness and sense of personal accomplishment are related to how successfully we make these transitions. One of those transitional moments is leaving secondary school. It is not only transition to 3rd level education but also transition to adult working life. Let us reflect a little on the school leaving moment. It is a reminder that the young people, who were toddlers only yesterday, are getting older and are getting closer and closer to the point where they must face all the challenges of adult life. That is not to say that some of them have not already begun to do so. One of the sad features of being young is when the young get old too quickly. Some children are forced prematurely into adulthood either by the way they treat their own bodies (for example by the abuse of drugs), by the hardships their families and the society impose on them, or by adults taking advantage of them.

Navigating the uncertain waters of today's world requires guidance from those who have gone this way before. The challenges that today's school leavers will face are not the same that those of a generation ago had to face. A generation ago, we were not preoccupied with text messages, e-mails and cellular phones. We did not have the internet; we did not know of HIV/AIDS. School leavers a generation ago would cringe when they heard of people being chopped to death or being shot to death. Those graduates did not know of the drug mules that swallow little sachets in Jamaica to give birth to cocaine in New York or London a few hours later. So the challenges were different. Despite these differences, though, those who have already faced the challenges of adulthood should count it a privilege, if not a duty, to share their experiences with the young for whatever it is worth. You might be an adult who have young people close to you who will sometime soon make this transition. Or, you might be a young adult about to leave school or who left school recently. If I can keep your attention for a little longer, and even at the risk of sounding paternalistic, I would like to offer some things for consideration from my insight into Psalm 1. It is an offer – accept it if you will, leave it if you will. No hard feelings!

Towards a Happy Life

I suspect that, like most people, you are interested in the happy life. What is the point of life anyway if it is unhappy from start to finish? Note that I did not say a trouble-free life. Note that I did not say a life free from hardships, difficulties and struggles. The happy life comes amidst the struggle to overcome the hardships, surviving the difficulties and avoiding the troubles. The happy life requires that we also make some tough decisions, for example that you will recognise and reject the advice that is contrary to your best interest. This assertion comes from Psalm 1 where the writer says, among other things, that happy is the person who does not walk in the counsel of the ungodly. By ungodly the Bible does not mean an atheist. In fact, the only allusion to atheism we have in the Bible is Psalm 14:1 – "the fool says in his hear there is no God." However, the Bible makes a clear distinction between the ungodly and the fool. The ungodly is no fool. The writer in Psalm 1 is not concerned about the fool. He is concerned about the advice that the ungodly gives – that is the person to watch; it is the advice of the ungodly person we must reject. Why does the Bible take such a radical position in relation to the ungodly?

Be Suspicious of the Ungodly

With a closer reading of the passage we get an idea of why we need to be suspicious of the advice of the ungodly. It compares the lot of the godly with that of the ungodly. According to the Bible the godly person has his roots firmly planted in the ground. The ungodly are not planted beside the rivers, thus ensuring that they are properly nourished. The lack of proper nourishment in the inner person means that the ungodly are barren. They do not produce fruit when the moment requires it and the things they produce do not last. The ungodly does not have good examples of success that people can follow. Moreover, when their deeds are placed under close scrutiny they do not stand the test. And so, the Bible says of them, they are like the thrash from the wheat, the chaff, which the wind blows away. They are the excess that serves no real purpose, except to give you work to clear them away. Such people are a burden to the spirit and must be avoided at all cost. Do not take the advice of such persons.

You will notice then that the graduate who takes my advice has also the task of giving careful scrutiny to the person who comes along with a suggestion about what they can do for them. In short, we must be suspicious and critical. And the advice I am giving you here should not be excluded. One weakness many young people have is that they are gullible, meaning that they accept everything they hear. This gullibility has led many into premature pregnancy, drug addiction and prison because some person comes along with many promises of good. We must maintain a level of suspicion about whatever we read and whatever we hear. Subject the message and the messenger to careful scrutiny. It is this due process of scrutiny that will expose the flaws and the ungodly nature of the counsel you receive. In another place the Bible also says, "Test the spirit".

The ungodly person is one who knows the will of God but deliberately gives advice to the contrary. A good example of this ungodly counsel is the advice that Job received when he was in a desperate situation. Job fell on hard times. He was a man of means and uprightness. He was respected for his material wealth as well as for his spiritual goods. Sadly, though, disaster struck. This is important to note. Disaster can come to anyone. His children died, his house was destroyed and he lost all his livestock. He was under the attack of the evil one. When his wife saw his condition she felt it was an embarrassment to his faith. In her view, there was nothing more worth living for, because she saw no way out of the pit of desperation in which he had slipped. Her advice to him was that he should curse God and die. She knew nothing of the counsel that God's strength is made perfect in our weakness. She never heard it said, "I am with you even to the close of the age." She did not hear the words of the songwriter, who said:

Where the many toil together, there am I among my own
Where the tired workman sleepeth, there am I with him alone.
I the peace that passeth knowledge, dwell amidst the daily strife
I the bread of heaven am broken in the sacrament of life.

She did not hear the words of the songwriter, who said,

Thy way not mine O lord, however dark it be
Lead me by thine own hand chose out the path for me
Smooth let it be our rough; it will be still the best
Winding or straight it leads, right onward to thy rest

Her counsel was a counsel of desperation. In effect she was asking him to denounce the truth he knew. She was in effect asking him to trample down and leave behind the principles of righteousness and justice that he was taught. She was saying to Job as if speaking to you, deal dishonestly, and deal deceitfully. Her position, which is the temptation this generation of school leavers face, was that we should yield to no authority beside our own. In her view, we should declare ourselves accountable to no one but ourselves – curse God and die. Be suspicious of this kind of counsel, even from someone who is close to you. When you find someone who advises you to act contrary to your conscience and convictions you must be suspicious. When you meet someone who would have you sacrifice the principles of honesty and fair play, be careful, it is a bad sign. When you meet someone who makes the argument that you can twist the truth; that you do not have to give account for your actions blow them away for they are only trouble. When you meet someone who believes that there is no God, who claims that hard work is a curse, do not make that person your companion.

Those people, then, who want you to turn your back on parents, on truth, on godliness, who want you to turn away from righteousness; those people who are not properly grounded, who produce nothing that can be held up as an example, if you desire happiness mark their advice as ungodly and stay clear of them. For as scripture says, they are like the excess thrash, the chaff that the wind blows away, they cannot stand up to scrutiny and happy is the person who does not walk in their counsel; they are the ungodly. Look out for them and reject their advice and this will give a good basis on which to assess what might be in your interest and the way to a happy life.

CHAPTER 11

Emancipation Day

So, if you have been raised with Christ, seek the things
that are above, where Christ is, seated at the right
hand of God. Set your minds on things that are above,
not on things on the earth. [Colossians 3:1-2]

Introduction

Slaves were formally set free in the Caribbean and the Americas in 1834 but the reality of captivity remains, not only for their offspring but also for offspring of former slave-owners. This is so because enslavement is not only a physical structure that sets limits on the rights of the economically weak but also a condition of the mind, which is not peculiar to any group of people. We are hindered by unjust structures that benefit some and disadvantage others as much as we are hindered by our mental state. The Reggae singer Bob Marley preserves this insight in one of his songs: "Emancipate yourself from mental slavery, none but ourselves can free our minds." Through the Biblical witness, we learn that it is possible to be enslaved not only by the political systems of the world, but also by our thinking and attitudes. Readers of the Bible will find that the theme of emancipation is used frequently throughout Scripture. In the OT, we find the theme in the story of the Exodus and in the NT it subsists in the idea of the resurrection. In Colossians 3 the challenge of living a resurrected life is presented as an analogy of being set free. Liberation is seeking after the things of Christ, and the setting of our affections on heavenly ideals. There is, then, a biblical imperative to be set free from those things and systems that enslave us. So, emancipation is not only about the dismantling of the political, social and economic shackles, which hold us down. It is also the inculcation of the tendencies and dispositions of a free and empowered life. Observing Emancipation Day, then, is to remember. In remembering we call to mind the fact that for well over one hundred years, Africans were transported to the Caribbean and the Americas to be used as forced labourers in the sugar plantations of what was then a British Colony. The Africans were forced from their homes and would be killed if they did not show willingness to work against their will.

The Ethics of Business!

The conspiracy to purchase and sell human beings was made possible by two factors. On one hand there were the traders, mostly but not only from England who, like the drug traders today, could not care less about the effect their trade was having on families. And why would they? They did not consider that these beings were human beings in the same sense in which white Europeans were human beings. It was an opportunity to make money; it was filling a demand, so it was business and so it was acceptable. As it was then so it is for the most part now, people are not appreciated when they raise ethical questions about the nature of business. It was not the first time entrepreneurs from the metropolitan areas of the world invaded and raped the resources of a region. In those days they raped the human resources; today they are raping the mineral deposits. If it were not the case that there was such a large deposit of oil in Iraq, then there would not have been a war for the flimsy reasons that were concocted by the Americans and the British. So it was the unethical and insensitive, greedy and wicked trader, on the one hand, which made the traffic of human beings possible.

On the other hand, though, there were the greedy tribal leaders in Africa, who sold their brothers and sisters. This was business! In much the same way today, young women and children are being sold in the prostitution trade, which is more extensive in Asia but from reports is also present in many Caribbean and European countries. There was an unwillingness to protect the members of the tribe, so they were exposed and families were disrupted and broken up. Maureen Warner Lewis in her book *Archibald Monteith: Igbo, Jamaican, Moravian,* reflects on what the impact of Aniaso's capture might have had on his family:

To have kidnapped the only son of a family was a dastardly act. As his father's heir, Aniaso's abduction rendered his family not only bereft of one of its younger generation, but also bereft of a future lineage head. Furthermore, the implications for Aniaso's mother were not only emotional but status-related as well, for the boy's removal is likely to have increased the possibility of his father taking another wife in order to improve the chances of male succession. In this connection, one wonders whether this act was not political and intended to belittle the family: there may have been jealousy or inter-clan rivalry between the captor's family and Aniaso's parentage, some intrigue of which the little boy was unaware.[7]

Can you imagine the heart-rending cries of those who knew they would never see their loved ones again? No wonder many jumped overboard, preferring to die than to face the indignity of slavery. It was for this reason that from the very start there were rebellions and revolts, which eventually erupted in the great rebellion of the 1820's.

When we speak of emancipation, then, we must not forget the experiences of our African forebears because we are their posterity. If we forget their experiences, we are more likely to be re-enslaved. Indeed, the struggles we have with crime, with drugs, with the economy; the trials we face, as we seek to overcome our own sinful and wicked tendencies; the struggles to build communities of hope result from the fact that we still need to free ourselves from some lingering shackles. So the message of emancipation, together with its challenges and privileges, are as true today as they were in 1834.

Duty of the Emancipated

Slavery is a system in which we are not free to follow the dictates of our convictions. In a situation of enslavement, we are not free to follow God; we are not free to worship. We are not free to be ourselves. Emancipation is the removal of the organisational rules that support the system of enslavement. However, when that is done, the individual must operate with the new rules. This is where we have problems. After a long night of enslavement, people do not readily walk to the open door on liberation morning. After a long period of powerlessness, we must learn to live as free people, who are truly empowered. According to Colossians, emancipated people have duties to perform, which will show that they are truly set free. This is the force of the "**if**" in Col 1:1. It is not a question of whether or not the situation exists; it is not a question of whether or not emancipation has come. It is not a question of whether Christ has been raised from the dead. The usage of the word is to be understood in the sense of an actual state of affairs. The word "if" could be translated **"since,"** which would imply, "You have been set free!" "You have been emancipated!" You are no longer slaves because Christ has been raised from the dead. The use of 'if' here reminds us of the challenge that Satan put to Jesus in the account we find in Matt 4:6, "If you are the Son of God…" The duty of the emancipated is derived from the fact of emancipation. Emancipated people must seek after the ideals of emancipation. This principle can be illustrated by reference to people who suffer from substance addiction. Once the addict begins to gain some mastery over the addiction, he must strive hard not to re-surrender his will. This will mean not only avoiding the substance but also staying clear of the situations in which the balance of power to resist the urge would not be in his favour. People trying to quit smoking may use the nicotine patch as a help to make the full transition. The aspiration at all times is to be fully free and so the ethical and moral decisions are meant to reinforce this. It is another way to say that the emancipated must set their affections on high things. In other words, emancipated people must become preoccupied with holy ambitions.

Holy Ambitions

Some people will naturally think of heaven when we speak of setting affections on things above. However, this is neither a licence for us to live with our heads in the clouds nor that we should imagine that this is a justification to be unconcerned about the experiences that people are having on a day to day basis – that is, things below. Years under tyranny sometimes restrict people in their drive to the full exercise of their freedom. Therefore, people who no longer need to live under the tyranny of a system of slavery, sometimes falter in their will to aspire for another ideal – the holy things, so to speak. This lack of drive for high ideals is often evidenced when they come upon problems in a new situation. A good biblical example of this is when the people who were set free from Egypt longed for the flesh pots of Egypt (Exodus 16:3) when they ran into difficulty in the wilderness. They preferred death at the hand of their slave masters than the struggles of emancipation.

One of the holy ambitions, which we must earnestly seek, is the freedom from the thinking and the values of the slave-master. The challenge is to be ambitious for a different frame of reference. According to Colossians 3, we must seek the things that are above, where Christ is. In other words, seek to operate in the frame of reference in which Christ operates; seek the values of Christ. Rely on the Spirit on which Christ relied. Seek the empowerment of the Spirit of God. If the Spirit of God who raised Jesus from the dead dwells in you, God shall also quicken your mortal bodies. It is probably true to say that we are more likely to achieve the things on which we set our affections because we will strive more earnestly for them. This is the truism of the statement, "Be careful for what you wish because you will certainly have it." The idea is that if you are going to develop a strong desire then you should desire the divine and eternal things of God. An earnest prayer of mine is that God will create in me the love for the things of God; that my desire will be after holy things. For I know and have seen the destruction that follows lusting after the things of earth, which grow dim and lose their value.

This idea of being ambitious for holy things finds its application in the social life of our country and our world. When we see the widespread violence in our country we have to ask whether non-violence is a serious ambition. It is not good enough for us to wish for peace we must pursue the things that make for peace. If there is a serious ambition for peace and if peace is to take root it requires the prepared garden of programmes and people, with the commitment of resources over a period of time. The place in which violence grows is one that suffers from lack of attention and poor husbandry. It is hard and fallow. Therefore careful and timely nourishment is needed for peace to come to fruition in such a place. We must challenge out fellow citizens not to allow the callousness of the time in which we live to kill the love for life and the ambition for peace, which God has placed so deeply in our minds and hearts. We therefore need the affection for justice as much as we need the ambition for peace. The vale of tears and violence is crying out for the affection of industry and investment and our churches need the affection for sinners and their salvation.

Conclusion

These reflections come at a time when many regions of the world are in turmoil and when, with a few exceptions, there is a dearth of political will to embrace peace. It must strike us as one of the greatest travesty of justice and peace that certain nations in the Middle East are supported and allowed to be so reckless in their policy towards their neighbours. It is clear that there is no ambition for peace. Enslavement and years of reliance on war has anaesthetized these leaders against the possibility of peace growing. To be emancipated then is to develop an ambition and to aspire for things beyond captivity – a new land, a new paradigm, things above, where Jesus is. Those who are emancipated must consider it as a duty to entertain holy ambitions and to set their affections in the highest place.

We place you at the highest place
For your are the great high priest
We place you high above all else
And we worship at your feet.
Ron Kenoly Lyrics

CHAPTER 12

Digging Deeper - Recovering Evangelistic Passion

The words of Jeremiah son of Hilkiah... to whom the
word of the Lord came in the days of King Josiah... in
the thirtieth year of his reign. [Jeremiah 1:1-2]

Introduction

In August 2004, a large number of Moravians from all over Jamaica came together at the Kendal Conference Centre, Manchester, Jamaica, to reflect on the evangelistic and missionary responsibilities that faced the church at that time. Being the year in which the Moravian Church in Jamaica was marking 250 years of witness in Jamaica, it was appropriate that there would have been some reflection of the Moravian heritage and its ongoing relevance for the Jamaican society. Using the theme, *Tapping the Resources bequeathed to us in Christ* the organizers threw out the challenge for us to give serious consideration to what gifts the present generation has received and the use to which these have been put for the further, credible witness of the gospel. This was an important call for the church of the day, recognizing its accountability to God, the forebears and the future generations, to pause and to think carefully about what it was doing. In this regard the Moravians in Jamaica were seeking to live up to an aspect of their heritage, the sense of call to evangelistic witness, which was the motivation for the commencement of the 18th century missionary movement in which they led the way.

Speaking of the impulse and commitment to evangelistic witness among the early Moravians, David Bosch said, "ordinary men and women, most of them simple artisans, went literally to the ends of the earth, devoted themselves for life, to people often living in degrading circumstances, identified with them, and lived the gospel in their midst."[8]

Throwing out this kind of challenge for us to think about the resources given to us in Christ is not unique to the Moravians but is an example of the kind of reflection that must take place in every church community. However, the reflection is really meaningless if it does not lead to a revision of work where a serious failure of responsibility is recognized. When I consider the idea of tapping into the resources given to us in Christ, the first thing that comes to my mind is the need to locate a source – that is, the place from which the resources come. Reflecting a little further, I came to the conclusion that the resources given to us in Christ and the knowledge of those resources are preserved for us in the faith of the church and in the Bible, as the word of God. The call to tap into those resources, then, is really a challenge to dig deeper into the faith of the church through the ages and to dig deeper into the word of God, to find those resources that can sustain us in these days.

The Biblical Resources

I am convinced that in the Christian tradition in general and in the Bible in particular, there are critical resources – but we have to search to find them, hence the topic of *Digging Deeper*. One way to read the theme is that it was seeking to bring the faith of the church and the word of God to centre stage, so that our nation, our church, the aged and the not so old, the young and the not so young, might be preoccupied with those things that can sustain our lives in these days. This is important because we must admit that there are certain preoccupations that have failed to sustain the well-being of our people. At this time, we are a nation preoccupied with the lure of gambling, guns and the GSM (Global Systems for Mobile phones) network. They all drain our resources; they all operate on questionable ethical principles of profit. The task we have then is to find credible resources for our time. We need to find resources that can provide an alternative to communities overtaken by violence; credible, sustainable alternatives for those who have lost hope.

In order to find these alternatives we must search, we must dig. Dig in the tradition of the Christian faith. Dig in the word of God. So, the exercise in which we are involved now is a digging exercise. The imagery is nicely captured for us in the story of Isaac in Genesis 26:18, where Isaac dug again the well that his father Abraham dug. The Philistines had stopped the well, thus causing a serious water crisis. For when there is no reliable source of water, when there is no well springing up, there will be a crisis. Today we face a crisis because of our preoccupations and because of other powers at work in the society, which taken together are starving us. We are longing for nourishment and refreshment and we thirst for righteousness and peace. It does not matter who has closed the wells needed for our refreshment- it may be the Philistines within our country or it may be those from outside; because we can say assuredly that though some of the difficulties we face are self-inflicted, others are beyond our control. We live in a globalized world in which it is hard to insulate ourselves from the happenings overseas – America sneezed and Europe caught the financial cold. It hardly matters now, then, who is primarily responsible for blocking access to critical resources. With a crisis before us we don't have the luxury of time to give priority to apportioning blame - we will come to that in time. The ethical imperative is to first address the crisis by clearing the blockade. However, if there is a crisis in our land, if there is a crisis in our church, if there is a spiritual crisis in our time, it is related to a refusal or a failure to tap into our resources; it is related to a failure to dig.

So the resources bequeathed to us in Christ are preserved in the faith of the church and in the word of God. I want to challenge you to make digging for the resources a priority. Ministers and leaders have a duty and privilege to lead this digging but everyone needs to dig. For its part, the Moravian Church in Jamaica must ask about the resources that have preserved the witness of the Church for over 250 years. After 250 years, the original three persons became thirty thousands. Now there is a desire, a longing, and an impatience for that witness to get stronger. Can 30,000 become 300,000? We want to tap into those resources that will enable us to fulfil this longing. So dig we must.

God's word and Human Words

We shall start digging at Jeremiah 1:4. No sooner than we tuck in, there emerges something important about the ground in which we have thrown ourselves. The immediate discovery that we make concerns the character of the word of God. The text here in Jeremiah is very deliberate in putting before us not only what the word of God is but also what it is not. First we notice that there is a distinction made between human (Jeremiah's) words and the word of God. We say there is a distinction because whereas verse 1 speaks about the words of Jeremiah, verse 2 speaks about the word of God. This is a curious discovery because the prophets are usually the ones whom we associate with speaking the word of the Lord. The fact is that it is not necessarily the case that the word of the prophet is the word of the Lord. No doubt the prophet is relieved that this is the case and so it should be for anyone who has the privilege of saying, "Thus says the Lord." Although it might fall to us to have to say that, we know that God's thoughts are higher than our thoughts, as that Psalmist declares, and God's ways are not our ways, so our words are different from God's word.

With this awareness you can appreciate why Bishop Desmond Tutu had to say to the President of apartheid South Africa, "Mr President, you are not God." You might have to say that to the pastor or to the Prime minister, to the police or to your partner – remember that you are not God, so don't expect me to treat your words as the word of God.

Recognising that we should not confuse human words with the word of God is important also because we live in a time of much speaking, which accentuates the difficulty of discerning the speakers and on whose behalf they speak. The advancement of communication technology will go down as one of the more important developments in this century and people are making good use of it to make their opinions heard. This must not be seen as a disaster but it adds to the task of discernment because ordinary, unknown people are contending to be heard and the irony is that often what they have to say is much more important that well-known people.

John Amos Comenius, one of the Moravian forebears, cautions us about refusing to listen to others – even people of other faiths. To refuse to listen to others is, in effect, to tie the hand of God by insisting through whom he should speak. At the same time it does not mean that those who control the airwaves and who have the power to be heard have greater command of truth. In fact, the contrary is often the case because those who find it necessary to monopolize what you must read and what you must hear in the media seem to have something to hide. Let us remember then that because it is written in a book or the newspaper or because it is broadcast on radio, TV or the internet that does not make it truth and certainly that does not make it the word of God. This digging exercise is an exercise of discernment and we must be careful how we dig. Digging and discerning are important if the Christian is to declare, "Thus says the Lord." So we must dig and discern before we declare.

The word as an event

When we start digging in the Bible for resources we find out not only that the word of God appears as something separate from human words but also that the word of the Lord is not empty. Human words can be empty since we are not always able to back up what we say. Our selfishness, boastfulness and insincerity mean that we sometimes tell untruths and make claims that we cannot substantiate. However, the word of God is never empty because, as the prophet Jeremiah himself also affirms, *"the Lord watches over his word to perform it."* [Jeremiah

1:12] We can trust the promises in the word of the Lord because, as the saints of old testify in 1Kings 8:56, *not a single word of the good promise of the Lord has failed.* It is this trustworthiness of the word of the Lord that underlies that well- known passage in Isaiah 55:10-11: *"As the rains come down and water the ground and cause it to bring forth and bud, so shall be the word of the Lord that goes out from the mouth of the Lord. It shall not return empty but shall accomplish what pleases the Lord and shall proper where the Lord has sent it."* Of course it is not all the time that human words are empty. We say, "Sticks and stones may break my bones but words cannot harm me," but that is not true all the time. Our words can have an effect on people. If you tell your child long enough that he is a fool he may soon become one. We make predictions and we speculate and sometimes our words bring things to pass. For example, the words of IMF (International Monetary Fund) can cause the stock exchange to worsen or improve. When the rating agencies make a comment on the economy, it can affect the decisions people make about investing in the country. The human words we hear can affect what we see and how we understand things. Even our mood is affected by the words of others. That is why the psychologists warn us about what we say of ourselves – we must not speak certain things into being because words have creative power. So it is clear that both human words and divine words have creative power. The difference is that human words can be empty and come to nothing but the word of the Lord is never empty, because the Lord watches over his word to perform it.

So the minute we start to dig for resources in the Bible, we find that the Bible makes a distinction between human words and the word of God. Though both have creative powers, only the word of God is never empty, as is sometimes the case with human words.

We should not imagine that the word of the Lord is just sound or letters because we find that the word of the Lord is **also an event,** like a visitation. If you check the Bible carefully, you will find that the expression the "word of the Lord" appears some 240 plus times in the OT alone, most of which refer to a moment in the life of a prophet. Of those references, in at least 123 times it says the word came to such and such a person at such and such a time. For example, we are told in Jeremiah 1:2 that the word of the Lord "came" during the 13th year of Josiah's reign. In 1:3 it came in a period from the days of Jehoiakim to the 11th year of Zedekiah and to the 5th month of the captivity of Jerusalem. In 1:4, Jeremiah says, it came unto me. To get the sense of this visitation of the word of God, we have to think, for example of the visit of the angels to Abraham (Gen18) and Lot (Gen19). The incident with Abraham is particularly noteworthy **(See Gen 18:19)**. The point of the visit was that the Lord might reveal to Abraham what he was about to do. More importantly, it was the intention of the Lord to bring to pass what he had spoken to Abraham. In other words, the Lord visited because he was watching over his word to perform it. This is the point also with the visit of the angel to Zechariah and to Mary in the NT. The visit to Zechariah we are told in Luke 1:13, was that his prayer had been heard. The angel was present to perform the word of the Lord. The word to Mary was that she had found favour with God. Consequently, the Lord was present to perform his word. If Zechariah or Mary were reporting on this visit, in the manner in which Jeremiah was speaking, they would say, "The word of the Lord came to me saying."

When we can see that the word of God is not just words, it is easier for us to appreciate the idea of the word of God becoming a human being. According to John, the word that was in the beginning and by which the world was created, became flesh, a human being that we could see. In Jesus a human being is the word of God. In him we have supreme access to the promises of God. This is an important resource that we find in Christ. The point I am making then is that when Jeremiah says, "the word of the Lord came to me", he was not just speaking of the words he may have heard. The word of the Lord was the event of the visitation. The Lord does not need words to make his word known. That is why Amos 1:2 says, the Lord will roar from Zion, the shepherds will mourn and the mountains will melt.

The Power of God's Word

Jeremiah understood from the visitation of the word of the Lord, which came at a particular junction in history, that God was enabling him to overcome his weaknesses, inhibitions and fears. That word was necessary for that time and that place. He received from God the assurance that he, Jeremiah, was not a "nobody". How could he be a nobody when he was known before he was conceived? How he could be a nobody when God ordained and sanctified him before he was born? The threat of "nobodyness" became a reality for the land of Israel and Judah, which moved from the secure days of Josiah to the uncertain days of the exile. Things started to go downhill after the death of Josiah (See II Chron 35:25). Jeremiah was greatly distressed at the death of the king. After Josiah's reign Israel became a vassal state of Egypt and then of Babylon, by which the Northern Kingdom was eventually destroyed and sacred vessels of the temple along with leaders were transported to Babylon. You can then appreciate the feeling of "nobodyness" that overtook Jeremiah, who was persecuted, mocked and jeered. It was during the desolation of the exile that the people began to think that they were nothing.

The threat of "nobodyness" is also a real threat today. It is not just the fear of being unimportant; it is also the fear of being non-existent – a nothing, a zero. It is the fear of being without worth. It is a fear of being an excess - the idea that I am only refuse. In many places in the world today, we not only have the fear but also the reality nothingness. It is the reality of "nobodyness" that fuels the machines of death, which work so well in the inner city areas of many countries – from New York to Kingston & Spanish Town, to Rio, to Johannesburg. Can you imagine the horror if there were transparent morgues in which bodies of the men and women killed in our cities were placed? Imagine the repulsion if the bodies were piled up so that we could see the effect of the death machine in stark pictures. Maybe it is only at that time that we would be face to face with the nothingness and "nobodyness", which thrives in our society. How do we get it into the head of those who take the lives of others with such consummate ease that each life is precious to God and should be honoured, respected and treasured? We are something! We aren't nothing! How do we convince those who put no value on their life that everyone's life is precious to God? You are not a nobody you are somebody. The word of the Lord is a hedge against that threat. The word is that God knew you before you even came into existence. If the Lord were able to engage the reality of your existence before you were conceived, then how much more now that you are conceived and born into the world? One thing is clear, you are important to God; you are not an after thought, you are not a nothing, and you are not a nobody.

A Threat Facing the Church

If the people of God live under the threat of nothingness and "nobodyness", it inhibits confidence and prevents growth. When churches experience decades of stagnation it is a temptation to ask whether it is because that church is a "nothing". This is the case with many of the historic churches, for example, the Church of Ireland (Anglican) which, until 2002, did not record a net numerical increase in membership for over 100 years. It is a sort of dilemma when a church has been in existence for over 500 years and in a small country for over 250 years and yet many people in that country know nothing about it. The tendency then is to blame the former generations that they did not do enough to promote the work of the church and expand its witness. The dilemma is whether more time should be spent promoting the ministry or should the energy be focused on doing those little things that can be done well but will not be widely known. The threat of "nobodyness" sometimes inhibits our willingness even to give time, money and energy freely for the work of the Church. The consolation is that although your church is not known that does not constitute "nobodyness". God knows you and God knows your church – even before you or your church came into existence.

This is what we discover when we dig in the Bible. We encounter the word of God and discover that the word of the Lord is distinct from human words. Human words are sometimes empty but the word of the Lord is never empty because the Lord watches over his word to perform it. We discover that the word of the Lord is not just words but an event, a visitation. Jeremiah found that the word of the Lord was also a hedge again the threat of "nobodyness", which was occasioned by the exile. That threat is a reality in our society and the church. However, you should know that God knows you; you are of worth; you are not a nobody. In order then to tap into the resources available through Christ, we must dig. Dig in the Old Testament. Dig in the New Testament. Dig in the Christian tradition. Dig, discern and declare. So when they ask you what are you doing with the Bible, say to them that you are going to dig. We need to discover afresh the resources bequeathed in Christ, which are kept for us in the Bible and in the faith of the Church through the ages.

CHAPTER 13

Taking a Stance

"To him who loves us and freed us from our sins by his blood, and made us to be a kingdom, priests serving his God and Father, to him be the glory and the dominion for ever and ever. Amen" Revelation 1:5-6

Introduction

One of the challenges church leaders face from time to time is how to respond to the issue of the day in a manner that leaves no uncertainty in the mind of the public about what the position of the church is. For example, when the executive committees of the councils of Churches meet, one of the questions often contemplated in the discussion on national issues is, "What statement can we make?" Often the statement is made more effectively by an act rather than by words. For example, if the church leaders were to join in a demonstration of workers at the ministry of finance, which is set to cut expenditure in the public sector, that would be a statement. There are numerous instances of Christians acting courageously under serious threats to their personal lives: the confessional church in Germany during the Hitler regime; the black churches in the United States during the civil rights movement of the 1960's; the churches in South Africa during the struggles against apartheid in the 1970's; Christians in Central and South America in the struggles against poverty in the

1980's and so on. These Christians not only participated in courageous prophetic actions but they also made sure that their worship services reflected the statement that they made in public action. The liturgies and celebrations, therefore, were not benign events but in them they were making a call to serious commitment. They were seeking to worship in a manner consistent with their convictions.

If the religious gathering we attend is to be more that some simple gesture, if it is to be more that just a tradition, then we must consider its meaning for life on the street today and tomorrow. When the church takes time out to gather for any event, be it a regular weekly service or a special service, it is a commitment to making a statement and not just an occasional gimmick to raise more money. What then is it that you would like to say to the world? I would hope that you do not participate in your next religious gathering under some notion of just participating. Each gathering is with a purpose and has potency. When we consciously reflect on it we come to the view that we must chose consciously because we need a certain amount of courage to participate in them. We choose to participate so that we can be part of what is said. Being part of the statement means we are the words and the punctuation. We are the text and context and the building and benches are the pages on which the pronouncement is written. In your next religious gathering you should be clear about the statement you make and what the words actually mean.

Whose Dominion is this?

Imagine a religious gathering in which the text in Revelation 1:6 is read. In this verse an assertion is made about something that belongs to God: *"to [God] be glory and dominion for ever and ever."* Dominion here is to be understood as rule, power or sovereignty. However, to say that the rule and power belong to God we are immediately faced with two challenges. The first is that Scripture also speaks of human beings as having dominion over the living things on the earth. In Genesis 1: 26 God said of the humans he created: *"Let them have dominion over the fish of the sea, and over the birds of the air, and over the cattle, and over all the wild animals of the earth, and over every creeping thing that creeps upon the earth"* [Gen 1:26] Similarly, in the post-flood blessing on Noah, God declares: *"The fear and dread of you shall rest on every animal of the earth, and on every bird of the air, on everything that creeps on the ground and on all the fish of the sea; into your hand they are delivered.* [Gen 9:2]. The Psalmist spoke in similar terms: *"What are human beings that you are mindful of them, mortals that you care for them? Yet you have… crowned them with glory and honour. You have given them dominion over the works of your hands; you have put all things under their feet."* [Psalm 8:4-6] If then power and dominion are given to the human being who, in any case, we see leading the nations and power structures of the world, in what sense does the power and dominion belong also to God. This is a biblical challenge and in that sense it is internal and peculiar to the community of faith that affirms the authority of all scripture.

The second challenge is not unlike the first but it is external to the faith community. In this modern age, even where people are prepared to acknowledge God as creator, they generally do not see God as having any right to glory and dominion – not over the earth and certainly not over their lives. For many, to speak of God as having dominion is to surrender their right to be responsible and accountable to themselves. In his book entitled *The Legitimacy of the Modern Age*, Hans Blumenberg argued that in the age of reason and rationality the human being came to realise that he was abandoned by God and was made responsible for himself. According to Blumenberg, when the human being came to this realisation of being accountable to himself alone, he did not express disappointment but rather celebrated the fact that he was "awakened from his cosmic illusion." In other words, only those who are still in their cosmic slumber will want to say, "To God be glory and dominion".

Faced with these two challenges, it is not easy to say in the hearing of others that the glory and the dominion belong to God. On one hand we must resolve the problem of interpretation in which God, to whom we ascribe glory and dominion, speaks of having given that dominion to the human being. On the other hand we have the problem where, even though God's existence is affirmed, there is no necessary acknowledgement of accountability to God. So what could it possibly mean to say that the glory and the dominion belong to God?

A Statement of Accountability

I want to suggest that despite the difficulty there is to say, "To God be the glory and the dominion", it is possible to say so with confidence and it is an important affirmation to make. The first way in which we can understand this statement is that it is a statement of ultimate accountability. To say that the glory and the dominion belong to God is not simply to return favour to God, who in the first place gave glory and dominion to the human being. The truth is we often behave as if we are doing God a favour.

For example, when as members we see our church activities as ends in themselves, we might be tempted to think that we are doing God a favour because others see us as doing the church a favour. When we have to ask people for their financial support, or when we have to plead with people to use their talents and training to further the witness of the church; when it does not come naturally to the church member that his or her allegiance is to the Lamb of God, it is possible to think that we are doing God a favour. But this is not the meaning of the affirmation that the glory and the dominion belong to God. Rather, it means that we recognise that whatever we have in terms of power, and influence arising from our material possession or technical expertise, whatever glory we receive from our work, whatever authority we have from our experience in life or experience in our vocation, it is due to God to whom all glory and dominion belong. To affirm that the glory and dominion belong to God is to insist that contrary to the cynical person we have not been abandoned by God because our God is *Jehovah Jireh*, our provider.

I am contending that the loss of the sense of accountability to God in the high Middle Ages, of which Blumenberg speaks, signaled the rise of the modern age. It was the thin edge of the wedge of the eventual loss of accountability to fellow human beings. It is an uplifted sense of self and blindness to the God, to whom we are accountable, which lies behind the wanton loss of lives that we have come to see in so many nations of the world. It is the loss of a sense of accountability to God that pervades the thinking of leaders for whom the death of the innocent in places like Iraq and Palestine are treated simply as the unavoidable consequence of a war. It is the loss of a sense of accountability to God why the political and financial affairs of many countries are treated as projects for personal gratification. Many countries, especially in the third world, are heavily indebted and are fast losing their capacity to borrow. In many inner cities large sections of the population live in squalor and the conditions reek with the stench of disaster. Why must so many people live in such squalid conditions? Does it have to be that way? I contend that it is all possible because of the loss of that sense of accountability. The conditions are this way because individuals in positions of power ascribe to themselves and the dominion to their cronies. Therefore when we today ascribe the power and the glory to God it is to undermine the claim to glory and dominion that ruins rather than empowers the lives of others. An affirmation as this is radical because it takes back power and wrests dominion from those who have misused their God-given capacities and opportunities.

When we affirm then, that glory and dominion belong to God it is to insist that we will not seek the glory for ourselves. It is to affirm that we will not seek to dominate the lives of others. We do not claim by this that what we have today is simply the result of our hard work and that people who have nothing are lazy (which is not to say there aren't lazy people). Rather it is to recognise that we have experienced the grace of God. Our children have experienced the grace of God. God has been good to me because I cannot claim ultimate responsibility for all that I have. In short, I am accountable to God. Let it not be imagined that to hold ourselves accountable to God is some kind of infantile or fanatical position. Rather it is mature, robust and courageous because is cuts across the grain of tendencies in modern society. It is a deep sense of accountability that will inform our environmental practices, out financial and monetary policies, as well as our personal moral and ethical conduct. Where this sense of accountability is absent the result is ruined lives, ruined homes, ruined communities and ruined countries.

A Statement of Accusation

To say that the glory and the dominion belong to God is not only a statement of accountability but is also a statement of accusation. In fact, by being a statement of accountability it becomes a statement of accusation. Once again I urge you to dismiss from your minds any feeling of innocence and harmlessness about gathering for worship services, as we do from time to time. Gatherings like worship services appear harmless only when we do not reflect deeply on their significance. When we meet in a service, for example to celebrate harvest, or a service to celebrate Christian unity, and in that service we read that the glory and dominion belong to God for ever and ever, is to accuse those who are seeking the glory. It is a word of accusation against those who are claiming the dominion. In our world, there are some people who have no glory and no power. Those who get the glory are usual the rich and famous, which is why people "worship" them. It is because they have the glory and the power why stories of their lives take front pages of magazines. In this world some people, the poor and marginalised, have no dominion. Instead they are dominated by the merchants, the utility companies, the police, the politician and the media. Even the church takes advantage of the poor and the powerless. How else are we to understand the litany of abuses visited upon children in their care? We take advantage of the poor when we give the impression in our theological statements and songs that they must wait for a time in the distant future to get justice; that they must be patient with the world because everybody can't be comfortable. Governments take advantage of the poor when their communities are the last to have proper roads, proper infrastructure and proper amenities. It is no coincidence the hot beds of violence and crime in the cities of the world are communities renowned for their poor infrastructure, poor housing and poor services for the residents. The media takes advantage of the poor when they show concern for their communities only when a crime has been committed. The media houses have aided and abetted the view that the poor are worthless criminals who deserve exclusion and avoidance. One of the fundamental problems in our society is that there is really no justice for the poor. When we take advantage of the poor we are claiming that we have the glory, that we have the dominion. Therefore when in our church services we read and affirm that the glory belongs to God it is to say to those who dominate the poor and take the glory from them that what they are doing is wrong. It is without justification. It is a sin. We undercut their claims and their credibility by saying to them we do not subscribe to their dominion; we will not worship at their altars; we will not bow to their power because the power and dominion belong to God.

If in your next church service you stand and say that the power and the glory, the dominion and the praise belong to God, you are accusing those who would claim otherwise. When a husband insists on making a statement like this it is an accusation against his wife if she thinks what he is saying is foolishness. When children joyfully participate in a worship service and say amen, when this text (Rev 5:1-6) is read, it is an accusation against their parents who may think it is a waste of time. When your co-worker is scornful at your testimony that you participated in worship service, in which power and dominion was ascribed to God, it is an accusation against your co-worker. When Christians say that the glory and the dominion belong to God, in a world as ours, we are calling attention to misplaced glory and misplaced honour. You will see then that you cannot truly participate in a worship service of that kind and remain neutral. When we say to the reading of this text, "this is the word of the Lord," we have crossed the Rubicon from innocence and neutrality to accusation. We have taken sides. A worship service is no longer a mushy kind of experience. It is a bold assertion of conviction that the glory and dominion belong to God. When we claim this in a society where the pundits have only testimonies of doom and gloom, when we reject the dismal predictions of the future by the realist we hear every day on the airwaves, we are insisting that we will not give glory to them; that we will not surrender to their dominion because in our view it belongs to God alone.

A Statement of Adoration

When we say the glory and the dominion belong to God it is also a statement of adoration because we are insisting that God alone will be the object of our worship. Situated as it is in the book of Revelation, this text is particularly powerful because the background of the book is the persecution of early Christians by the power holders of the day. The persecution was as cruel as it was prolonged because the powers would not countenance Christians "raining on their parade" or tampering with their absolute dominion. The sad irony of this assertion is that later a smaller group of Christians had to use it to remind the larger, more powerful group of Christians that God and not the church over which they had control, was the holder and owner of the glory and the dominion. So co-opted were those church leaders by the idolatrous political system of the Roman Empire that it became impossible to distinguish between the church and the evil powers of the world. So blinded they were by influence that they lost sight of the true object of worship.

There are still many places in the world where Christians and other people of faith have to be insisting that they will worship God alone – not political power, not religious superstructures, not people, not political leaders, not celebrities, not systems, not deteriorating secular values, not moral ineptitude, not political correctness, not class, not movements, not discourses, not theology, not philosophy, not scientific discovery, not economic theory, not social theory, not the environment, not political system – God alone.

To say the glory and the dominion belong to God is a political statement and a statement about the future of the world. It is a statement about who has the final say in our lives. When you attend your next religious service bear in mind that you are making a bold statement when you say, with conviction, that to God be the glory and the dominion for ever and ever. It is a statement of accountability; it is a statement of accusation; it is a statement of adoration.

CHAPTER 14

A Timely Reminder

It was I who fed you in the wilderness, in the land of drought. [Hosea 13:5]

Introduction

W hen things are going well in a country's economy, there are many people who feel their efforts should be recognized. When things are bad, however, no one wants to take the blame. Where the prophet Hosea had difficulty was that the people felt it was due to their efforts in seeking the intervention of the fertility gods of the Canaanite religions that Israel's economic life was prospering. Let us thank Baal, they would say, who has responded to our call. Our wise investment of time to Baal was worth it after all. Israel did not credit the Lord for providing the grain, the wine, oil, silver and gold. The cardinal problem, to which Hosea called attention, was the disloyalty of the people of God – their misplaced love, their misplaced gratitude, their misplaced prayer. Hosea, who was based in the Northern Kingdom of Israel, during the divided kingdom period, speaks in the same vein as Isaiah 1:3, who was at the time in the Southern Kingdom of Judah. This is what Isaiah said: *the ox knows his owner, and the ass knows his masters crib, but Israel does not know, my people do not consider."* The problem was how to get the people of God to own the one who was truly their provider and protector. The people were preoccupied with their own achievements, without making reference to the grace and kindness of God. You will notice that in the older versions of scripture, we have the rendering: "*I did know thee in the wilderness.*" Another way of translating this section, which the NRSV prefers, is "*It was I who fed you in the wilderness.*" The idea is that God sustained the people in the time of want. The message to the people of Israel was clear – don't forget the God who provided for you. It would also be accurate to say that the people were being cautioned about the weight they were putting on their own efforts because they were being blessed not simply by their own strength. How shall we receive a text like this today? The convenient amnesia of forgetting God makes it necessary for a little reminder to be given – a timely reminder.

Remember the Wilderness

The first thing of which Israel was reminded was that there was a wilderness, through which they had passed. It is understandable that a people would want to forget a traumatic experience like the wilderness. There is hardly a way to travel from Egypt to the Promised Land without passing through the wilderness. We know from Deuteronomy 1:2 that it should have taken only eleven days to go from Horeb to Kadesh Barnea, which was on the border of the Promised Land. Yet, it took the children of Israel forty years to make the journey. They got stuck in the wilderness because of unbelief and because there were things they needed to learn about God. In Hebrew, the word for wilderness is *midbar*. It is surely interesting that the root of *midbar* has the meaning as "speak" or "word." God speaks to us in the wilderness. God also humbles and proves us in the wilderness (Deut.8:2). The wilderness period can last days, or years, depending on how quickly we learn its lessons.

When we notice that there are over 307 references to the wilderness in scripture, it serves to underline the significant place of the wilderness in the life of the people of God. The wilderness was the place where Hagar hid from Sarah and in that sense it is a *place of hiding*. It was the place to which the children of Israel went after leaving Egypt. They worshipped in it but they also wandered in it for forty years. The wilderness then is *a place of wandering*. Joshua 5:4 reminds us that the wilderness is also *a place of death* because all the men of war who left Egypt died in the wilderness. From the experiences of Jesus we are reminded that the wilderness is *a place of threat and temptation*, for it is in the wilderness that Satan came to him with offers Satan thought he could not refuse. For Hosea, the wilderness was *a place of encounter*, to which God lured Israel so that he could speak tenderly to her [2:14]. It was the place where the Lord found Israel, ready to be plucked like a bunch of grapes [9:10]. So the text is reminding us of our wilderness. Some of us have passed through extremely trying times and it may be that today you are going through your wilderness. Maybe even now you are hiding from God. Maybe you are wandering to and fro, not knowing where to rest. Today, you may be under the threat of death and loss; you are probably in the place of grief. You may be faced with a moment of great temptation that you find hard to refuse. If you are in the wilderness today, then let this text speak to you: It was I who fed you in the wilderness or I knew you in the wilderness. You are not alone in your wilderness. You have a journey partner, who will walk with you and talk to you, who will tell you that you are his own. I thank the Lord Jesus that there was a wilderness in my life.

Remember the Drought

The text not only reminds us of the wilderness but it also reminds us of the time of drought, during which the Lord fed his people. This is probably a peculiar experience of the wilderness that the prophet wanted to emphasise, though it is not the only kind of experience we can have in the wilderness. Think of the **drought** and the rugged times in our lies. The text would have us see that even in drought, God does not abandon us. It was I who fed you in the time of drought, said the Lord. This is somewhat ironic because if God continues to supply our needs how then can it be called drought? However, the issue of drought in Israel is a critical part of both its ancient and modern history. The climate of the country is significantly affected by the region to the South called the Negev Desert, which accounts for about 50% [12,000 Sq kilometres] of the land mass. The Negev is effectively an extension of the Sinai desert, which sees serious droughts each year because it receives on average one-tenth of the rainfall that is seen in the North. For this reason only one-third of the land can be cultivated today and there is an extensive irrigation programme and water is conserved by using recycled water for agricultural purpose.

That experience of drought is not only characteristic of the modern times but was also a feature of life centuries ago, as we can discern from the book of Genesis. We see, for example, that it was the experience of Jacob when he worked with his uncle Laban [Gen 31:40]. Drought, serpents and scorpions were also part of the experience of Israel in their wanderings in the wilderness. Drought is also used in a metaphorical sense because according to Psalm 32:4, drought is the experience of the person who lives with unacknowledged sins. Haggai the prophet called for a drought upon the land, when he saw that the people neglected the worship of the Lord. So there is a spiritual significance in the drought. It is the experience of the people who are far from God or the experience of a people under discipline. It is time when there is no growth or a time when we find it hard to pray. Drought is evidenced when we've lost interest in the word of God; when we cannot muster the courage to gather with the saints for worship. We are in a time of drought when we have no pleasure in justice and peace, or for things pertaining to the kingdom of God. When we cannot rejoice at the repentance of a sinner we are in a place of spiritual drought. It is times of drought in our lives when there is greater pleasure in sin than in righteousness. In these times it is important to remember that God is able to sustain you. God is not prevented by your sin because while we were yet sinners Christ died for us. God is not hindered by our anger because the Lord says, "vengeance is mine and I will repay" [Deuteronomy 32:35]. Even as he is God of the valleys and the mountains, so too God is a God of the wilderness, in which also he provides.

Remember God

Since there was a wilderness and since there was a drought, we are reminded also that there is God. God is in the midst of all our experiences whether or not we know and whether or not we care. Today we have the reminder that God undertakes to provide. So when we come through the hurricane, when we come through the drought, when we come out of our wilderness we are not to say that it was simply our wisdom and strength. We are to say all power, glory and thanksgiving to God. The Psalmist (139) speaks eloquently of the presence of God. God is present and I cannot but be in God's presence. God knows where I sit down and where I get up. Where ever I go there God is.

We have memories of our wilderness and we can still remember our droughts. We are also aware that it was our Lord who journeyed with us and fed us abundantly during those days of need.

O Lord of heaven and earth and sea, to thee all praise and glory be;
How shall we show our love to thee, who givest all?
For peaceful homes and healthful days, for all the blessing earth displays,
We owe you thankfulness and praise, who givest all.
To you from whom we all derive our life, our gifts, our power to give!
O may we ever with you live, Giver of all.

C. Wordsworth

CHAPTER 15

The Communication Age

Charge them that are rich in this world… that they do good, that they be rich in good works, ready to distribute, willing to communicate. [1Timothy 6: 17-18]

Introduction

The Jamaica Association of Open and Distant learning (JADOL) has the following as their mission statement: "Persuaded of the need for sharing experiences and for networking… JADOL will promote, enhance and develop the practice of distance and open learning." If this part of the mission statement were written in the 1st century, a single word in Greek would be used for the expression "the need for sharing and networking." That word κοινωνια (koinonia), which we find for example in I Timothy 6:18, is translated in the NRSV as "ready to share" and in the AV as "willing to communicate." Κοινωνια may also be translated "liberal" or "generous." The root word κοινvια also means association, fellowship or communion. In other words, it is a complex word that was used to describe all kinds of interaction and sharing in business or professional relationships. In what follows we will explore the meaning and application of sharing in a communication age.

Choosing to Share

Each person has the final say on whether or not he or she shares information or anything else. People cannot really be coerced into sharing if they don't want to do so. They may indeed be forced to give up some of what they have but then that is hardly sharing. Some people are committed to the principle of sharing and do so even when they seem not to have the means. They would hold the view that what they have is part of a larger store of provision to which they are privileged to have access and over which they are only stewards. Recognizing the need for a sense of accountability on the part of those who have a fair share of the world's resources, the writer of 1 Timothy 6:17-18 addresses those who are rich. They were charged not to be haughty but rather to set their hopes on God who provides everything for us. They were to be rich in good works, generous and willing to share. This willingness to share has come to be regarded as good economic and social principle, as well as a necessary principle of communal life. Sharing will help to guarantee a certain quality of life for all. The people to whom 1 Timothy was written were to be governed by this imperative of sharing "so that they may take hold of life that is really life."

In the agrarian society to which the writer of 1st Timothy would have belonged, the rich were for the most part traders and owners of livestock. However, since our age is an information age, the rich in our time would include those who hold access to information and traders whose commodity is information and information systems. The powerful also include people who have or hold access to technical information. Those who are rich with information and have unlimited access to information in this information age must read carefully the address here in 1 Timothy. They were not to trust in riches. The caution is for us to be mindful of the uncertainty of riches. Along those same lines the writers of the gospels caution about storing up and building our hope on corruptible treasures in places where thieves have access. Rather, the rich must put their trust in the living God.

This caution is worth applying to our time because of the uncertainty of information. The truth is that people are more prepared to give homage to the information systems of the age than they are to the living God. 1Timothy then poses a serious challenge to our time, which is an age when people find it more plausible to trust in the tangible, the visible and the verifiable. In such an age as this Timothy says trust in God, who is intangible, invisible and whose existence and work we accept by faith not by proofs. To us who live by the riches of the information age Timothy says that the information that you have cannot save you. In an age where access to riches is directly related to access to information Timothy says do not put your trust in riches. In an age where information is power Timothy says put your trust in God the Almighty. In an age where people go to the information highway for pleasure, Timothy says look to God who richly supplies the things we need for living. In other words information is uncertain so put your trust in the living God.

Information is Power

If we apply this principle to the education sector, for example, we can assert confidently that in the truest sense education is possible only where there is a willingness to share experiences. More and more institutions of learning are becoming sensitive to the importance of sharing information and of networking. The principle of sharing and networking is symbolised by the existence of various forms of social media in the information superhighway or the World Wide Web. It is becoming a matter of basic infrastructure for educational institutions to give unlimited, free access to the internet. Smart cities are those in which, among other things, everyone has free access to the internet. It is believed that this open sharing of information counter balances the power of media houses and retains power in the masses. It is no longer necessary to rely on media moguls to filter news through the lenses of their own interests. This is people power – or so it is believed.

With increased awareness of the power of the social media, aspirants for political power are seeking to harness them to boost their campaigns. Life in our time involves a liberal crisscrossing of information, some of which is very harmful, not least to children, who are equally exposed to the liberality. People demand ready access to information and those who hold or hoard it do so to their own detriment. What this age has taught us is that information has economic value, which explains why media houses, especially in USA & Europe, have no difficulty in paying handsomely to get a story. The media houses know that if they are the first to carry the story and if they have exclusive rights, it will translate into increased readership or listenership and, in the final analysis, will increase their profit. So it is clear that committing money to the getting of information, as we do in paying school fees and purchasing books, is an investment. We assume that those who expand their knowledge base, who develop the capacity to add value to goods and services, are in a better position to compete in the market place. In an information age, those who have access to information and those who know how to treat information as a commodity are rich because they have the thing on which this age thrives.

Sharing Experiences about God

One of the ironies of our time though is that amidst the readiness to share information there is not equal willingness to communicate. Some people are happy to put information into the public realm but some people are not allowed equal opportunity to share. This is one facet of the information age that institutions of learning must address. We need to revisit whether sharing information about experiences of God is not a worthy aspect of the things to be shared. Since the age of the Enlightenment, ironically, there has been a suspicion of people who have a Christian worldview. The suspicion was later expanded to include all religious worldview. Of course, the suspicion of the power and potential negative impact of religious views on society is not without some justification. Countless atrocities have been committed in the name of religion and only very few of the religious communities can claim a clean hand. However, religions are not unique in this respect. Many atrocities have also been committed in the name of political and economic theories yet these have not been excluded from public discourse. On the other hand, religions have contributed much to the welfare of society and continue to do so. The argument was put forward that a person's religious view is a private affair and should not be propagated in the public sphere. It should not be that a case has to be made for the inclusion of religion in education and social discourse.

With the radical shift in values, however, the things that were thought to be private are occupying prominent places in the public arena. We have all sorts of personal opinion being paraded as topics of public interest. In countries like the USA and France, for example, people are barred from making overt references to religious convictions while it is acceptable to espouse an anti-religious point of view. The prejudice against theories of experiences about God is not justifiable. France has made it a criminal offence for Muslim women to wear a veil covering their face in public, even though this has been part of their religious practice for centuries.

One of the things that the Christian faith emphasizes is that God has undertaken to share and has initiated a conversation with the human community. "Come now, let us reason together." [Isaiah 1:18] It is in this sense of a divine conversation that we should understand the witness of Hebrews 1:2: *in sundry times and diverse manner God has spoken to us by the prophets but in these last days he is speaking to us through his Son."* The incarnation is God's invitation to humanity to participate in a divine conversation or the broadening of the divine discourse to overlap and intersect with human discourse. In the incarnation the human being is challenged to make a re-assessment of the human and divine realities because of the interfacing of the two. The incarnation is an invitation to dialogue with God because with it a fundamental statement affecting divinity and humanity is made in a language that human beings can understand. God speaks concretely in the (body) language that we know most intimately – the human-form. In order for the dialogue to be ongoing, a human response must be made to the divine assertion. Instead of reckoning with Jesus, however, our inclination to self-hate means that we prefer when dealing with the divine to hear an assertion that has to do with "something incomprehensible, unfathomable, and transcendent… than to hear of an incarnate Creator, of a God who is of [our] own flesh and bone."[9] Consequently, in the conversation with God, the human being is inclined to take objection to the incarnation as human discourse being presented as divine discourse.

It is ironic then that we live in an information age where, on one hand, there is an unwillingness to hear and on the other hand you have people of faith who are not allowed to share. The challenge that the text puts to us is to overcome this irony. The task that institutions and organizations of learning must seek to perform is to overcome the prejudices against sharing religious views in an information age.

Something More
A Crisis of Faith

Introduction

O ne of the questions concerning the New Testament, about which scholars are preoccupied, is the chronology of gospels. The issue of which was written first has been the subject of much research and discussion. The traditional view is that Mark is first and John is the latest. According to that view, the author of the Gospel of John borrowed material from Matthew, Mark and Luke (the Synoptic Gospels) in writing his Gospel. However, that view has been questioned as far back as Gardner Smith's *St. John and the Synoptics,* which was published in 1938. Since the persuasive argument of C. H. Dodd in his book *Historical Tradition in the Fourth Gospel* two decades later in 1963, New Testament studies have been shifting more and more to the view that the fourth Gospel gives evidence of very early original material, maybe even earlier than Mark's Gospel.

The story of Peter's denial, which is recorded in all four gospels, is not only interesting in and of itself but might actually throw some light on the question of which Gospel was first. If for example we assume that Mark was the earliest, we come to an interesting situation when we read the account of Peter's denial. According to the story in Matthew 27:69-75, Mark 14:66-72, and Luke 22:55-62, Peter goes away and wept bitterly after denying that he knew Jesus. In John 18:15-27, however, we have a shorter ending to the story with no reference to Peter's weeping. It is more probable that the idea of weeping was inserted later than for the later tradition to exclude the sign of Peter's remorse. Another interesting feature of John's account of the story is that where as the Synoptics have the damsel and other persons making comments about Peter's discipleship but not directly to him, in John's Gospel questions are put directly to Peter. This direct questioning of Peter by the young girl might be evidence of a very early tradition in which Peter had not yet come to be held in the high esteem that we see later.

From the reading in John's Gospel we are justified in calling the story Peter's trial, which means that his faith was being put to the test – hence the topic of this meditation. On closer reading you will see that John places the story of the trial or questioning of Peter in a way that accentuates the irony. The scene moves from Peter to Jesus then back to Peter again. In the first scene with Peter (John 18:16-17) he is asked whether he is not also one of his disciples. (More time would be needed to explore the interesting inclusion of "also", which incidentally makes more sense in John than in the Synoptics. In John it seems to relate to the fact that there was another disciple there who was known to the high priest. No reference is made to another disciple in the Synoptic account.) Nevertheless, Peter's answer is no. In the first scene of Jesus before the High priest, Jesus is asked about his disciples. Jesus' response is that the high priest should ask those who heard his preaching, since he preached openly. But where are the disciples? The scene shifts to Peter again and the same question is put to him as at first, "are you not one of his disciples?" Once again Peter answered no. A third question is put: "Did I not see you in the garden with him?" In order to emphasise the strength of this evidence, John tells us that the person asking the question was a relative of Malcus, whose ear Peter had cut off. Yet, a third time, Peter answered no. The questioning of Peter ends. There is no cursing and swearing as in the Synoptics, no crying, and no evidence of remorse. The trial of Jesus continues.

This brings us to the question of whose account was the earliest. Could it be that John's account was the earliest and that the later account found the lack of remorse in John too harsh? For this reason I want to keep the focus on the way John relates the story – the questioning and the remorseless way in which the account ends.

Awkward Moments

The moments of questioning, awkward moments one might add, reveal something of the challenges we face in our own discipleship. These are moments when questions are put to the person of faith. The first question was from a little servant girl. The word in Greek (παιδισκη, *pronounced paidiské*) emphasises the childish simplicity of the one asking the question. She may have asked the question out of sympathy for Jesus and Peter. Incidentally, you will notice too that in the story in Acts 12 it was a damsel called Rhoda that recognised Peter at the door after his escape from Prison. So here is Peter before the discerning, doorway damsel. This kind of moment may not at first seem awkward because the threat that the disciple faces seems somewhat benign. He might have considered that the damsel was out of her place to be questioning him. He might even have considered that he was not under any obligation to account to her – she was only a damsel anyway. On the face of it there is no danger. Here the disciple treats the question simply as an inquisitive damsel seeking information and she would not be considered to have the sophistication to draw any consequence from the answer she received. He could get away with giving any answer because it's just information not accusation. However, the appearance that the situation is benign quickly evaporates because the disciple must consider the implications of his answer. The damsel may be innocent but his response cannot at the same time be insincere. All of a sudden the situation that at first appeared to be benign turns out to be a moment of ethical dilemma. Being preoccupied, as we often are, with our own sense of security or insecurity, danger is perceived even in a doorway damsel. Often when we find ourselves in these situations we construct fears and we imagine the worse when the situation does not justify them.

The significance and yet irony of this doorway moment with the damsel is that the disciple imagined that there could be no progress unless there was the suspension and setting aside of his beliefs and convictions. In a real sense his faith was in crisis because he imagined that there was no way out. You may have been in such a moment when you believed the only way to get on the inside of a certain circle you must leave aside what you have on the inside; that is to set aside your convictions, values and beliefs in order to feel included. It is a serious crisis of faith when one of the options the disciple contemplates is the denial of the faith.

The second moment of the crisis of faith was in the social gathering at the fireside. The disciple is here having a social moment – not a drink this time but a warming by the fire. It could well be the case that they were sharing in a cup of something. The concern seemed to have been about identifying those at the fireside – a kind of "getting to know you." The social moment is one in which the disciple wishes to remain in the circle but perceives that any claim to know Jesus will threaten that. The doorway moment is about getting into the club, group or circle but the fireside, social moment is about remaining. The fireside moment is one in which the disciple does not wish to lose the social or class privileges. When the disciples believe, for example, that their badminton, their tennis, their watering-holes and their club take pre- eminence over their Christian convictions, they are having a fireside moment. When the young Christian finds a greater sense of security with their drug-abusing, sex-abusing companions than in a Christ-like company, they are having a serious fireside moment.

The third awkward moment for the disciple was the eye-witness moment, with the relative of Malcus, whose ear, according to the writer, Peter had severed. This relative was there and saw the incident. We call this the eye-witness moment, which in this context is the moment in which the disciple is faced with a serious ethical decision. The question was coming from one whom the story portrays as an eye-witness and as you know, this is reliable evidence that can stand in a court of law. No doubt you can further appreciate how this account can be called faith in trial because here we are allowing for eye-witness perspective.

This moment is different from the damsel moment, in which someone, out of interest, raises a question. The damsel was wondering about this, probably because of the demeanour of the disciple. The eye-witness moment is also different from the fireside moment, where the question is based on suspicion. By the fireside the individuals with Peter were suspicious as to why he was there – somewhat like the story of Jonah where the prophet brought suspicion by his very presence. The eye-witness moment is one in which the evidence of the eye-witness comes face-to-face with the testimony of the defendant disciple. It is an ethical moment because only the disciple knows for sure if the eye-witness is right. To answer no, which is the option he chose, not only made him to be a liar, as in the other moments of questioning, but also made the eye-witness out to be liar. It is an ethical moment because the disciple may have faced a situation of real danger. Unlike the account in the Synoptics, John does not have Jesus replacing the ear that Peter cut off. Peter may have imagined that to own up to his past actions would put him at great risk. To admit knowledge of Jesus would make it more difficult for him to extricate himself from the situation. The only easy way out is to relax his convictions. The eye-witness moment called for a courageous ethical stance but the disciple found it easier to water-down, change, or relax held convictions in order to keep the peace and his sense of security. Often this is the line of inner rationalizing and reasoning we pursue when faced with an ethical decision. The issue that we must resolve internally is what the consequences are to us. The eye-witness moment then is one in which the disciple feels the greater sense of danger and acts to preserve himself in the eyes of others, although he knows within himself that his reputation has plummeted.

Like Peter, then, we face our moments: the doorway damsel with a benign threat, the social servants with questions of social privileges and the eye-witness moment, which throws up a serious ethical challenge. Like Jesus, the disciple is on trial and often we fail but with no weeping and no remorse. May God help us in our moment of crisis when our faith is on trial!

CHAPTER 16

The Resurrection

*Those who are considered worthy of a place in that age
and in the resurrection from the dead neither marry nor
are given in marriage. Indeed they cannot die anymore,
because they are like the angels and are children of God,
being children of the resurrection. [Luke 20: 35-36]*

Introduction

In the Christian calendar November 1 is observed as All Saints Day, which gives an opportunity to reflect on the extended community of saints, including those who have died. However, from a Christian point of view talking about the dead makes more sense if we are talking also of the resurrection of the dead. There are as least three reasons why Christians must be clear about what they mean when we speak of the resurrection of the dead. The first relates to the tradition of Halloween, which presents the idea that the spirit of the dead is ugly and to be feared. Have you ever wondered why the Halloween images are so fearsome? The second reason is that there is a plurality of beliefs about life after death. Thirdly, and may be most importantly, we must be clear because for many today, the idea of the resurrection is simply ridiculous. In the same way in which we find Jesus in this story defending his position in Luke 20: 27-38, the early Christian community had to provide a defence for its belief in the resurrection. I would like us to look closer at the answer Jesus gave because it may provide us with some clues about how we may respond to the Halloween caricatures and trickery, the plurality of beliefs and the charge that the whole idea of the resurrection makes no sense.

Against the Status Quo

The first response on the lips of Jesus is that in the resurrected life people neither marry nor are given in marriage. This response was given to a scenario that was painted by the Sadducees to underscore something illogical about the idea of the resurrected life. The scenario described an ancient Eastern practice where, when a man dies before his wife, she would pass to his brothers. In the unlikely scenario, seven brothers died before the woman, who had been wife to all of them. The question then was to whom she would belong in the resurrected life, since they all had her as wife. The full implication of this response cannot be appreciated without reference to marriage practices in first century Palestine. In the first century Palestinian society marriage was not simply a matter of love between two people, though it would normally include that, even if not at first. Instead, it was the coming together of two families in a socio-economic bond, for the stability and longevity of the community. Marriage was a public ceremony where the whole community, led by the families involved, gave its approval to a couple to partner each other for their mutual well- being, to live together and to raise children. Marriages were generally arranged by the elders who were more aware of the financial and social implications of the union between the couple. The man who gave his daughter in marriage was expected to benefit by the receipt of the dowry. This practice is not as overt today as formerly but it is still in use. Former president of South Africa, Nelson Mandela, had to pay some 70 heads of cattle to his father-in-law but he said his wife was worth every hoof. Parents today still calculate the financial implications of the marriage proposal given or received by their children. Having three girls, my wife and I would sympathise with them. In Eastern societies, also, marriage was one of the ways in which the social relations in a clan or tribe were maintained. We can see remnants of this practice in families today, where the "gate-keeper" of the family tradition (usually a senior female) does not allow persons of a certain social class, ethnic group of educational and professional background, to get close to their eligible spinsters and bachelors. So marriage was about love but more so about political and social relations; it was a covenant that had important economic implications.

When Jesus therefore said that in the resurrection people neither marry nor are given in marriage, it was a way of saying that the resurrected life is one in which the social relations that we want to maintain on the basis of money, class and ethnic background would change. The resurrected life radically transforms our social structures; it turns our lives upside down and inside out! That life would differ from the present in that it would lead to new patterns of relationships and new values placed on individuals, especially women. No longer would it be possible for us to treat the young women as property on which we would speculate. Mind you, speculating on people, as we do on merchandise, is not something of a bygone era. One of the realities of our time is that the bodies of young women and men are used as a basis for speculation and financial transaction. Read again the stories of how the models or the pop stars are made. Look at the way in which advertisers use the bodies of men and women to advertise their products, even when the products have no direct connection to the human body. Belief in the resurrection, then, was a way in which Jesus called attention to the fact that the patterns of relationship as we know them in this era would change, although not in a way that would favour the exploitation of the weak. In the resurrected life, people are not treated as we do commodities, where their value is judged in economic terms. People are valuable and have worth apart from the fact that they may have economic power. People are valuable and have worth even when they are not sex symbols. People are valuable and have worth even when their physical appearance is not what is paraded on TV as the ideal. People are valuable and have worth apart from their capacity to bear children. When we see the resurrection in these terms, it may be seen as a threat to those who do not know how to place a limit on their importance and power. Those who benefit, often unfairly, from the present status quo should not imagine that the resurrected life is designed to preserve it for their benefit. Those who are considered worthy of the age to come, Jesus said, neither marry nor are given in marriage. They have a different understanding of human worth and the value of the human being. They do not use people as a commodity to further their economic interests. People neither marry nor are given in marriage because they have matured beyond the need to be preoccupied with the dynamics of male and female relations.

Beyond Death

The second response Jesus gave to the question of the Sadducees is that in the resurrected life people do not die anymore. In Christ, the Resurrected One, "there is neither male nor female, Jew nor Greek, bond nor free. They do not "die anymore... and are children of the resurrection." One wonders why Jesus needed to say this, since the question the Sadducees raised was whose wife the woman would be. The point is, the question of what the resurrection is, calls for further thought beyond the question of marriage. Beyond the issues of social relations, economy and power, which lie behind the question, there are other issues about life and death. We live in a society where there is a strong belief that we are in a cycle of death. The argument is that we are born and the life form reappears in a new way after we die and after that forms dies, the life appears again in yet another form, and so on. This is what is called reincarnation. The Christian belief in the resurrection though is that in the resurrection we do not die anymore. This statement is important because we live in a society that sees death as the last word. The ethic of death says if you want to silence someone who stands for justice, kill that person and so lay the matter to rest. If you want to get rid of the excess people then kill them. If people trouble you, kill them. If people threaten you, kill them. The ethic of death is that which drives the need for war, the need for hate crimes and the like. It does seem backward but we live in a society where the leaders resort to war and the killing of people to solve the ills of the world. Those who do this, terrorists and non-terrorists alike, do not yet know the way of peace; they do not yet know that God is not a God of death. They think that death is the last word and as children of death they are seeking to have the last word. Those who manufacture equipment to perfect the art of killing people need to hear again the word of Jesus: in the resurrected life people do not die anymore because death is not the last word.

The famous 17th century Moravian Bishop, John Amos Comenius, challenged the angels of death in his day to melt the war implements and use them to make church bells. We would urge the angels of death in our time to use the resources to help people instead of using them to kill people. It is simply mind-boggling the amount of effort and resources we spend trying to kill each other. That is the nature of the culture of death; it has no conscience. Its single aim is to eliminate. Christians must not live for this culture even though we are living in it. It is not only that the children of resurrection live in a society based on a different set of human relations but the children of the resurrection do not regard death as the last word. One of the reasons the Church of Jesus Christ must oppose the culture of killing is that our God is God of the living. To the Christian death is not friend but a foe and so we do not see killing as part of the solution to problems. The culture of death is a problem and so cannot factor as a solution for those who want to live.

Angels

The third part of the response to the Sadducees was that the children of the resurrection are like the angels; they are children of God. We should understand from this that the beauty of resurrected people shows the creative hand of God. Of course the question of what is beautiful is a relative thing. I'm often amused at the way aliens are portrayed in the movies. For the most part they sort of resemble us, although just a little less attractive. The fluid in their body is not red blood – usually

118

green. We can't imagine that other beings might outshine us in beauty. We also have a task to help children to form positive, beautiful images of the resurrection and not the ugly faces they see at Halloween. The idea of the dead being raised has been so misused and manipulated for commercial purposes, to the effect that our children are more inclined to believe in ghosts than to believe in God. Halloween is being promoted as ugliness and facial disfigurement, the concealment of personality and trickery. With that caricature of those who are raised up, it may not be easy to associate the children of the resurrection with beauty, goodness and truth. I would like to challenge the churches to begin a Halloween celebration in which the figures we see are more attractive. So that we insert goodness where there is evil, truth where there is insincerity and untruth, beauty where there is ugliness and kindness where there is trickery. This would be a Christian Halloween, in which we capture the wonder and the beauty of the resurrected life. For, as scripture says, the children of the resurrection are like angels, they are children of God. Let us then portray godliness and the beauty of the angelic host.

The faces of Halloween are meant to say that the idea of people being raised for the dead is really nonsense. In an interesting way, however, it evidences the culture of death in which we live. It reminds us that we live among people who are angels of death. We need a counter-culture to death. We need a culture of life; a culture that recognises that God not the devil, not death but life is the last word about human life.

Those who know the new life in Jesus Christ have already entered into the resurrected life. In this new life people are valued apart from what may be their social standing or economic worth. As those who have tasted of the resurrected life we can affirm that death is not the last word on human life and so we are against the rampant killing machines and the culture of death in our time. We say to those who kill and order the killing of people – killing cannot be the solution when it is the problem and God is not a God of death. The children of the resurrection are not children of death or the devil. The children of the resurrection are like angels; they are children of God.

CHAPTER 17

Discipleship

*You did not choose me but I chose you and appointed you to
go and bear fruit; fruit that will last, so that the Father will
give you whatever you ask him in my name. John 15:16*

Introduction

One advice I picked up from a late Bishop of the Moravian
Church is that I was to give thought to the Lectionary reading
appointed for the day, even when I didn't like what it said. On
several occasions this was the case –the appointed readings were at times
difficult to handle and at other times were at variance with my mood.
The text that forms the basis of the reflections here is one of those texts.
It does not lend itself to easy interpretation. Nevertheless, it is imposed
sufficiently on the mind to merit a considered response.

On first appearance it might seem that this passage is about
predestination, that idea that God decided before hand those who
will be saved. This idea got a fair bit of attention from church fathers,
Aquinas, Duns Scotus, Ockham and others in the Middle Ages.
However, it became primarily associated with John Calvin during the
Reformation period. Predestination is based primarily on passages like
Rom 8:29-30 and Ephesians 1:5, which allude to decisions made about
the life of the individual even before birth. I do not have to delve into
this problematic issue because the word that John uses here is completely

different from the word that is translated "predestined". Nevertheless, there is something still mysterious and special in these words which, according to John, Jesus spoke to his disciples in part of his farewell speech. Already in an earlier chapter, in what seems to be an allusion to his betrayal, a similar word was used: he told the disciples that not all of them were clean; for the writer noted that, he knew that one of them would betray him; nevertheless, he knew whom he had **chosen.** Also in John 15:19 he used the word in saying he has **chosen** the disciples out of the world. We find the same idea also in 1Cor 1:27-28: God chose what was foolish in the world to shame the wise; God chose what was weak to shame the strong; God chose what is low and despised, so that no one might boast in the presence of God. It is in this sense that we must understand being chosen; you did not choose me but I chose you.

Chosen for a purpose

I think that the Moravian Pietist, Nicolas Ludwig *von* Zinzendorf, was right when he said that the mystery of discipleship was not about those who had not been called but rather about those who have been already called. In his *Twenty-One Discourses on the Augsburg Confession*, he wrote:

> *Another mystery, which we cannot well account for, is not so much why the gospel is not preached to the African?... no; but the mystery lies rather here, Why the gospel is preached to the Europeans?... that in the situation wherein the present Europeans are, since the year 800, the gospel is everyday preached unto them... This I cannot understand."*[10]

If then you would today acknowledge you are a disciple of Christ this is a fundamental issue to appreciate. Your discipleship is an act of divine mystery and an act of grace; for if the word to the apostles are true, then so it is also to us; we did not choose him but he chose us. My discipleship, then, is not something about which I boast, because I was chosen as one low and despised. My discipleship is not evidence of my wisdom, for I was chosen as one foolish. My discipleship is not an indication of my strength of mind or character for I was chosen as one who was weak. When I consider my call and discipleship I must then say, like my forebears in the faith; this is a deep thing; this is a mystery. Zinzendorf said of this, "O the abyss!"

Note though that the call to discipleship is not an end in itself and it is never without its challenges. Indeed, immediately after reminding the disciples that it was he who chose them, John reports that Jesus said to them, "that you might bear fruit, fruit that will last. This can be called the purpose of our discipleship. The question that Paul asked, when he was confronted with discipleship on the road to Emmaus was, 'what will you have me do Lord?' Our walk with the Lord is made more difficult when we are either unclear or confused about our purpose, or where we have forgotten or abandoned it. This was the charge against the church in Ephesus, according to Rev 2: 4 – "But this I have against you, you have abandoned the love you had at first. Remember then from what you have fallen." In John 15:16 Jesus emphasizes that the purpose of their calling was that they would bear fruit. Already they were told that fruit-bearing was not possible unless they were connected to the vine. They were warned that branches that bore fruit were pruned to increase their productivity and that where there was no fruit the branches would be cut off and burnt. Therefore, emphasizing that the reason they were chosen was to bear fruit could not have filled them with glee but with awe and maybe anxiety. When we consider our discipleship do we not ask:

> *I wonder have I given my best for Jesus*
> *Who died upon the cruel tree!*
> *To think of his great sacrifice on Calvary,*
> *I know that Lord expects the best from me.*[11]

The purpose for which I was chosen is to bear fruit but am I bearing fruit? And where I am bearing fruit, are they of the quality that will last? You are probably still searching to know your role as a disciple. This one thing is sure: it is not without a purpose that you were chosen; this of itself is a mystery for none of us can boast of our fine qualities that so impressed the Holy Spirit. Beyond that though, your purpose will not exclude bearing fruit that must last.

The Privilege of Selection

Discipleship is not without its privileges, as Jesus assured his disciples here in John 15: 16: *So that the Father will give you whatever you ask in my name.* Some community of Christians today have insisted that clear evidence of improvement in one's material and financial wealth is a necessary outcome of a close walk and fellowship with the Lord. Some have based this claim on the assurance given in this passage. With chronic poverty among many Christians all over the world, other community of Christians have insisted that the prosperity and fulfilment of any request for alleviation of need will only be fully realized in the world to come. Both these extremes have their problems and I would caution against insisting on either. It is a privilege that we have access to the Father in Jesus' name. I want to celebrate the joy and privileges of this access and I want to use this access to the full. I want to know how I can fulfil God's purpose for my life so that I can testify to the experience of abundance. It has been shown again and again that the abundance of things is no guarantee of security. The abundance of things does not convert to a happy and abundant life. If there are sad, rich people as there are sad, poor people, then it is clear that there is no absolute correlation between happiness and having things in abundance. The converse of this is also true: if there are sad, rich people and sad, poor people, then there is no absolute correlation between being poor and being sad. So what is the benefit of having access to the father? It is important to know that although this is a privileged access it is not privileged in the same way we might have access to a private members club. This privilege of access is shared with every one of the over 6 million plus people on the planet, as well as any other being that may be on any other planets, who through Jesus Christ also have the right to be called children of God. It is privileged because the right we have is by virtue of creation and God's gracious redemptive work. At the very least I want to use my access to the Father to better understand the mystery of my having been called.

Chosen at a Price

As there are privileges so too there is a price. Prepared to be hated by the world Jesus told his disciples. This is not a joy ride. The famous theologian, Dietrich Bonhoffer, who was charged and hanged for being part of a plot to assassinate Adolph Hitler, said in his book about the cost of discipleship:

> *The cross is laid on every Christian. The first Christ-suffering which every man must experience is the call to abandon the attachments of this world. It is that dying of the old man which is the result of his encounter with Christ. As we embark upon discipleship we surrender ourselves to Christ in union with his death—we give over our lives to death. Thus it begins; the cross is not the terrible end to an otherwise god-fearing and happy life, but it meets us at the beginning of our communion with Christ. When Christ calls a man, he bids him come and die. It may be a death like that of the first disciples who had to leave home and work to follow him, or it may be a death like Luther's, who had to leave the monastery and go out into the world. But it is the same death every time—death in Jesus Christ, the death of the old man at his call.*[12]

I cannot but contemplate what price I have had to pay for my walk with God. I am humbled by stories about those who were prepared to die and others who chose death rather than to deny their Lord. I have never been faced with such a choice and I fear that I don't know how I would respond it I were. I pray that the Lord would give me the courage not to deny him, which I have already done even when faced with lesser consequences. For this reason I must not complain about the small inconveniences that I encounter and I must be resolute in commitment, unless, of course, my having been chosen has come to mean nothing to me.

Having been chosen for discipleship, then, is not about predestination. It is about understanding that there is a mystery and a divine initiative about our walk that we should not fail to contemplate. As a disciple you were chosen with a purpose – to bear fruit, fruit that will last.

CHAPTER 18

The Dead Shall Hear

Very truly I tell you, the hour is coming, and is now here, when the dead will hear the voice of the Son of God, and those who hear will live. John 5:25

Introduction

Many families have known grief but not many mothers have had to carry the weight of grief associated with having to bury a husband and three children.[13] Those who have not had to carry a burden like this can only speculate about what that feels like; they truly do not know. We pray then for families that carry such a weight, that your faith will not fail and that your heart will mend. When we stand, as we now do in the face of such grief, we turn to the word of God for consolation and hope. I have chosen John 5:5 as consolation because this text says something hopeful for those who carry a great burden of loss: *"The hour is coming and now is, when the dead shall hear the voice of the Son of God: and they that hear shall live."*

The Dead shall hear

The first issue I found necessary to clarify when I read this text was whether this was a figurative reference to the dead, as we find in Matt 8:22 *"let the dead bury their dead"*. The idea in the figurative sense is that those who are spiritually dead, that is, those who are alive but do not know the way to life eternal, can be called dead. In fact, some of the commentators seem to think that that is so. A closer reading, however, suggests that this refers to those who are physically dead. Indeed, lest we might think otherwise, the writer says again in verse 28: *"marvel not at this: for the hour is coming, in which all that are in the graves shall hear his voice."* The writer has good reason to say "marvel not" because such a statement is a fantastic and marvelous thing to hear. It is marvelous and it is hopeful.

This discourse about the dead has behind it a dispute about the authority of Jesus and it should not surprise you that in a similar way people question Jesus' authority and find claims Christians make about him to be ridiculous. In the background to this saying there is a story of a man who had been healed by Jesus and was accosted by the religious leaders of the day because he was seen carrying his bed on the Sabbath. The man did not know who healed him but after Jesus saw him again he was able to tell the religious leaders that it was Jesus. The religious leaders made a plot to assassinate Jesus because, according to them, he was making himself to be equal with God when he said, *"My father is still working so I am also working"*. According to Jesus, when you see the work of the Son you will marvel because what the Father does the Son will do also. Just as the Father is able to raise dead so also the Son is able to give life to whomever he wills. The point of all this is that how you feel about the saying that the dead who hear the voice of the Son of God will live is at the same time how you feel about the authority of the Son of God. When we face death, it forces us to think again about what we claim about the power of God and what we believe about the authority of the Son. The text is putting before us the view that not even death is beyond the reach of Jesus' authority. The faith of the Church, the faith by which we live, is that even though we no longer see our loved-ones whom we bury, death is not the last word about them. Jesus is able to cause them to hear!

You will notice that this idea of hearing Jesus is mentioned several times in this section of John's Gospel (v. 24). Those who hear Jesus' word and believe have everlasting life (v. 25). The dead shall hear... and live (v. 28). Those in the grave shall hear... and come forth. If those who live and those who are dead can hear the voice of Jesus, it means that Jesus is speaking among the living as well as among the dead. In this we affirm the power of God and the authority of the Son of God who can speak beyond the grave. This is a marvelous thing because normally we say that the dead cannot hear. But if what the text says is true, and I believe it is, we have to say that the dead can hear the voice of Jesus! The saying in John's Gospel, that Jesus' sheep hear his voice takes on new meaning. In his early ministry, the Apostle Paul was faced in Thessalonica with the question of what will happen to those who die. We have him writing similar words of consolation in 1Thessalonians 4:16: "*the Lord himself shall descend from heaven with a shout, with the voice of the archangel, with the trump of God: and the dead in Christ shall rise first.*" The voice of the angel and the trump of God shall summon the dead and they shall hear. In the stories about the resurrection in the Gospels, Jesus speaks to the dead and they respond to his voice. In the story of Lazarus (John 11:43), "*[Jesus] cried with a loud voice, Lazarus come forth.*" In the story of the damsel (Mk 5:41), *[Jesus] said unto her, Talithacumi, Damsel, I say unto you arise.*" I wonder then, whether our faith in the power of God and the authority of the Son of God, can give us the assurance that God will not abandon those who die in Jesus. Can we find consolation in this, that Jesus will speak and the dead will hear, so that we can say with Paul that when we are absent from the body we are present with the Lord? Do we not have a reason for consolation, believing that our God speaks to us who are alive in our grief and speaks to our dead in their grave? We grieve for our loved ones who we put in the grave but whether in grief or in the grave, God speaks to his own people and they hear.

The Dead shall live

The idea that the dead can hear the voice of Jesus is one part of this marvelous saying. The other part is that those who hear shall live. To see this only in a figurative sense is to miss the thrust of the story. To begin speculation about whether the dead can hear us now is fantasy. The thrust of the text is that God can cause the dead to hear – don't ask me how. Moreover, the dead who hear will live – ask me why but don't ask me how. They live because God is able to speak life into their dead being. They live because God is God of the living. I admit that on this question we do not have much in terms of verifiable proofs. According to the account in the gospels, Jesus called Lazarus and Lazarus came form the grave. This is the witness of believers. He called the young child who was dead and she got up as if from sleep. This is the witness of scripture. He whispered to the only son of the woman of Nain, and touched the cot on which he was being carried and he got up. This also is witness of scripture.

Whether or not you believe that the dead heard and lived will also depend on what you think about scripture. It is perfectly reasonable for you to be suspicious of the witness, especially if you did not learn to trust it. It is therefore your choice to believe or not to believe. What is the reason for your choice – since it is not a matter of proof? Why have you chosen not to believe? Why have you chosen to believe? I chose to believe and "every time I hear a new born baby cry, or touch a leaf or see the sky, then I know why, I believe." I believe because it makes sense to me. I accept the testimony of the believers through whom this account has come. Can you?

To say that the dead who hear will live is an affirmation similar to saying God created the world. It is something we believe and accept as a ground principle, which means it is not amenable to proofs and it cannot be disproved. Whether or not we accept this as a truth by which to live and in which to die will depend on what we believe about God. If the God in whom you believe does not speak then this will not be truth for you. Some people prefer the kind of God who does not speak, who asks no questions and holds no one accountable. If this is your kind of God then in that case you are living without hope and for that reason must answer the question, "Why am I living?" For if your life at the end comes to nothing and in the end is nothing then what is it now? But we believe in a speaking God. The world as we see it is evidence of his speech because he said, "Let there be… and there was…" As James

Weldon Johnson says, "he uttered his voice and the mountains clashed, he clapped his hands and the thunders roll." The witness of scripture from beginning to end is that God is speaking. We have a faith because God has spoken – "in time past he spoke to the fathers by the prophets but in these days he is speaking to us by the Son" (Hebrews 1:1). God speaks. In the witness of Daniel, the dead will hear and live because *"many of those who sleep in the dust of the earth shall awake, some to everlasting life, and some to shame and everlasting contempt"* [Dan 12:2]. In the witness of Paul the Apostle, the dead will hear and live because *"the Lord himself, with a cry of command, with the arch angel's call and with the sound of God's trumpet, will descend from heaven, and the dead in Christ will rise first."* [1Thess 4:16].

When we affirm then that the dead will hear and live it is also to say that the dead in Christ will not be forgotten. The view that the dead are buried and eventually forgotten is held as normal for some people today as it was in the day of Job, about whom we read in the Hebrew Bible (Old Testament). Indeed, it is only when we visit the cemetery, as I did recently, that we remember that such and such a person was once alive with us. Although concerned about this issue for a different reason, the book of Job expresses the dilemma:

> *For there is hope for a tree, if it is cut down, that it will sprout again, and that its shoots will not cease. Though its roots grow old in the earth, and its stump dies in the ground, yet at the scent of water it will bud and put forth branches like a young plant. But mortals die, and are laid low; humans expire, and where are they? As waters fail from lake, and a river wastes away and dries up, so mortals lie down and do not rise again; until the heavens are no more, they will not wake or be roused from sleep.* [Job 11:10-12]

The circumstances faced by Job led him, however, to ask to be hidden in the grave until the wrath of God is passed. He wonders whether God would appoint him a time when – and this is the crucial point – he would remember him.

O that you would hide me in Sheol, that you would conceal me until your wrath is passed, that you would appoint me a set time, and remember me! If mortals die, will they live again? All the days of my service I would wait until my release should come. You will call and I would answer you; you would long for the works of your hands. [Job 14:13-15]

He does not want to be forgotten in the grave. He imagines the possibility of being released. It is this hope of release that we proclaim to those who, though not living in Job's time, hold Job's ideas and labour under the burden of Job's fear of being forgotten. People may indeed forget you! Your children's children may not even be aware that you existed – though if they paused for a little they would realize that their existence is contingent on their parents, whose existence is contingent on their parents before them, and so on. They may not remember you but an awareness of themselves would lead them to imagine you because in a certain sense they will be "the works of your hands." We have sprung from our forebears yet we may forget that and we may forget them. So you may be forgotten by your relations and acquaintances but what we affirm is that with God you are not forgotten because when God calls, in the manner Job imagined that he would, we who lived in Him and who die in him will hear and live. Therefore, comfort one another with these words.

CHAPTER 19

Catch the little foxes!

Catch us the foxes, the little foxes that ruin the vineyards –
for the vineyards are in blossom. [Songs of Solomon 2:15]

Introduction

*I*f you have not read the book of Songs of Solomon I want to encourage you to do so. As you read, you are likely to see a number of very interesting things. You will see that although it mentions Solomon and David, Jerusalem and Mt. Zion the book does not mention God or the Holy Spirit. You will see also that the writer was preoccupied with issues of male and female relationships. You will see references to the human body: to the lips, and legs, cheeks, breasts, neck, arms and hair. The writer makes extensive use of images known to a farming community to convey the message couched in the language of a love song. You will see references to vineyards: to apples, raisins, figs, pomegranates, grapes, mandrake and wheat. You will see references to scented plants: cinnamon, aloes, crimson, frankincense, myrrh, rose and lily. You will see references to the animals: the gazelle, the stag, goats, sheep, leopards, lions and foxes. But even though the book never mentions the name of God, it is not void of allusion to the divine and the messages have spiritual significance. One such message is in the words of our text 2:15: "Catch us the little foxes that ruin the vineyards – for our vineyards are in blossom."

132

Vines in blossom

Let's see whether we can discover the symbolism in this verse. When your father is a coffee or citrus farmer, as it was for me growing up in South Manchester, Jamaica, you may run through the citrus grove as a short-cut but try never to do so when the trees are in blossom. It is from the blossoms that the fruits come, so if they are knocked off at their most vulnerable stage the yield will be affected. I know from personal experience what that feels like because we had a citrus grove. It was a major source of income for the family and we all took pride in what was the largest citrus farm in our little district. Care had to be taken to prune the plants and weed around the roots. Interestingly, it was during one of those weeding sports, in the summer of 1978, that I had the call to full time ministry.

There was a short-cut through our citrus grove but we were discouraged from using it, though I did not at first appreciate why. I realized the reason when the citrus trees were in bloom. Coming home late from school one day, a constant sore point in those days, I took the short-cut hitting blossoms off the trees as I dashed through the grove like a panther. Well my dad who was sitting at the end of the grove near the house was livid! Needless to say, that kind of recklessness never took place again – Papa Luther saw to it!

That was the imagery that came to mind as I read this account from the Song of Songs. The foxes are a danger to the vineyard because they run recklessly through it. So then, we must catch the little foxes. It was not until I went to Ireland I realised the extent to which farmers despise the fox, which is often the subject of wonderful stories. However, they are a bane to farmers, much like the mongoose in Jamaica because they will kill any farm animal or birds they can manage. Farmers in Jamaica would have a celebration ritual when they caught a mongoose, for which cremation would be a sure end.

The context in which the writer uses the expression gives it more than one meaning – but then, that is the nature of symbols and metaphors. You can pour all kinds of understandings into them. *(Speaking about metaphors let me digress to illustrate how dangerous they can be. The most severe punishment I ever got was about age 12 when I told a man who didn't allow me to climb his apple tree, "is not one day monkey is going to want a wife." In disgust at what to me was meanness I used to metaphor to express my unhappiness to him. In my mind it meant, OK sir, one of these days you will ask me to do you a favour. It was years after that I came later to appreciate the other ways in which we could understand this idea of "wanting wife," as reference to sexual intimacy. It was only then I appreciated the anger of my poor Mother, whom I embarrassed with my uncouth comment to the apple tree owner.* However, let's return to the metaphor in this story. There is a dialogue going on between two persons in verses 8 to 14. In verse 8 and 9 the woman speaks and the man speaks in verses 10-14

> *[Woman]The voice of my beloved! Look, he comes, leaping upon the mountains, bounding over the hills. My beloved is like a gazelle or young stag. Look, there he stands behind our wall, gazing in at the windows, looking through the lattice. My beloved speaks and says to me: [Man] 'Arise, my love, my fair one, and come away; for now the winter is passed, the rain is over and gone. The flowers appear on the earth; the time of singing is come and the voice of the turtledove is heard in the land. The fig tree puts forth its figs and the vines are in blossom; they give forth fragrance; Arise, my love, my fair one, and come away. O my dove, in the clefts of the rock, in the covert of the cliff, let me see your face, let me hear your voice; for your voice is sweet, and your face is lovely.*

The intriguing thing is to discover who is speaking in verse 15: "*Catch us the foxes, the little foxes that ruin the vineyards for the vineyards are in blossom.*" Is it the woman, or the man, or the writer making a parenthetical comment? On first reading it would appear as a parenthetical comment inserted by the writer. We see examples of such kind of comments in 2:7: *I adjure you, O daughters of Jerusalem, by the gazelles or the wild does: do not stir up or awaken love until it is ready.* This same phrase is repeated in 3:5, 5:8, and 7:4. It could also be that the phrase was in the mouth of one of the persons in the dialogue. Otherwise it could be a comment that is addressed to both persons in the dialogue and hence to us the reader. Whatever the source of the comment, it seems clear though that this "Catch us the foxes" expression in 2:15 is loaded with meaning. It speaks of guarding against the destruction of meaningful potentials and cautions against ruining opportunity. It is my contention then that you, as reader, must consider the opportunities and the potentials before you and *catch us the little foxes.*

We are accustomed to the metaphor the fields being white and ready for harvest. This metaphor is making another point – the trees are in blossom, they are ready to bear so catch the little foxes that ruin the vineyard when it is blossom. It speaks about being mindful of threats to the yield of the harvest, which we have a sense of because the trees are ready for bearing.

Ceasing Opportunities & Nurturing Potentials

However, you may then say I should speak clearly, not in parables, so that we can understand what all this really means. There are two points that I want to emphasise. The first is that we must discern the opportunities for growth and for fruit-bearing and to nurture them. Or to put it in the imagery of the text, we need to discern when the vineyard is in blossom. For example, when the pastoral staff are united in their desire to see a change of direction in the life and witness of their church I would say that the vineyard is in blossom – something is about to happen. When there is an obvious change in the work ethic of the pastoral leader and more time is being given to respond to the needs of the worshipping community, I say, the vineyard is in blossom. When there are calls coming from all sections of the church, urging that we move out into places where the witness of the Church is not known; when I see the enthusiasm of members, especially young people, for developing new ministries, I say our vineyards are in blossom. When I hear the cry for liturgical reform, for us to make our worship services more culturally relevant; that we should re-work, re-express and re-create the liturgies and traditional heritage of the church we have received into our own imagery, I say the trees are in blossom. When I hear the call in the media for the voice of the Church to be heard; when I come to the awareness that the society values traditional, ethical and moral principles of the Church; when I hear speaker after speaker calling attention to the critical significance of primary education, which many churches have maintained as a fundamental hedge against societal decay, I say, the vineyards are in blossom. When I see the zeal with which members of the Church take on its outreach programme, whether the health clinics, feeding programmes, outreach into the inner city areas, vocational and agricultural programmes, scholarship funds; when I see more and more people wanting to go into full time ordained ministry or when I hear ministers of Government speaking with sincerity about the extent to which they rely on the partnership of the church for the effective building of our society, I say, the vineyards are in bloom. These are some of the signs of the times. In these we have the evidence that God is creating opportunities for us to bear a credible witness. In these I see the vineyards in blossom. In other times other signs will emerge and we must read the signs of the times. So the first point is that we must discern when the trees are in bloom because failure to do so, for which we have countless examples, we will destroy the potential and miss the opportunities.

Despair and Cynicism

The second point is that we are faced with some clear and present threats to opportunities. In the words of the texts, there are the little foxes, which we must catch, because they are a danger to the vineyard. They are the threats that we must neutralise. One of the threats, which for example the church in many countries face, is the ever-rising tide of violence and crime in the society and this is indeed a threat to the blossoms. We see this threat in South Africa, Jamaica, Brazil and Columbia. The situation is equally dire when we think of countries like Iraq, Afghanistan, Palestine and Libya, where there are those who believe that only violence and war can end violence and war. Related to that is an even greater threat in the growing sense of despair and numbness that is creeping up our limbs towards our heart. We seem to have become so accustomed to the daily toll of murders that we run the risk of thinking – that is life. That is not life. Rather, this is death. We must refuse to give in to the idea that things have gone so bad that they cannot change. We dare not despair. We must refuse to give into the idea that nothing can be done. It may be true that we have lost a generation to the violence and crime. For a small nation like Jamaica, the numbers of Jamaican men in prison in Jamaica, the UK, the USA and Bermuda is an embarrassment. It is a shame that the name Jamaica has in some places become synonymous with extreme cruelty and criminality. It is a shame that so many see no opportunity for them to advance through peaceful means. It is sad that other people are perceived as obstacles that must be eliminated for progress. The attention of the Church, then, must be focused on creating opportunities for social advancement. The church has the task of building communities of hope and to demonstrate how people can dwell together in unity. The church must not retract from the message of peace and non-violence and of respect for lives. We have to summon our energies and organise our human and material capital to address this problem. It cannot be an option as to whether or not the churches have a programme that is aimed at crime reduction. It is not only a mandate that is crafted in church Synods but we also have it as an imperative of the Holy Spirit to stand up and be counted in the cause against crime. The church must challenge the government, the private sector and itself in the use of corporate resources. I recently visited an inner city community where I saw a nurse walking to work but there was so much water on the road, the potholes were filled with mud; mud was everywhere. It was difficult for the poor nurse in her lovely white shoes to find a place to walk. I said to myself that this would not be allowed to happen in the communities of the rich. Why then would governments allow it to happen in communities of the poor? Why should the people of those communities accept that their roads must be in that condition? It is reprehensible how the resources are apportioned to communities. The church has to join forces with the communities in the inner cities and insist that we want better community infrastructure. Churches that are located in the inner city areas have a particularly difficult task but maybe we have come to the kingdom for such a time as this. We must arrest the fox of despair. We must catch the foxes that are a threat to life and well-being.

There is another little fox that we must catch. Amidst the blossoms of opportunities I see a little fox of public cynicism that is directed at the Church. People take church leaders for jokers and think that what they claim, as church under Christ, is foolishness. The cynicism is born out of ignorance and prejudice. Ignorance about what the church is and prejudice against the insistence that people must be accountable to God. Mind you, the churches have themselves contributed to their being perceived sometimes in a negative light because of the questionable use of their human and financial resources and the priorities that they espouse. Also, although there have been ongoing efforts to improve the relationship between the churches, the competition between many for prestige and members has led to people seeing the churches as just another set of small businesses. When the churches in a given area pool their resources and develop joint projects there is likely to be a greater impact and a greater perception of credibility in their work. I also believe that when the churches and members of the churches live according to the gospel we preach we will catch the little fox of cynicism that ruin the blossoming of opportunities.

There is yet another little fox. In their zeal to emphasise the managerial responsibility that the ministers have in the congregation, some people have suggested that we must see the work of the Church as business. However, a major issue that the Church must clarify for itself is whether the gospel is a commodity that we package and sell according to popular taste. Don't misunderstand me. There is the need to keep our witness credible even if it is not popular. The issue I am raising is whether we are under a demand of the marketplace to cater to the changing religious taste and values. Since people have become accustomed to shopping around, is it then our task to understand what people want, what they are looking for, what will sell, and deliver on these things? The frequent changing of theological and doctrinal positions, while this may illustrate the flexibility of the churches, it also reflects the tendency to treat the ministry of the church as a commodity we sell. When we live in a time of shifting values and taste, we must determine if the gospel we bring is something negotiable. Treating the gospel as a commodity, as something we adjust to changing taste, will ruin the vineyards that are in blossom.

This parable of the vines in blossom is about guarding potentials and making the best of opportunities. Whether it is the ministry of the church or the witness of the gospel, there are things that pose a threat to the future growth. In more recent times we have also seen a sinister threat in how disputes in the church have been resolved. The stress on a dictatorial approach and the over reliance on law courts is threatening to abort any emerging competencies in skills in dispute resolution. And so we say, "catch the little foxes."

CHAPTER 20

Hiding from God

*They heard the voice of God walking in the
garden at the time of the evening breeze,
and the man and his wife hid themselves from
the presence of the Lord God,
among the trees of the garden.* [Gen 3: 8]

Introduction

I sympathize with the feeling of wanting to hide from God because there are times when our openness and vulnerability to God is simple overwhelming. The story of the ancient prophet Jonah teaches us though that we can run but in truth we cannot hide from God. Knowing this, it is hard to miss the irony in the story of Adam and Eve in the Garden of Eden, where we see the couple trying to hide from God. This all came about because in direct opposition to the command of God the couple had tasted the fruit in the middle of the garden. The story is very well-known, so much so that you may even consider it boring to have to focus on it again. Mindful of that, I will limit myself to consider a few lessons that we can draw from this story.

In search of Wisdom

The first thing is that it may come as a shock to you that according to the story what the serpent had to say to Eve came to pass – in part. The serpent told the woman that her eyes would be opened if she ate the fruit and that is exactly what happened! They ate the fruit and the Scripture says, *"The eyes of them both were opened and they knew that they were naked."* We should note, though, that before the woman took of the tree, she became convinced of the serpent's argument. We are told in verse 6 that *"she saw that the tree…was desired to make one wise."* This brings us to the first important observation. It is that knowledge or awareness must not be mistaken for wisdom. The woman was zealous in search of wisdom but what she received was knowledge and awareness. The intensity with which she yearned for knowledge is similar to our time. People are urgent about the need to know what's going on in the world and in the lives of others. It is this zeal to know that fuels the exponential growth in internet use, especially social media. It seems equally common among the young as it is among middle-aged men and women. We are inclined to go into depression if we cannot access the internet – not primarily for business, as the research tells us, though that too is increasing, but more so just to be in the know.

The drive for information is critical because we are living in an age when information is a commodity, which means, it is something we buy and sell. People speak of it as the commodification of information, which drives all the industries that rely extensively on the internet. One does not have to pay directly for all the information one needs. In fact, much of transaction is indirect. For example, we get to access the internet and others pay for the advertisement and other information that comes to us online. With immediacy we can access information related to any subject, though not all the information is reliable.

In the same way we have the commodification of information we also have the commodification of misinformation. People earn their keep by posting and circulating misinformation, sometimes in the form of viruses that are harmful to your computer. However, having knowledge of what is available, or even that for which the information may be used, does not amount to wisdom. People treat having the capacity to purchase information and information devises as a symbol of their status. The consequence of this is that certain information, for example, the things that pertain to our salvation, about which we can know without having to pay, are less interesting. Yet everyday large sums of money are exchanged for information on other people, especially information about their private lives. The problem with having information is to know how to use it. Teachers see this played out in their classes daily. There is a difference between one student who learns by rote and has the information and the other who reads and understands. The first has information but the second has understanding and so is wiser. This was the problem Adam and Eve ran into. They bought the serpent's story with the hope of gaining wisdom but what they received instead was awareness and knowledge. What were they going to do with it now?

Let me urge you then to be careful about the source and content of your information. Watch your source and watch the content. When you hear some news, check the source. Whether or not you accept it as a true account will depend on what you think about whom it comes from. Every piece of information has a bias; every story you hear is influenced by somebody's interest. That is why there are always different accounts of the same event and why it may be useful to get different sides. Unfortunately for the Eden couple they committed themselves to a single source. It is not just a matter of what we see but also on whose perspective we rely. It is for this reason people have different understandings of the Bible: it depends on who does the teaching! The point I want to make then is that Adam and Eve bought the information from the serpent. That information, like all information, came with a bias. They knew the source but they did not consider the bias in relation to their own values and certainly not in relation to the express command from the one to whom they were accountable. This brings us to the second thing I want to mention from the story: the need for wisdom.

Hiding from God

Another point to note is that with the new information they did not know what to do when God came a-calling and so they tried to hide from God. They played the ostrich, which in fear is less concerned about the exposure of its whole body providing its eyes are in the dark and the head covered. The couple was now embarrassed and had reason to be suspicious of the serpent's story, which in reality was only part of the whole story. Half-truths are as good as lies! There were critical things that the serpent left out. The serpent did not warn them that God would hold them accountable for the fulfilment of His will. To mention that part would not coincide with his programme. Like some journalists the serpent was not interested in being balanced. There was no virtue in accurately representing the other points of view. The couple discovered that there was indeed another point of view with which they had to reckon; that they were indeed accountable, as God had told them. It all came to a head when they heard the voice of God. The serpent also did not tell them that what they would get would become a burden to them. They were made to believe that what mattered most was having information. They were now discovering that for God obedience is more important than knowledge; that standing in awe of God, standing in the fear of God, not being afraid of God, was the beginning of wisdom.

Hiding from God is a great human pastime but it is also a great irony. We can only try to hide from God when we do not understand that God is all seeing. We hide from God when we do not understand that God is all knowing. We hide from God when we do not understand that God is present everywhere. We should consider this matter a little further because some people are hiding from God without even realising that that is what they are doing. Some people go to worship not because they have answered the call of God on their lives but because they are tired of being called. We are sometimes in church to appease our consciences rather than to express our commitment. Some people even go to church because they think that the demand God makes for their obedience will be lessened because they are in church. You may be shocked to realise that the trees of the garden, among which people hide are also growing in the church.

It seems we must try to face this question of why, like the Eden couple, people try to hide from God. A ready answer to this might be that people hide from God because they know they disobeyed and are guilty. One of the consequences of sin and disobedience is shame. Many of us carry this shame of sin and disobedience as a heavy burden that oppresses us. It would kill us to have to tell. Many of us carry these burdens longer than we need to because we have not fully discovered that burdens are lifted at Calvary. What a joy to know that we can tell it to Jesus!

There are other lessons that we can draw from this habit of hiding from God. The aim of this is not simply to give information, but to help us to hear God calling our name, asking the question, "where are you?" and to challenge us to come to terms with this tendency to hide.

Excuses and Mockery

We learn from this hiding incident something about excuses. According to the story, the aprons they sewed from fig leaves were meant to cover their nakedness and so to give them a greater sense of security and covering. We know that this is so because according to verse 6, they hid because of fear and nakedness. They must have said how wise they were in coming up with what amounted to a workable solution for their crisis. It seems that we should commend them for their creativity but it would amount to commending someone for covering the evidence of fraud. Like us they were led into a false sense of security in their own covering, their own way of doing things. They settled for aprons of fig leaves because they did not know that is it God who would clothe them with his robe of righteousness. When confronted with the presence of Almighty God, what they had stitched up as covering could not suffice. The aprons of leaves were their excuse for a proper covering. So it is with us. Many times the excuses we give are really attempts to cover up – just like using fig leaves. So making excuses is one of the ways then that we hide from God. We clothe ourselves in excuses and feel secure in the excuses that we make. Despite these excuses, however, God comes and God calls.

We also hide by seeking the covering of the crowd. We run to the bushes and concrete jungles of the world when we realise that the covering we have made is no shelter for the all-seeing eye of God. The lesson, then, is that our covering will not do. What we need is not aprons of excuses, not the covering of the hills but the robe of righteousness, which the Son of Man will give us. If you are wearing an excuse today you need to come out of hiding and face God. Don't make excuses for an absolute and unconditional commitment to the cause of God and righteousness. Admit your nakedness and seek the only dress with which we can stand before God – the robe of righteousness. The leafy excuse for a proper robe is not sufficiently secure. It does not offer sufficient cover.

There is yet another lesson from this hide-and-seek story. One of the things we know in hide-and-seek is that if the person seeking does not find, then they will go away. Could this be what Adam and Eve expected of God? The author of the story has a good sense of humour. He paints the picture of God as a man walking in the garden with the two people hiding. It is like the little boy who when he could not find a proper place to hide in his hide-and-seek game just covered his eyes. When we hide from God we turn our eyes away but God is not caught by that trick. If I refuse to look to God it does not make God blind. Hiding, then, is just another name for what people do when they make a mockery of God. We mock God when our attitude to God suggests that God does not know what he is about. We treat God as blind, believing he does not see us; we treat him as deaf believing he does not hear; we treat him as disabled believing that his hand is too short to save. It is a mockery when people resign themselves to the idea that there is no God because they cannot find ready answers to the perplexing problems of human life.

There are those who, though they cannot properly account for their own existence and the existence of the world, prefer to live with the false notion that there is no God. This too is a mockery. There are those of us who live in the comfort of the charity we show to others and feel that we ought to be commended by God. This is to make a mockery of God who gives us all we have and in whose stewardship we stand as unworthy stewards. There are others of us who are satisfied with the very least of the effort we can make in the cause of the gospel. We say, the demand of Christ and the gospel on me I can live with, providing it does not interrupt my important schedules. This is to make a mockery of God who provides us with life and gives us strength to labour. There are those who are prepared to delay any commitment to God, as if they know better than God does about the time for a decision. Yet it is the Lord who said in his word, today, this very day, when you hear his voice harden not your hearts. It is the Lord who said in his word that now is the acceptable time; today is the day of decision and salvation.

Conclusion

The lesson from this story is that God comes and walks into our hiding places, where we stoop among the trees so as not to be seen. God will come again and call our names. Don't be ashamed if you hear what seems like God is calling to you. When you hear your name it means God sees you as one who needs to come out of the place you are stooping. You are hiding because you know that the aprons of excuses you have sewed together will not do and you need a more secure shelter, a better covering. Move your hands from your eyes because God sees you as you are. God offers his robe of righteousness so that we can say with the Psalmist, you Lord have been my dwelling place; you are my hiding place; you are my rock and refuge. What if you do not hear your name? It could simply mean you have stopped your ears. Ears that are stopped cannot bear to be troubled with the voice of God. Ears that are stopped are of those who make a mockery of God, who believe God is satisfied with their goodness; who believe they are in heaven because there is no more need to grow.

Those who cannot hear the voice of God are the "Eli's" whose compromises have blocked their ears and blinded their eyes and hardened their consciences that they cannot be challenged. Adam and Eve in the Garden hiding represent us. We make excuses and we mock God because we live in the illusion that God does not see us and will go away. However, God calls us and is determined to find us. Those who answer and come out have the opportunity to be clothed afresh and will find that God is only seeking to rescue us from self-destruction.

CHAPTER 21

The Unworthy Servant

So you also, when you have done all that you were ordered
to do, say, 'We are unworthy slaves; we have done only
what we ought to have done. [Luke 17:10.]

Introduction

Many of us might find it difficult to put ourselves in the places of domestic helpers because their experiences of life are often far removed from ours. It should not miss our notice though that Jesus did not overlook them and drew on the life of servants to expound some important truths of the gospel. The story of the servant in Luke 17 is a case in point. From all appearances the word, which in Luke 17:10 is translated worthless in the NRSV, was used mostly in relation to slaves. We find a derivative of the same word in Matt 25:30 in the story of talents. The servant who is called worthless, wicked and lazy, who was to be thrown into outer darkness, is the one who made no investment of what he was given. The word also appears in the story of Onesimus in Philemon. The literal meaning of the name Onesimus is "useful", and so a careful reading of the story reveals the play on words. Onesimus was considered useless. In effect, he was not his true self and so his name was a misnomer. Paul returns him to Philemon as someone valued, as useful, though Paul seems to mean it in more than just an economical sense. In using the term unprofitable in Luke 17:10, the AV was attempting to keep the meaning of the word in the context of the economy of the day. An alternate meaning is in a moral sense, as in Rom 3:12. The challenge then is for the servant to admit of having no great importance.

According to the account in Luke the servant refuses praise and commendation because he was not going beyond the call of duty. He was only doing what he was asked to do. If he did not do it, he seems to imply, then another servant would have done so. The servant is dispensable and so one could question the economic value of the servant. The servant who appears to be non-essential is not being commended for his creativity and managerial savvy. He considers that he is of no significant value and is only doing what he was told to do. It is not the first time that this writer has focused on this idea of indispensability and so I must regard it as a ground principle. I find the idea sobering and at the same time consoling. Awareness of my own dispensability frees me from any uplifted sense of importance. I don't have to be afraid to fail and I don't have to preoccupy myself with performance. Awareness of my dispensability frees me to be faithful. As I read this text, I see a number of lessons, of which I will consider three, that are relevant for society today.

The Dispensable Servant

The first lesson is that no one is indispensable in the Lord's work. Although the text alludes to the importance of being obedient to the Lord's commands, to focus on the issue of obedience alone would be to miss the major thrust. It also challenges us to concede that the Master's project does not need us, even though we love to say we are the hands and feet of the Lord. One might even get the impression sometimes that some classes of people in church and society are indeed indispensable. Take the pastoral and administrative staff for example. In some churches these are the paid servants in others they are volunteers but their role would relatively be the same. It might be hard to imagine the witness of the gospel proceeding without them. One might even ask if their role is not indispensable then why is so much time and money put in their preparation and training and why such a large percentage of the church's income is devoted to their salaries. When one makes a critical analysis of the way financial resources are used in some churches, it is most alarming. In some churches, with which I'm familiar, the ministries of the congregations are organised in a way that most things depend on the pastoral leadership. One young minister, when he realised that there was a great weight of expectation on him as congregational leader protested that it seemed to him that he was being treated like a little god on a pedestal. Ministers seem to be indispensable because they have the powers of veto in the work of their charge. Even in the religious communities that have no formal cleric, there is an individual or a group of individuals who function in that way. Yet, it is precisely because church life tends to be organised the way it is why the text today has relevance. The ministers as servants, or the members for that matter, should realise that they are dispensable. What we do is an offering that we make to God, who may not even use our offering in the manner in which we believe it is usable.

The Uneconomical & Inefficient Servant

The second lesson relates to the tendency in church and society to rate people in economic terms. When the text speaks of the unprofitable servant, it is to say that the economic importance of this servant is doubtful. We should not for a moment imagine that the wealthy person is less deserving of pastoral attention and care than those who are not wealthy. However, churches tend to give more attention to the wealthy of the flock and there is also a tendency for the wealthy to consider that their wealth is indispensable to the witness of the Gospel. The same is true for the wider society, where the wealthy sometimes appear to be a law unto themselves. The point is that we must resist the temptation to judge our value in economic terms.

One of the larger, wealthier congregations of the Moravian Church, Southern Province, USA decided to withhold its financial contribution to the Provincial board because it disagreed with a decision taken by the Board. They found that they could try to penalise the executive by withholding financial support. This is indeed the way of the world. The point of the text, however, is that the servant should not think anything of his/her economic significance. In fact, we are to concede that in terms of economic value we are nothing. From a financial point of view this servant is a detriment. Don't consider the financial value I have to your work because I am really zero. No doubt you see the irony in this position. The fact is that the slave in Jesus' story had economic value but to hinge your worth on your economic value is to miss the point of being a servant.

Some of the translators use the term inefficient rather than useless, which makes a fresh point. In a world that is inclined to think of the managerial quality of the servant/minister, the third lesson is an even harder sell. The revolution of the social and business sciences has affected how we see the work of the church and the witness of the gospel. The managerial competencies of the minister have come to be of greater weight than an emphasis in an earlier generation on the minister as servant. It is of importance that the decline in the numerical strength of the historic protestant churches seemed to have occurred at the precise moment the switch was made to this managerial ethic. The new managerial ethic has tended to put more weight on the efficiency of the management system rather than on the needs of the persons receiving or delivering the service. The message of the text can be seen as a corrective to that trend. We should re-think the managerial skill-set competencies that we bring to service. In fact, the servant is being challenged to say that in managerial terms, I am inefficient. The servant should say I am dispensable, I am of no economic value; I only did what was my duty.

One of the ways in which the churches ensure that there are minimum competencies for the delivery of the service of the gospel is to subject their ministers to similar levels of training. From the point of view of this text one wonders how to deliver training in faithfulness in the witness of the gospel, which is an issue for urgent consideration today. The truth is that faithfulness to the gospel, which is a basic requirement of the servant's role, is not something that one will learn in a classroom. Rather, it is hewn out of the experiences of the Lord in life situations. We learn and practise to be faithful to both Lord and duty. This is the lesson of the unprofitable servant. He was seeking to be faithful to the Lord and duty and not to preoccupy himself with performance. He was focused on his character as a servant and less so on his performance.

CHAPTER 22

The Days of Noah

But about that day and hour no one knows, neither the angels,
nor the Son, but only the Father. For as the days of Noah were,
so will be the coming of the Son of Man. [Matt 24:36-7]

Introduction

One of the benefits of modern technology is that meteorologist are able to track hurricanes and other weather systems with a fair degree of accuracy. Recent hurricanes have taught us, though, that people do not necessarily act according to the information they have. The knowledge of impending danger does not necessarily make people more cautious. In fact, people often disregard the warning. It is sometimes hilarious to see people being rescued, by the emergency services, after they had spurned the warning to leave their homes to higher ground for safety from approaching floods. Similarly, in order to ensure that people who smoke do so with full awareness of the risks, most countries now insist that cigarettes are sold with health warnings, for example, "Smoking can cause cancer". Despite this, people still smoke, ignoring the risks. The point is that the news or even knowledge of danger or disaster is not sufficient to alter attitudes or courses of action to which people are committed. Our text speaks of the warning in Noah's time where, according to the story, people simply disregarded the warning of the impending flood. This is the challenge we face when we speak about the coming of the Son of Man today. People simply do not pay much attention to it; they do not take it seriously. As it was in days of Noah, so also it shall be at the coming of the Son of Man.

It is becoming increasingly difficult to speak of matters like these. There is growing doubt and suspicion about the whole idea of God and people are even more doubtful and dismissive about being accountable to God. Speaking of the coming of the Son of man, then, is for many people simply meaningless. It should be kept in mind that when we speak of the Lord today, the message we bring must compete with other points of view and convictions that people hold. According to the story in Genesis, at the time of the warning concerning the flood, people were simply going about their business. Many years later a New Testament writer took an interest in their attitude because it reflected attitudes in his own time and it is also hard to miss the similarities with our time. Let's consider in further detail the kind of responses people today have to the Christian message, in particular the message about the Lord's coming, and let us see what to make of the attitudes.

Disregard

One way in which people respond is to **disregard** the message when it does not make a connection with the day-to-day problems they are facing. For example, whereas Christians observe the seasons of Advent, as a way to highlight accountability to the Lord, many people simply couldn't care less. People observe the Christmas season as a time of giving gifts – although it is probably more a time of buying and consuming. In the Christian message, the idea of Christmas stems from the promised Advent of the Lord. However, that connection between Christmas and advent is missed altogether. Therefore, when attention is called to the need to prepare to meet the Lord, it goes into one ear and comes out the other. There is nothing between the two ears that can make sense of it. Like the people in Noah's time, people just continue to do all what they are accustomed to: eating, drinking, and making merry, marrying and being given in marriage. In other words, they pursue their regular pleasures and business as usual. The coming of the Lord, which emphasises the need for us to give account to God, is not received as urgent.

Of course the problem is not that people do not understand the need to be accountable. In fact, people who have no religious interests understand that being accountable makes sense. The trampling of peoples rights, the destruction of the earth's resources, the waste of the taxes that people contribute from their hard labour, the embezzlement of public funds and the unregulated run of private business to the detriment of the public welfare, all stem from a lack of accountability. People get extremely aggrieved when public funds are used to rescue private corporations, which are not known for their corporate responsibility and are accountable to no one. What the message about the coming of the Lord does is to tune our consciences to the awareness that we will have to give account for the stewardship of our gifts and opportunities and therefore the need to have an ethical compass to guide our daily lives. This generation has the need for a crier; one who announces the day of reckoning. The disregard of the day of reckoning accounts for waste and corruption. It is the disregard for the day of reckoning that explains crises that have arisen again and again in the financial markets and local economies. This is true of the sub-prime markets in the United States, the deterioration of the Irish economy, the crisis in the Greek economy as it was for the 1990's banking crisis in Jamaica. When people disregard the day of the reckoning for their actions, they are prepared to gamble if there is a slim chance of getting away with it. In some of the cases above, which are drawn from the financial sector, it is clear that there were external regulatory bodies that failed to do their job. In others, however, what seemed to be missing was the internal sense of accountability. Key players either figured they could get away with doing as they like or figured that even though their actions might come to haunt them, they didn't care. In either case they disregarded the signs and warnings.

Contempt

Showing disregard is bad enough but it is even worse to show contempt, which is the response some people have to the message of the gospel. According to the story, people did not find the warning of the man of God important enough for them to disrupt their regular schedules to pay attention to it. It does not seem that they were singling out the message of the man of God for contempt; they were simply going about their business. It was not that the warning was judged to be meaningless. Rather they didn't count the pronouncement as being sufficiently meaningful to distract them from their preoccupation. To put it in today's terms, the media did not pick up on it, it was not on the main evening newscast; it did not make the front page of the newspaper. Recently we were inundated with the news in print, electronic and internet, of the closure of a major newspaper outfit in the UK. Some people saw the irony of the media making the closure of a media house the news. It was everywhere – the media houses were making themselves news because they have the power to determine what makes the news. Imagine when the news media determines that something is a non-event. Such was the case in the story of Noah and so it will be in the time of the Son of Man. It was a non-event, a weak message that was unimpressive and not likely to generate sales.

It could be that the Christian message is lacking for smartness in the way it is presented but that does not make it irrelevant. Once people take time to hear it they might well readily admit it does make sense. The point is that people do not make the time to listen. Herein lays a challenge to make better use of the available means of the communication for purveyors of the gospel. In former generations the missionaries put time and energy in getting the message to people in far off lands, who spoke different languages. Their task was to ensure that people could understand what they would hear. We live in a society in which we have to direct our evangelistic task as we would to strangers. No longer can we assume that people know what we are talking about when we say the Christian message. Our challenge is to present the gospel in a manner that cause people to hear because any message that does not challenge the hearer will be treated with contempt. The witnesses to the gospel are not those who the world is inclined to obey. The world will hear the pop star, the world will take notice of the beauties and the models, the world will listen to those who have political power and those who have money are sure to get a hearing when they speak.

What amazes me is the radical courage of the gospel bearer, who presses forward with Paul's encouragement to the Corinthians, telling them that God uses the foolish things of the world to confound the wise. He uses the simple and the ordinary to bring critical issues to the attention of the powerful. The question then is this: what are those simple things of the world that will confound the wise and powerful of our time? What are those foolish things that can be put to the service of the gospel that will make people stop and listen? What are those simple things that will help to focus the mind? This is a challenge for gospel practitioners not to think in terms of grand designs but rather of the simply things on which everyday life depends.

Conclusion

The situation in which we bear witness today, then, is a situation of competition. It is a context in which there is a disregard for the message. Moreover, people show contempt for the message and maybe even the messenger. This situation calls for creativity and consistency; it calls for persistence and patience. People will continue living as enemies of the cross of Christ if we do not point them to another way. We must say to our world, there is a Lord to whom we must account. When we say he is coming again we mean to stress that the Lord has not surrendered his right to hold us accountable. That is part of the reason that the Christian calendar observes Advent, which is not simply about the coming of the Christmas season. More than that, it reminds us that Jesus is standing at the door. It challenges us not to lose sight of the Saviour. In the same way in which we put time into preparing to meet our relatives at Christmas, prepare also to meet your Saviour. For one thing is sure the Lord will come, as he has promised, and call us to account even if we are unprepared, as it was in the days of Noah.

Something More Doubt

Thomas was with them

In the Christian calendar, the 1st Sunday after Easter is called Low Sunday. The probable explanation is that it is considered less significant when compared with the height of significance attached to Easter. In the Eastern Church it is better known as Thomas Sunday. The reading from John 20:19-31 is usually set in lectionaries as the reading for that day. There are many aspects of this story that deserve our attention. However, given the brevity of this reflection, I want to focus your attention on the expression, "Thomas was with them." The "them" in question, of course, refers to the disciples meeting a week after Easter. Their lives descended in uncertainty and confusion with the death and burial of Jesus. For a moment everything that sounded plausible in the preaching of Jesus seemed to have collapsed. Thomas, who has come to symbolise doubt and uncertainty, was this time present with them.

We should probably see Thomas not only as one of the twelve but also as a state of affairs. He remains a symbol of doubt not only at the personal level but also as descriptive of the state of affairs that can overtake a Christian community. It is probably descriptive of the state of affairs your church is experiencing. The Thomas moment takes hold in the midst of change and calamity. All these possibilities are bound up with the expression, "Thomas was with them."

It is quite possible that many of us – maybe most of us – have experienced that Thomas moment. When we were not privy to an important occurrence, we feel a sense of suspicion or even full blown doubt. This is similar to what happened when Thomas missed the first appearance of Jesus but on the next gathering he was there with the rest. The remark that Thomas was with them was not said with dejection and sadness but with delight because the expectation was that something would happen to make him also believe. So when we say that Thomas is with us, we should not imagine that this is some unmitigated disaster. It is more like, thank God, Thomas is with us. Praise God, Thomas is with us this time. So, unlike what we are apt to think, the presence of doubt and of the doubting one in our midst spells opportunity, as we shall see.

The Reality of Doubt

Bear in mind that when John's gospel was written the end of the story, which is the high point of the resurrection and appearances of Jesus, was already established in the Christian tradition. Some therefore see the story of the resurrection as providing an impetus for the gospel. This part of the story, ironically called "Low", where Jesus appears after death, was in the foreground of the writer's mind at the outset. The experiences of the early Christian community gleam through this story. Even though they bore witness to the miracle of Easter, there were many who had problems with the idea of Jesus appearing alive. Indeed, it might well be the case that in this story we see the difficulty with believing that early missionary efforts faced. The story is written with us in view; we who like Thomas were not there at the first appearing. By placing ourselves in the centre of the story, it is not necessary to consider Thomas as an outsider. This is not Easter. It is now after Easter and after Easter Thomas is among the disciples. That is why I say "...Thomas is with us." This is not to point the finger at my doubting neighbour. On the contrary, it is to recognise a reality within the body of believer's after Easter. When the height of Easter is passed Thomas, symbolizing doubt, is among the disciple.

I hope it is clear that Thomas is not an outsider to the community of believers. He, or she for that matter, is among those who have come to faith. I can identify with Thomas, not because I do not believe Jesus appeared to the disciples but because like Thomas I was not there. Furthermore, like many others in the faith, there are times when I have questions. These questions relate not only to how the resurrection might have taken place but also questions about God. I have questions about God's intention for the world, especially in relations to people of other faiths, who put their trust in the one they worship as Lord and creator of the world and saviour of their lives. Questions do arise in my mind about the traditional claims concerning the special place of the Jewish faith. I wonder at times whether that special place has become a burden for us and whether it has trapped us into believing that we in the Judeo-Christian tradition are more special that others. I can therefore identify with Thomas. I am Thomas but I am not the only one in the community of believers who has these questions.

Opportunity Missed

By emphasizing that Thomas was with them the week after Easter, the writer is reminding us of the fact that an opportunity had been missed. By having to single him out for mention, the one who missed the opportunity became the centre of the story. What was the opportunity missed and what were the consequences? We are not told why Thomas was absent at Easter. More than likely it was due, as we often say, to unforeseen circumstances. This is an interesting irony because later he will insist that he needs to see. For his sake, I hope his absence was for a good reason because the most wonderfully unbelievable thing happened when he wasn't there. Something unforeseen and quite likely will not be seen again. The Disciples said, "We have seen the Lord."

Thomas missed an opportunity for an encounter like we do when we miss the gathering of the saints. I believe that the writer of Hebrews

10:25 had this missed opportunity in mind when he urged the saints not to neglect the gathering, as is the habit of some. It is sufficient warning for us to weigh carefully what we are likely to miss in the gathering. Although the presence of the Lord is not confined to the gathering of the saints, it is certainly one of the places of encounter. I want us to place great significance on the manner of our gathering and our attitude to and expectations of it. It is also critical that we come with a clear mind about who we are looking for and who we are coming to meet. Not everyone who arrives at church to worship. Not everyone is keen for an experience of the risen Lord. Therefore, it is quite possible that he is missed when he puts in his appearance.

The disciples grasped Thomas' missed opportunity and turned it into an opportunity for witness. This is important because witnessing must not be construed as something we do only to outsiders who have not heard of Jesus. Witnessing happens within the community because members of the community of faith also experience missed opportunities and descend into doubt and uncertainty. We sometimes wonder how to witness but the crucial thing is timing; it is all about ceasing opportunities. If we had been following John's story we would have seen that the writer already had Thomas connected to another missed opportunity relating to the resurrection. We first meet Thomas in John 11:16, where Jesus expresses delight that he and the disciples had <u>missed </u>seeing Lazarus before he died because he had in mind to turn the missed opportunity into an opportunity for witness; for glory of God. The writer wants to underline the fact that Thomas was there so we hear Thomas speaking: "let us go with him…" It was important that Thomas did not miss the raising of Lazarus. It was important that Thomas did not miss hearing Jesus say "I am the resurrection and the life." From the point of view of John, it was preparation for a future moment.

Thomas found himself in a unique position. Unlike the disciples he did not have the benefit of sight and direct experience so he must now decide what to make of their experience and testimony. His profile as an individual believer is raised by his having to decide. It is this position as an individual who must decide after the fact that throws Thomas amongst us. Thomas is a modern, thinking, rational individual, who is not keen to be swayed by what others say. He is not under any obligation to accept their testimony. He is not under any obligation to line up with the received tradition. He has the power of choice and he exercises that power. In so doing he constructs obstacles in the form of conditions for faith. This brings us to another point I want to make: in response to opportunities missed, obstacles are mounted.

Obstacles Mounted

So let us consider the obstacles mounted by Thomas when he realised he missed an opportunity. The first obstacle to faith is the ego: the individual Thomas himself. Listen to him: "Unless I." It's not "unless we." It is not "unless they." It is not "unless the Lord". It is "unless I." Truth for him is not preserved in a tradition or what others have witnessed. It is not something received and shared through the community of trusted witnesses. He makes himself the primary judge of truth. That is why I say he is a modern person. Thomas anticipates the modern person who treats religion and religious truth as a commodity for which we are the consumer. The modern person says "I decide what I accept as truth." "I choose to believe this." "I believe this but I do not believe that." The shopping and hopping attitude of Christians today have led sociologists to term us "consumers of the holy." In their view, we believe more in ourselves than in God. It is a sort of practical atheism, which is characterized by a striving for control over reality by rational-technical means and an inflated view of human potentials and abilities. How many times have we placed our ego as an obstacle? With an uplifted sense of self we place ourselves above others disciples. We believe that we can determine the truth but they can't! This is Thomas' ego.

Another obstacle mounted by Thomas was the obstacle of evidence. He called for verifiable evidence: insisting on the necessity to "see the marks of the nails in hands." One fascinating thing about the Greek, in which the NT manuscript has come down to us, is the capacity in the language to express ideas with precision. Where English has a single word to describe all love relations, for example, there are three different words in Greek. The same can be said of the word "see" in this context. For example, the word used here is different from the one which means to stare [*orao*] and from the one which means to see from a distance [*skopeo*]. The word used here connotes the idea of seeing something as evidence or proof of its presence. Thomas' call for verifiable evidence anticipates the modern age, where for a long time it was imagined that scientific evidence was the only way to determine truth. If it could not be proven scientifically it was to be doubted. The rise of this approach to truth happened at the same time that revealed truth, to which the Christian faith bore witness, was gradually pushed to the outskirts of public conversation. It is still the case in much of our western, civilised world that the talk of revelation is pushed into the realm of fanaticism. People find illogical an approach to life that moves forward on trust in God, whose existence is beyond scientific proof. The affirmation of the person of faith though is that God, who reveals himself in the Lord Jesus, resists every effort to be confined to our narrow consciousness and narrow definitions. Belief in such a God is considered to be pre-scientific, meaning backward. However, Christians should not be surprised at this because doubt has been in the community of believers from the beginning. Thomas has been with us for a long time. Thomas is not a new comer to the Christian community.

It is ironic that this agnostic, practical atheistic attitude tends to apply only to revealed truth. Our time is on the brink of being shipwrecked by those who find it hard to admit that scientific theories are also based on prejudices and that a scientific approach to life must subject itself to the questioning. Moreover, the frequency with which scientific theories on the same issue change is reason enough to question the next theory. People who put forward the theories believe in them, even though others may question them. Therefore neither believing nor questioning is a difficulty. The problem is that a scientific approach to life is often paraded as void of belief, which is the basis of revealed truth.

Another obstacle to faith mounted by Thomas was that of <u>experience.</u> He insisted that it was a necessary prerequisite for him to "put [his] finger in the mark of the nails and [his] hand in his side." Thomas was not content with hearing about what the disciples saw. He imagined that because he was absent the Lord owed it to him to come forward with something more than just showing himself. The disciples did not say that they had placed their hands in the hole in Jesus' side. They did not say that they had placed their finger in the mark. They simply bore witness to the fact that they had seen Jesus. So why does Thomas mount this Eiffel tower-like obstacle? He did not stop at his ego. Sight was not sufficient proof because like the famous philosopher Descartes argued, his eyes could have fooled him. He did not just want the evidence; he wanted a certain feeling! This is not just beyond reasonable doubt this is a call for an unusual experience. How many times have we constructed this as our obstacle? How often have we turned away because we did not get the feeling? How much do we make the feeling the pre-requisite of proof that Jesus is with us? One of the banes of the Pentecostal and charismatic movements is their insistence on a feeling as proof of Jesus' presence. One could add that our Protestant heritage, which has emphasised personal experience or pre-requisite to faith, has contributed to the expansion of the Thomas-like attitude in the Christian faith. So what experience are we now requiring as proof that Jesus is truly alive and amongst us?

Confronting Doubt and Questions

Having missed an important event and opportunity the previous week, Thomas doubted the story. Like the modern person, he established obstacles and put forward criteria for believing. How will the risen Lord respond to our obstacles of doubt? Let us remind ourselves of this: Thomas is the disciple who was not there at Easter but Thomas is with the disciples after Easter. I was not there when Jesus appeared in the flesh neither were you there. So what will we make of the witness given by those believers who were present?

One can sense the expectation filling the air as the disciples met after Easter. They gathered in hope to see the Lord. The fact that Jesus appeared, disregarding the doors and walls does not detain the writer and need not detain us. The writer is not sidetracked, nor should we, by Jesus' quick greetings to the other disciples who, like the 99 sheep in the parable of the lost sheep, are safe within the fold of faith. The writer keeps focus on Jesus who, without distraction, moves immediately towards the man of the moment; the man in doubt; the one with questions, the one with obstacles to faith, the man of missed opportunities; the one with uncertainties. It is as if Jesus is here especially for that one. To Thomas' surprise, Jesus is aware of his questioning and uncertainties and comes directly to him. This is the moment for which he asked. This is his moment and this is our moment. This is his opportunity for the vision he insisted. This is the opportunity for the experience he requested.

It boggles the mind to imagine what Thomas felt and what exactly he saw. I believe we have no account because those details would be missing the point. What Thomas saw was more than he asked for and what he experienced was more that he expected. One thing for sure is that in the end his uncertainties melted, his obstacles to faith were removed and his faith came to life. His conviction was ignited and a foundation securely founded for us, the Thomas' of the future who missed the opportunity of the first appearance; who would have the same questions, who would mount the same obstacles. We arrived more than two millennia later but we need not count the missed opportunity a disaster. We can understand that obstacles to faith are mounted over and over again but of this we are sure, those who come after Easter with an expectation, looking for something to ameliorate their loss; those who come with a need; those of us looking for answers to our questions; those who come with a desire to tame their ego; those of who come in search of a reason for faith and an encounter, will have our expectations surpassed for Jesus appears to us in faith and like Thomas, lost for words we hear the declaration, My Lord and My God.

CHAPTER 23

The Threat of Unbelief

"He called the place Massah and Meribah because the Israelites quarreled and tested the Lord saying, 'Is the Lord among us or not?' [Exodus 17:7]

Introduction

Unbelief is a threat even among people of faith. In many countries there are growing numbers of persons who chose to define themselves as belonging to no religious faith or not having any faith at all. If we take a traditionally religious country like the Republic of Ireland for example, the largest change in the religious/non-religious section of the census is of people who belong to no religious faith. Part of the reason for this, it would seem, is that the society is in transition from the domination of one religious group to having a diversity of religions and philosophies. It seems that part of the modern "Irishness" is to steer clear of religion. The threat of unbelief then, is a feature of societies in transition to a different way of life and different values.

Unbelief is a real threat also because the worldview from which Christians and other people of faith operate are at times out of sync with mainstream views in society. The question that people of faith face is whether there is need to change their view of the world, so that their message can be heard and understood. For what is the point of speaking if no one is hearing? The clash of worldviews then can also lead to unbelief.

The threat of unbelief is clearly not a new thing. Although a great distance separates the world of the ancient Israelites from ours, there's a story in the Hebrew Bible that is of value to this threat of unbelief because it shows in a very simple way what happens when a society is caught in a vortex of change and when there is the challenge to do things differently. Although generally there is an impulse to move forward, it might appear things are moving backwards as the new generations seek to reoccupy places from which their predecessors have long moved.

The story in Exodus 17 reaches back to the earliest phase of the development of the people of Israel. According to the story, the group of people who associated themselves with the migrants who went into Egypt, followed Moses out, believing that it was possible to find a new life as an alternative to the hardships and persecution they were experiencing in Egypt. That event, called the Exodus, became the most important formative experience of the emerging people of faith. Their self-understanding would henceforth be constructed around this event, which formed them into a new people. We pick up the story in Ex 17, after they had gone a relatively short journey towards a destination, of which they had little or no idea and which many who started in hope of reaching would never see.

The problems that this little band of nomads faced seem quite similar to the problem that a group of Christians in today's societies in transition face. The problems relate to the role that faith and belief can play in solving a practical problem. Today a practical problem might be housing for the poor or sanitation. It might be violence and crime. In the case of that ancient society, it was a problem of water. In their response to the problem, which itself became a point of reference for future generations, the reality of the threat of unbelief was exposed.

Problem-solving

How we approach a practical problem is important because, as we shall see in this story, the incident became an example to future generations. It is a normal thing when faced with a problem that we would look at how others dealt with the same problem, to see what could be learnt and to avoid "re-inventing the wheel". So how did the incident appear to subsequent generations? What were the lessons?

Reporting on the incident in Numbers (20:13), the subsequent generation argued that it was a case of lack of belief. Moses and Aaron didn't trust the Lord and the people quarreled with them and with God. Similarly, we are told that as a result of how they handled the problem (Numbers 20:24), Aaron lost his priestly role. He was penalised for his disobedience at Meribah. In a "tongue in the cheek" question to the crowd he is believed to have asked, "Do you want us to bring water out of the rock?" However, that was precisely along the lines of which Moses was told to find a solution. It would appear then that Aaron was making mockery of God. He doubted that the Lord was able to work a miracle.

In another report on the Exodus incident (Deuteronomy 6:16) the whole assembly is charged with unbelief. In this reading of the event it was not an issue about the leadership but that the whole group was to be held accountable for their unbelief because they provoked God (Deut 9:22). The succeeding generations were warned against the behaviour reported in Exodus 17, where the Lord was put to the test (Deut 33:8). They were urged to choose the Lord, with whom their fore-parents contented and whom they tested. The same idea can be found in the Psalms, where it is said that the ancestors tested the Lord and were in unbelief, despite what they have seen the Lord do (Ps 95:8-9). Let us consider then how this emerging religious community approached the problem they faced to understand why their succeeding generations were so unhappy with them.

The fact was that there was no water. To make matters worse there seem to have been no preparedness to deal with this situation. For that reason some suggested that rather than die of thirst with the animals they should return the way they came. This was not an unreasonable proposition because death faced them and their livestock as a real possibility. This was not a game. Life was at stake. Desperate as they were they had to consider all possibilities. In the midst of the contemplation, they ruled out any expectation that the Lord was going to be part of the solution. It is this ruling out of the Lord, this decision not to look to him, which became the point of reference in subsequent years. To ask whether the Lord was among them or not was in effect to say there was no point expecting from God when there was no justifiable reason to do so. In other words, "What was the point?"

It is this questioning of the wisdom of hoping in the Lord that we call unbelief, which in my view is the threat we face today. The question we ask and the question people in our context ask is, "Where is the evidence that the Lord is able to be part of the solution?"

Difficulty

Three things emerge in this story as reasons for unbelief. The first had to do with a difficulty they faced, the difficulty of the location. It strikes us as curious, and of course we don't know the whole story, that they camped at Rephidim since there was not water there. The word Rephidim literally means a place of refreshment, which means there was probably water there but it had all dried up by the time they arrived. Nevertheless, it tells us something about the problem that they would encounter, relating to where they pitched their tent. For a nomadic people, their fortunes and problems were related to where they set up camp. A good example of this is the problem Lot ran into because he pitched his tent towards Sodom (Gen 13:12). The same was the case with Isaac. He pitched his tent in the Valley of Gerar and ran into a fair bit of bother with his neighbours who were prepared to murder him. We see innumerable problems faced by the children of Israel as they moved about in the wilderness of Sinai (Number 9). The problem had to do with their physical location; where they pitched their tent.

Thinking along those lines, we can observe that the problems and fortunes of Christians in one country will be different from those of Christians in another. By the same token, our problems and our fortunes are not unrelated to where we live, where we work and so on. The lesson for us then, which is also a lesson in faith and problem-solving, is this: take time to understand where you set up camp; where you spend time.

The threat of unbelief will arise from the context in which you live and the places from which you seek refreshment and comfort.

The issue of values is relevant here. You will of course be asking yourself about the values of the place where you spend time and how these are affecting the state of your faith. When societies are in transition one of the changes we experience is changes in values as people reach for new understanding of who they are. It is in this context we must consider same sex relations, which is a real problem for many Christians. In an earlier generation the church was much more exercised about issues relating to fornication, adultery, gambling and drunkenness. These have become more acceptable as the values and emphases in the society have changed. With the changing values in the society comes also the change from belief to unbelief. It is a question of the context. The warning then is to study your context. Know where you have pitched your tent.

Disappointment

A second reason for the unbelief was the disappointment arising from unfulfilled expectations. "Why did you bring us out of Egypt to die in this place"? This is neither what we expected nor what we were led to believe. Is it not also similar to our cry that we had hoped for our prayers to be answered? You can appreciate here the song writer who wrote, "Teach me the patience of unanswered prayer." There is of course a co-relationship between disappointment and expectations. This is true not only for the relationship between friends and partners but also true for our relationship with the Lord. In the people's mind neither Moses nor his God was proving to be helpful.

How do we respond to the person who says he finds no point following the expectations of faith anymore. There is of course no easy answer. The only response is really to act in faith and hope, which is what we do when the absolute power is not in our hands. The expectation of the people that Moses would provide an immediate solution to their problem was part of the reasons for the disappointment. We soon find that our parents and our leaders are no less powerless than we are. We find that they are as vulnerable to loss of faith as we are. Part of the maturing in faith we experience is when we come to hope in God rather than hope in the parent, the leader or the pastor; when we see the idolatry of expecting that they will solve our problems. There is really no solution for broken faith other than to exercise faith. When faced with the situation where we know the absolute power to make a difference is not in our hands, we act in faith and hope. This is the story of striking the rock. Drawing on the resources at his disposal and acting on the basis of his faith tradition, Moses struck the rock. He did so not because he was absolutely sure but because he was hopeful. His hope didn't disappoint him. When faced with disappointment, strike the rock, which means a bold and courageous action in faith and hope.

Death

The third reason for the unbelief was the reality of death facing the group. Why did you bring us here to kill us? When faced with their mortality they had every reason to hope in God, since absolute power was clearly not in their hands. For some people it is the fact of the death of their loved one unexpectedly that leads to unbelief. If there's a God, the argument runs, why would he not intervene to heal or help a vulnerable child? However, faith in God is no guarantee that we will escape the ravages of our mortality, for we are only human. Idolatry is the imagination that absolute power resides in human hands and the expectation we have that it will be exercised in our favour.

Conclusion

The experience of the nomads camped at Rephidim and the event at Meribah and Massah became a point of reference for future generations. In the face of difficulties, disappointment and the threat of death they lost faith and descended into unbelief. Their difficulties were situational. Their disappointment was due to unfulfilled expectations. The threat of death was unavoidable. Faith is courage to take action in the face of difficulties, disappointment and the threat of death. The refusal to act in faith and hope is unbelief.

CHAPTER 24

When the Soul is Bitter

I loathe my life; I will give free utterance to my complaint;
I will speak in the bitterness of my soul. [Job 10:1]

Introduction

Bitterness sometimes arises from disappointment and many people are disappointed when they feel that God has not come through for them. I felt that way when my mother died. She was a woman of strong faith and trust in God. When she was diagnosed to be terminally ill, she had the hope, to her last breath I believe, that God would miraculously turn her condition around and make her whole and well again. She would have heard or read stories of miraculous healing and she had nothing to lose from that child-like trust. I imagined then that she would have been quite surprised that God had other plans and did not come through for her the way she expected. Although, now that I think about it, she might have been willing to say yes Lord, if that is what you wanted for me. Nevertheless, in my grief at her passing I felt angry at God and angry for the way we had been led to expect miracles. I felt that there was something insufficient in the way we spoke of God and faith. I also found however, that it was not easy to express these thoughts among my fellow Christians. Why was it so difficult to have a conversation about this matter? Could it be that we are not accustomed to that kind of rugged questioning? I wondered too whether people would become uncomfortable to the point of despair. I also imagined people saying, "If the minister of religion is having those questions what are we to say?" So I was probably fearful that it would weaken rather than strengthen faith. In short, there is not a culture of questioning God.

However, the contemporary Christian cannot afford to live in a religious bubble untouched by the realities of life and unchallenged by the difficult questions that life throws up. In fact, the Christian today, living in the postmodern world, needs a robust faith community that is not afraid to ask and be asked difficult questions. It became clear to me that without the space to vent their feelings people will not only lose faith but may also waste their lives. There must be space for the bitterness of soul.

From Bitterness to Contempt

People who are bitter because of suffering have the consolation that, if it pleases them, they can speak their minds freely to God. This is one of the functions that the book of Job plays for the people of faith. It creates the space for us to be bitter, if only for a while. This section of the word of God was evidently hewn out of a crisis of faith resulting from inexplicable suffering and hardship. It faces the hard questions that people of faith raise in the quietness of their loneliness about what it means to suffer and yet to hope in God. From the account in Job 10, we learn that when the soul is bitter it can lead to contempt for life. *My soul is weary of my life*, Job says, or as it is translated in the NRSV, *I loathe my life*, I am sick of it. If this is what life has to be then we might as well forget it. What Job was in effect saying was that he was tired of living. Earlier in 6:8ff he wished for death: *O that I might have my request,... that it would please God to let loose his hand and cut me off.* Later in the chapter (v. 19) he argues that it would have made more sense if he went straight from the womb to the grave.

It must be clear though that the contempt Job is showing for life is not a general contempt. He is sick of his own life. He is asking God to take it from him if that is what it has to be. Some people find in Job a justification for wanting to end their life but the whole issue of suicide or assisted suicide is another matter altogether. These too are difficult and complex questions that must be addressed by the community of believers. However, Job gives no encouragement to suicide or assisted suicide here. He does not threaten to take his own life because he is not against the principle of life. Neither is he asking his peers or family to do so. He believes that only God has the right to take life. He is bitter in his soul and wishes to be relieved from his suffering. It would seem that God, who in his view is the proper one to take life, is not willing to help him. His talk about the burden of his life arises from his despair that no help is coming to him. So his original call is a call for answers and a call for help. Understanding this is important.

The suffering of Job is indicative of the experience of those who were not afraid to question the things they used to believe about the might and love of God. This kind of questioning is only possible for someone who is keen to deepen faith. There are those who have not moved beyond the Sunday-School version of their faith to take account of the adult discourse. It is clear that those childish conceptions cannot stand the weight of their daily experiences and will crumble under the weight of questioning because they are no longer plausible. People who are keen to mature through hard questioning do not see it as their business to defend God, as if their life depended on it. They are struggling with the meaning of their life and the book of Job gives them the vocabulary to accompany that struggle. Job is helpful then for the person of faith who has to think in a new way about the privileges of the righteous. Freedom from suffering is clearly not one of those privileges. It might appear that the rich and the famous are less likely to suffer and that the poor bear an uneven amount of suffering. However, the bitterness in the soul caused by unjustifiable and inexplicable suffering is a common denominator that does not have regard for class or creed. It is a sobering moment waking up to the reality that the righteous, who are called righteous because of their trust in God, are no less exposed to suffering that can cause bitterness in the soul.

The contempt for his life therefore leads Job to question and contend with God. This awareness might give us another understanding of how it relates to ancient Israel, as the people of faith. It was Jacob who was renamed Israel because he contended with God. In that story in Genesis 32, Jacob was about to meet Esau whose birthright he stole but he was distressed and afraid for what might happen in that meeting. We are told that while on his own he wrestled with a man all night until daybreak, pressing the man to bless him. Although he was struck on his thigh, Jacob prevailed and was blessed and had his name changed to Israel. Jacob called the place Peniel, being convinced that he had seen God face-to-face. In the same manner as Jacob and certainly as Job, people contend with God when they imagine him as the respondent to the questions they have. Sometimes this conversation is in the privacy of their thoughts. Sometimes, as it was with Job, it is expressed in prose and poetry. Other times people rant and rave to their peers or to anyone who will listen.

In this story though, Job perceives his suffering as unjustifiable punishment from God. His challenge to God was to justify this suffering. How could the work of God's hand be the object of God's oppression? Is it not inconsistent with whom God is and plays nicely into the hands of the cynic and the wicked? Or was it that God really has human/fleshly eyes and sees as humans do? The suffering makes sense if God is a bully. It makes sense if God is like mortals and in a moment of amnesia has forgotten that it was he who fashioned us out of clay. The suffering makes sense if God is playing the hypocrite and behaving as if he were not the one who cared, spared and preserved the faithful in steadfast love.

Courage to Speak

For those who have these difficult questions about life, we soon discover, as does Job, that there is no ready answer and God is not tripping over himself to find an answer for Job. In fact the first respondent to his questions is one of his friends – another person of faith. This is important because often we are the ones who hear the questions and see the struggles of fellow pilgrims. When a person of faith begins to struggle in his/her faith, or with faith, it becomes an issue for the whole community of believers. One might say that the questions, which the person of faith puts to God in the privacy of their thoughts, in prose or in poetry, are questions also addressed to the whole community. His conversation is also with his own people, who he challenges and by whom he is challenged. Our questions are also questions to people in our hearing who sometimes believe the same things as we do and have the same struggles. Other times they believe differently and do not have the same questions and we wonder how it is that they can go on believing the things they do.

In those moments of deep questioning one should be slow to speak. Quick speech serves only to make matters worse sometimes because people are not looking for nice sounding phrases and responses that try to smooth over the rough edges of what they are experiencing. Sometimes people want just to be able to express their thoughts in our hearing. It is not necessary to feel we have to rush to find a ready answer because the first question we hear might not be the most crucial. In the conversation with those who are bitter in soul being slow to speak is recommended because we must allow the person to formulate their questions fully and what we hear might only be the first draft. We must take a leaf out of God's book and be slow to speak.

So then, we are the respondents in the questioning that people in their bitterness of soul put to God. How we respond is critical. However, the response is not because God has made us his emissary but rather because we dare not keep quiet. Being slow to speak does not mean absence of response because we cannot be unresponsive and remain true to our claim to be a people of faith. Rather, we allow for the person to fully formulate the questions they wish to raise, questions that they sometimes want to revise. Yet, we cannot remain silent forever because, as people of faith, we are in conversation with the bitter soul and must consider carefully the neighbour's contempt for life. We are the one to respond when the neighbour questions and contends with God. We are the respondents not because we are God or because we are deputizing for God. Rather, it is because the question is at the same time being put to us. Suffering does not necessarily lead to bitterness but where there is bitterness there is no point wishing it away with nice sounding rhetoric. Our aim must be to face honestly the tough questions that people raise in bitterness of the soul.

The Late Rev Trevor Palmer

Reflecting here on the book of Job makes me think about the later Rev Trevor Palmer, who died in late 2011. We spent a year together in seminary and I worked alongside him for several years in the ministry. He was a friend and a brother. When I think of Trevor Palmer the words theodicy and importunity come to mind because he was the first to explain them to me. Theodicy is a subject matter in the book of Job and refers to the way people of faith account for the presence of evil in the world, while at the same time affirming the love and omnipotence of God. Importunity is about persistence in prayer and is illustrated in the story in Luke 18, where the widow wearies the judge in persistent pursuit of justice.

I have the sense that these words were themes in Palmer's life: he wrestled with the frailty of human life and its vulnerability to illness and decay without retreating from faith or hope in God. He was also tireless and persistent in prayer, believing that God was able to do even more than he could ask or imagine. His passing obviously filled us with sadness but I hope his family and friends would have been consoled in the character of the man. His hope in God was not undermined by the reality of evil or the illness to which he was subjected and to which he eventually succumbed. We might also be consoled in his importunity, which was founded upon the rock of his faith in God.

CHAPTER 2 5

The Tree of Life

*So when the woman saw that the tree was good for food, and
that it was a delight to the eyes, and that the tree was to be
desired to make one wise, she took of its fruit and ate; and gave
to her husband, who was with her and he ate.* [Genesis 3:6]

Introduction

T he story of Adam, Eve and the Serpent is a well-known
story and yet its relevance to daily life may not be readily
seen. Different interpretations have been put on the text,
especially in terms the meaning of the tree at the centre of the Garden,
and what it might mean that Eve picked the fruit. The long tradition
of interpretations, which have tended to focus on the failure of the
couple, makes it hard to lift the story out of a moral straight jacket. My
invitation is for you to let go a little of what you already know and try
to see something else in this story. I will not focus on any of the three
characters, (Adam, Eve or the serpent) *per se*. Rather, my interest is in
the fact that their action together amounted to them reaping a harvest –
fruits were found and fruits were picked. Adam blamed Eve; Eve blamed
the serpent. Amidst the blaming game there was a plan in the human
community to make a harvest of everything. When we look at the story
in terms of reaping a harvest, you will see that the act of harvesting is
a primary and fundamental activity in the human community. For no

matter in which society we live, whether modern urban or ancient rural, finding food is critical to meeting a basic human need.

Many people in urban societies may not know where their food comes from but they must eat. The beauty about living in the rural area is that we see where our food is coming from. Disconnection from the source and the means of production is in large measure responsible for the waste so characteristic of urban societies. It is ironic how agencies run by people in urban societies want to lecture rural dwellers about environmental awareness and water conservation. Growing up in rural Jamaica we did not need legislation to manage water properly. We knew that we had to conserve water because we could look into the tank and see that the water level had gone down and that we were in the dry season. When we are close to the source of food we have a keener awareness that the resources of the land are not unlimited. Not only so but we were always aware of God's provision. That might explain why from ancient times farming communities would have a celebration to mark the harvest. The traditional harvest celebrations were really moments to say thanks to Jehovah Jireh, God the Provider, who was affirmed as the one providing the food. The farmer planted the crops but did not cause them to grow. The farmer watered the crops but was not responsible for the increase. People with this awareness would gather to celebrate the mystery, the miracle and the wonder of God's provision. Today when you pause to have your meal, you might want to think about the source of your food. Where was it planted and by whom? How did it grow and who reaped it at the source?

Divine Provision

In the story, we are told by Eve (Genesis 3:2) that the trees in the Garden were meant for food. This was a recollection of what God said earlier (Gen 2: 16), "Of every fruit of every tree you may eat, except the one in the centre". So, there were several trees in the Garden of Eden, God's preferred place for the human being to dwell. These trees were available for food. In the mind of the people of faith, God provided adequately for the whole human community – this is the first lesson - God provides. When we sit for a meal and we say our grace, it is a rehearsal of this lesson – God provides. When people go to worship and we give tithes and offering, it is also a rehearsal of the first lesson – God provides. When out of our own labour and bounteous blessing we give to our friends, neighbours and to those in need, it is a reminder to them and us that God provides. When we take a day of rest and when we pause for prayer, we are saying that the things we have and our accomplishments do not all correlate to our effort but there is something for which we need to give thanks. So the very act of worship is itself recognition of the mystery of life and of our sustenance. So this is the first lesson we can draw from this story, God provides.

It is however a reasonable question to ask whether God has provided adequately for all the peoples of the world. Or to put it another way, why do we have pockets of need and pockets of plenty in the world? We must either claim that this idea of God's provision is nonsensical, or that God is partial in the way he provides. This is indeed a difficult issue because we know of starvation and malnutrition. We know of poverty and hunger. It seems to me though that whether or not we have food for everyone depends on us. What we see is that in the same world, in the same country, sometimes in the same community, there is hunger, want and waste. Until we can resolve the issue of human waste in the world, in our county and in our community, we cannot put the blame for want at the feet of God who provides. This matter of human waste brings us to another lesson.

Human Consumption

The second lesson is about human consumption: God has not only provided but in the understanding of the people of faith, God has also set certain limits to consumption. That is how we might understand the saying, *"The fruit of the tree in the middle of the Garden you shall not eat of it."* Everything is not to be used up; we do not have to make everything in the garden a commodity. Every tree is not for harvest, and everything is not to be eaten. There are limits to the extent we can drain our resources. Gen 2:17 calls this tree the tree of knowledge. Eve said of the tree that it was not only pleasing to the eyes, not only good for harvest but its fruit was also desired for wisdom. The error she made and the error of the human community is that she imagined that the wisdom and the pleasure were to be found in the exhausting the harvest. So let us consider this mistake about human consumption. We are not the wiser because we eat more; we are not the wiser because we deplete everything. What if the Irish potato farmer ate all the potatoes from the harvest? What will he have to plant for the next season? What wisdom is there in the farmer eating all the peas that he reaped? What would be the wisdom of eating the yam as well as the yam head, which must be planted for the next crop? This is a simple lesson of life. Everything is not to be eaten. Even if you are not a farmer the lesson holds good. What wisdom is there in the teacher using all her monthly salary to buy food? Is it not true that we need to save something? There must be limits to expenditure. One of the reasons for the crises we face in our economy has to do with our levels of consumption – not only the food we eat but also other commodities on which we spend our hard earned resources. This propensity to exhaust all in our garden or all our income is a millstone around the necks of many developing countries.

There is a close relationship, even if it is not direct, between consumption and poverty. People who exhaust the sources of food will soon have nothing to consume and the more each individual uses the less others will have because there is a limit to what can be produced. When we do not respect the limits of our use and expenditure we are paving the road to poverty and destruction, if not for ourselves then for others. We lose the benefits of living in the Garden of God when we do not set limits. The task then was to identify the centre of the Garden, that is, those things that must be preserve as a sign of awareness of limits. By refraining from harvesting one tree in the Garden, the human community would have left a relic of God's provision, a sign. When all the fruit has been eaten from all the other trees we would be reminded that there was a harvest. That tree in the midst of the Garden would stand also as a tree of hope and faith. It would stand as a witness of God's provision. However, by harvesting that tree, it amounted to killing the witness. What will be the evidence to share with the next generation? To what will the human community point when people begin to doubt the ability of God to provide? So the harvesting of that sign was not only an act of disobedience, it was a malicious act designed to make God a liar, thus leading people to unbelief. It was an act that had the effect of planting the seed of doubt and mistrust in *Jehovah Jireh*, my provider.

False Harvest

The reaping of the forbidden tree brings us to the third harvest lesson. We have seen the virtue of recognizing divine provision and the importance of setting limits to what we consume. Given those lessons, it should be clear that there can be a false harvest. When human beings reap what is not meant for food we say that they have reaped from the wrong tree. For the couple in the garden it was a false harvest because they reaped what was not meant for reaping – at least it was not theirs to reap. So, when it comes to reaping the produce of our efforts, when it comes to harvest-time, the question we ask is not only how big the harvest is but also whether the harvest is true. When one man steals another man's goat and sells it, does he take home that money and give thanks to God? Yes he might but that is a false harvest. When one man reaps another's field of potatoes or pineapples, he may even use the money to help his children and get food for his family but this is a false harvest. When the fisher destroys the coral reef, which is breeding ground for the fish, he may bring in a wonderful catch but that is a false harvest. When the fisher steals another's fishing-pot and takes in the young lobster, thus endangering the future of the species that is a false harvest. When the gambler or the cocaine dealer brings in a large sum of money he might put up a wonderful house for his family and may even help people in need but that does not make the harvest true. When the employer presses the workers to the limits of their productivity, pays a low salary and reaps a bountiful harvest through oppression, can that be a true harvest? When the multinational company puts in the capital to set up a business to mine the minerals or oil in a country, and reaps a bounty while paying little in wages and no capital gains taxes, that is not a true harvest. Our business is not only to harvest but our harvest must be true. It is true when it is honest, beyond ethical and moral question, and when limits to production are respected.

The tree of life is a sign of God's provision and to clear it is to destroy that which points to the provider. The tree of life is a reminder of human need and human consumption, as well as human attitude to both. Everything in the world does not have to be turned into a commodity and everything does not have to be reaped. Not everything was put at our disposal to be depleted. Life is not only about consuming but also about enjoying what has been created without thinking how can it be broken down for our use. Beauty and wisdom also lie in being able to enjoy the presence of the created order and not only in our capacity to turn it into waste, which is what happens when it is consumed. Moreover, not every reaping is ethically and morally justifiable and not every harvest is true.

CHAPTER 2 6

Reliability and Reality

Those who swear by Ashimah of Samaria and say, "As your
god lives O Dan" and "As the way to Beersheba live" –
they shall fall and never rise again. [Amos 8:14];

Introduction

*R*eading that passage in Amos 8 I can't help but think of the small rural community called Beersheba, which is in Westmoreland, Jamaica. The community is named after a little church, which has been there for over 100 years. The church boasts an attractive building, which is testimony to the hard work and the dedication of the members and ministers over the years. Also living at Beersheba was a kind woman called Mrs Louise Meyler, whose husband predeceased her by a number of years. Mrs Meyler was principal of the school in the community and a leader in the church. So deep was her involvement in church and community that her name soon became synonymous with the community. Mrs Meyler was long retired when, as a newly married couple, Jean-Marie and I went to live in the nearby community of Springfield. Like many other young families, we were beneficiaries of the many acts of kindness from this Beersheba stalwart. Among the kindnesses received from Mrs Meyler was her willingness on many occasions to forego the use of her reliable Ford Cortina car, so that my family could have had the use of it when our Russian-made Lada was close to giving up the ghost. In thinking of Beersheba, it would be remiss of me not to recall such acts of kindness from Mrs Meyler, who was such a reliable rock of support for our young family.

The Way to Beersheba Lives

How apt it is that Beersheba conjures up these memories, considering the story behind the biblical name. Beersheba is the name of an ancient city, which was particularly famous in the history of ancient Israel for several reasons. First, and probably foremost, it had a well, which is still there, believed to be about 66ft in depth and about 7ft in diameter. It is safe to say that the city was built up around the well. As a watering hole for animals, it was the place of meeting for the communities and the wandering tribes. The name literally means a *well of swearing*. In each generation of the leaders of ancient Israel, covenants and agreements were made here, between contending tribes, as everyone wanted free access to the water. According to Gen 21, the covenant Abraham made there with Abimelech, King of Gerar, was one of the earliest.

Beersheba was famous for another reason: it was the southern-most city in ancient Palestine, and so became a point of reference in geography and population census. In fact, in scripture you will find the reference "from Dan to Beersheba" in several places. Dan was the northern-most city.

There is a third sense in which Beersheba was famous. People would swear by the way, which leads to Beersheba, saying that it was a path that would not be overgrown with weeds. It was a sure, persistent and reliable path. We find allusion to this in Amos 8:14: "as the manner of Beersheba liveth" or "as the way to Beersheba lives." In other words, the way to Beersheba would never be overgrown with weeds. People will always want to go there because of what was there. There was a well, a watering hole, a well of sustenance, something by which lives were saved. I was delighted to discover this third sense because it is this sense of a way that is sure, in which we can find both hope and challenge, that I find relevance for today.

"The way to Beersheba lives," the saying goes. It was always bustling with the movement of people going to and fro to get water from the well. To capture the symbolic meaning of the word there are many places that could be called Beersheba because these places are renowned for their support to families and individuals. They are accessible, reliable and even when they may charge a fee for service they are affordable. I wonder what place you would call Beersheba. Whatever it is, I hope that your Beersheba will live up to its name of being a place where people will always visit because of what they are likely to get there. It is about an authentic experience, which is more than just optics. Beersheba is a place or maybe it can be someone on whom you can rely. Where then is your Beersheba?

The Shadow and the Substance

These are only a shadow of what is to come, but the substance belongs to Christ. [Colossians 2:17].

The Way of Christ

The reliability of the way to Beersheba is reflected in Colossians, which has a saying that was popular in the literature of the early church. *These are only a shadow of what is to come, but the substance belongs to Christ. [Colossians 2:17].* This saying, which speaks of the shadow and the substance, probes to reach the bedrock of reliability in the Christian faith, as the way of Christ. Older versions of the Bible, for example the Authorized King James Version (AV), reads, "Which are the shadow of things to come; but the body is Christ." The Revised Standard Version (RSV) reads, "These are only a shadow of things to come, but the substance belongs to Christ." I prefer the RSV rendering because it captures the play on words, which we have in the original text. In the original text, the word for shadow is *skia*, (σκια) and the word for substance (or body) is *soma* (σωμα). So, the things are only a *skia* of things to come but the *soma* belongs to Christ.

This expression, "the shadow and the substance," is meant to convey the idea that some things are only appearance and a reflection of the true and the real thing. As I think about the difference between shadow and substance, I recall an incident when as I student I was assigned to the Gracehill congregation, in the district if Content, near Balaclava, St Elizabeth, Jamaica. A house lizard spent the whole morning trying to fight its reflection, which it saw as it passed by a piece of mirror on its way to gather food. After hours of trying to bite its reflection in the mirror, the poor, exhausted lizard not only gave up the fight but gave up the search for food and returned from whence it came, only to repeat the whole thing the next morning. It is a true story with a good message; if we mistake the appearance for the substance, then we will spend our energy fighting and achieve nothing in the end.

The point that the writer to the Colossians was making is that the religious practices, which people in his day were insisting upon, were only a shadow of things to come. Some people were insisting that certain food and drink had to be consumed; that certain festivals had to be observed; that special days had to be kept. The contention of that day was that unless these religious practices were observed, then true worship was not taking place. The writer of Colossians was insisting, on the contrary, that these religious practices were not to be allowed to blind the worshiper to the object of our faith, the one true God. The ceremonies are to be seen in an instrumental way; they were only a shadow of the real thing. It was because of similar experiences in the early days of the Bohemian Brethren in Czechoslovakia that there developed the very famous distinction between the things that were considered essential for salvation and those things that we should consider as being either auxiliary or accidental. The **Essentials** were divided into divine essentials, on one hand and human essentials on the other. Divine essentials included the grace of the Father, the merit of Christ and the gifts of the Holy Spirit. Human essentials included faith, love and hope, which is similar to the framework in which the Catechism of a century earlier was written. The **Auxiliaries** included the Word of God, the keys of authority and the sacraments. These were given as the means whereby the essentials became known. For example, the word of God reveals eternal truths, it is by the keys of authority the church ordains and the sacraments is a sign and seal of the security in our relationship with God. The auxiliaries serve the essentials to ensure that the purity of the faith was kept intact. For the Bohemian Brethren the **Accidentals** of Christianity were those things relating to the time, place and mode of worship, which included the ceremonies and the external rites of religion. These things, which John Amos Comenius later called the accessories, should be practiced with liberty and prudence, and in a manner that they would not prove to be an obstacle to faith, love and hope. The Essentials and the Auxiliaries were commonly held among Christians but the Accidentals were drawn from practices in the primitive church and various indications in Holy Scripture. Although they were to be treated with a measure of flexibility, at the same time the recognition of Accidentals was not a license for individuals to change and introduce ceremonies and opinions without subjecting them to proper general examination. In this way the Bohemian Brethren seemed to have found a formula that allowed them to make a distinction between the shadow and the substance of the Christian faith.

The need to be clear about the things that are essential to the practice of the Christian faith reminds me of an incident in one of the churches I had the privilege to serve. I found there a system where each member would get a ticket (a little card with a verse of scripture) at the Speaking Service, which was a service of preparation for Holy Communion. The practice of holding a Speaking Service goes back to the earliest days when it was a slave society and the missionaries wanted to have opportunity to dialogue with those coming forward to participate in the sacrament. It was also a time of counselling and the hearing of disputes. Usually, persons not attending the Speaking Service would not participate in the Holy Communion. The ticket that was given at the preparatory service would also indicate that the individual had made a contribution to the benevolent fund for the needy and had given their monthly financial contribution to the church. After a time and certainly at the time I got there, several people began to think that they were paying for participating in the Holy Communion and the ticket seemed to have come to function as a receipt for payment. So deeply entrenched was the practice that it became difficult to cut the association between participating in the sacrament and receiving the ticket. In fact, one young person who had shown much piety and commitment, and who was encouraged to come forward for full communicant membership, said she was not ready for communicant membership because she did not have the money to pay for the ticket. An accessory practice had taken the place of the something essential.

Substance and Innovations

The challenge for the people of faith is to appreciate the substance of their faith, which is reliable and real, and to distinguish it from the shadow or accessories to it. We are not short of temptations today to imitate and focus on the shadow of things to come. In many places we hear more about form that about substance. For example, the Pentecostal revolution has made us see the importance and value of free participation and responsiveness in our services. It is commonplace to hear the shouts of praise the Lord and to see the dancing, to hear the drums and the tambourines. I welcome the liveliness of our worship services and want to encourage our ministers and worship leaders to ensure that people will want to come to worship because it is not a drag. We must continually infuse our worship services with new life, new forms and new instruments. However, while we do this, let us not lose sight of the substance and the object of our faith. The new innovations in worship are helpful but they are not sufficient to ensure and sustain growth in faith.

The Sunday Schools, which are or the nurturing of children's faith, must be given as much attention as the preparation for adult worship. The youth in their meetings must focus on Christ and issues of faith as much as they do on sex education, social media and the like. The men and women in their meetings must give time to teaching the faith. My appeal, then, is that all the activities and ceremonies of the church, which are only a shadow of things to come, will be used as means to focus on the substance and object of our faith, which is Jesus the Christ. It follows that we should not confuse the sanctuary, which is a shadow of things to come, with the substance of our faith in Christ, who is reliable and real.

Conclusion

The members of the little church called Beersheba worked hard and made many personal sacrifices to build their little chapel. However, in true awareness of the meaning of the name, they seemed concerned to ensure that the way of Beersheba would last. They didn't confuse the place of worship with the one whom they worship. The attractive little chapel was not the object of worship. They didn't worship it, but only worshipped in it. Their eyes were set on the substance, which is reliable and real, and not on the shadow. For them the way of Beersheba was to live for the substance of their faith and not for the shadow because the things that we use, and these places in which we gather, are only a shadow of the things to come but the substance is Christ.

I hope your Beersheba, the place where you worship, or your home, or your company, will live up to its name, as a place where people will always want to be because they can be sure they will be refreshed. Let them say that being at Beersheba is always a time of refreshing and renewal. Our God, who is revealed in the person of our Lord Jesus, is the object of our faith and the one on whom we focus. Being preoccupied with the shadow, the religious rites and ceremonies, is to miss the point of a life of faith. People should say of your Beersheba that it is not only a lively way but that it is also the way of Christ. To live for the shadow is to be preoccupied with the ceremonies and the instrumentals. The way of Beersheba is one that is reliable and Christ is the reality by whom we live.

CHAPTER 27

What is your Question?

The disciples asked him, "Rabbi, who sinned, this man or his parents, that he was born blind?"[John 9:2]

Introduction

A group of young men sitting on the street corner heard a loud bang and crash. They ran to see what had happened. Some way along the road they noticed that a very expensive sports truck, an Avalanche had crashed into the light pole. As they move towards the vehicle they each had different questions in their minds about the accident. Is the driver injured or killed? What was the driver doing? Is the driver alone? Whose truck is it? Isn't this a brand new truck? Can it be repaired? How much will it cost to be fixed? This might be a good start for a conversation between car fanatics. The questions that they ask themselves will probably depend on how they see themselves in the situation.

In all likelihood that was the case with the disciples, according to the story in John 9:2 about the man who was blind from birth. As Jesus and his disciples came around the corner they saw a man who was born blind. As they walked towards the man, they started to question themselves and Jesus about the situation. What was the cause for this and who must be held responsible? The questions they asked revealed how they saw themselves in the situation. Let's consider the question these disciples asked because I suspect that these questions might well have a bearing on the kinds of questions we are asking ourselves today. What is your question?

Who is the cause?

The disciples had good reasons for asking about the cause of the blindness. They were Jews who would have recited the commandments in Exodus 20. Verse 5 reads: *I the Lord thy God am a jealous God, visiting the iniquity of the fathers upon the children to the third and fourth generation.* In their understanding, to be born blind was evidence of God's retributive justice. Several stories of the OT demonstrated to them that God did not overlook sin, even if the punishment were to come in a later generation. The story of Joab in 1 Kings is a fine example – *Their [Abner and Amasa] sins shall therefore return to the head of Joab and upon the head of his children for ever.* (1 Kings 2:33) So this was the concern of the disciples: was the situation before them not then evidence of someone's sin?

The issue of whose action in the past was the cause for the man's condition is relevant. The difference between their day and ours is that we do not say that God is visiting punishment for sin (although some still see that way). Rather we say that the actions of the past have an impact on children in far reaching ways. The social psychologists tell us that the attitudes of parents and communities can predispose the succeeding generations to certain conduct. Indeed, in an attempt to understand the cycle of violence in the society sociologists have considered the violence and abuse to which children have been subjected. Studies (for example Horace Levy, *They Cry 'Respect', Kingston,* UWI Press, 1996) have shown that children who have witnessed violence in their homes are themselves likely to be predisposed to violence, and so perpetuate the dysfunction.

It would seem that for Jesus, the event presented him with an opportunity to bear witness to God rather than to find the cause, which was a primary concern of the disciples. Given our keenest to pass judgment, this is an important lesson. However, the Christian is challenged here to consider seriously the situation as it is before him/her in terms of the lessons it brings and the opportunity it offers rather than seeking first to be quick to pass judgement.

The disciples' questions revealed that they were aware of human failing. The religious context in which they lived had strict laws about what and what not to do as well as where to go. The law creates awareness of failure. This is probably not the case today because many of the traditional moral codes have been set aside and the standards for what can be called sin or moral misconduct have been relativized. This poses a challenge to evangelistic efforts today because people are less likely to have a notion of sin. There is a recent incident in which one parent took a priest to task for suggesting that her child was a sinner. As far as many are concerned, what they do in their private lives is their business and no authority of any sort should make it their business to pass judgement or to comment. The individualism of the time, the deterioration of community organisations and the weakening of the family structures, have all led to a change in the moral/ethical climate in which we live. It is a climate of "anything goes." In the interface between the young and the old those values that have stood the test of time are beginning to crumble in the threatening atmosphere of neglect. The questioning or berating of the church today is evidence of an ever-broadening point of view that each individual is their own, highest moral authority on any matter. The disciples asked about sin because they were aware of the possibility and reality of human failure. They were aware of sin. What would be your question, when faced with a man born blind?

What is the consequence?

The question of the disciples revealed not only that they were aware of sin but also that they were aware of its consequences. For them it was a moral issue. They saw the blindness as a consequence of sin. They read it to mean that God was not overlooking any act of wilful disobedience. To them it meant that God was sure to act even if it looks a little late and a little out of place. If we speak about Jesus as Saviour, as the one who saves us from sin, then it is necessary that we speak also about the consequences of sin. So the disciples had a question for the situation that presented itself. Their question revealed their preoccupation and the way they saw themselves. They recognised the presence of sin and they saw the consequences of sin. Their question was about sin and its consequence. They were quick to raise a question about how this blind man stood before the almighty God. Later in this story we will see that the Jews threw the man out of the synagogue because he was not welcomed among God's people. No blind or lame person could enter the temple. In other words, they held the man accountable for the sin and its consequences which, to them, were reflected in his blindness.

What about God?

Unlike the disciples who saw the blindness as an issue of morality, Jesus saw in the same situation an issue of ethics. The story does not tell us exactly but from his response we can reconstruct the question he seemed to have had in his mind. Jesus' concern was about how God would be manifested in the situation of the blind man. He did not focus on the possible cause of the blindness. His preoccupation was with the solution and how in finding that solution God would be glorified. Where the disciples were keen to secure the cause and pass judgement, Jesus was keen to discover the opportunity and to clarify what could be done. They asked, "Who sinned?" He asked, "How will God be manifested here?" Jesus' implied question was an ethical one, meaning it was about determining the kind of action that might be taken in the situation as it was. This may be a helpful question to ask ourselves when we are faced with a situation in which an ethical decision is to be made: "How will God be manifested here?"

Many of the problematic situations we encounter today, situations which cause strife and tension within the community, might be more easily resolved if we didn't first try to resolve it in terms of a moral failure. This is not to suggest that morality is out the window. On the contrary, it is to accept it for what it is but also to recognise that, given its propensity, preoccupation with it will not bring a solution. This is the point of Jesus' approach. Instead of seeking a moral solution, he based his response on the ethics of love and witnessing to the grace of God. In his word, the issue was not the man's sin but God's glory. His question then was about God's glory.

There are a number of issues which have become problematic for the church and Christian community, in which a Christ-like response might be of value:

- When we encounter the HIV/AIDS victims in the society, what is our question? Rather than ostracise them it may be helpful that we consider this: How will God be manifested in their lives?

- When we discover that members of the church have chosen to be known as homosexuals, what is our question? It might be wise not to try to approach them first as a moral problem but to see them as individuals in whom God can also be glorified.

- When the young people in the community have become parents prematurely, what do we ask? Instead of visiting our anger upon them, it might be useful to consider the ethical character of our own response. The Christ-like approach would be to ask how God might be glorified in that situation.

- When we meet a poor family, with little means, where alcoholism and drug addiction are present and they have taken to begging as a lifestyle, what is your question? Their situation might well be the result of moral failure but how will preoccupation with morality help them? The Christ-like approach would be to ask ourselves about the action and response to them that might bring glory to God.

Chapter 28

Jesus' Prayer

And now I am no longer in the world, but they are in the world, and I am coming to you. Holy Father, protect them in your name that you have given me, so that they may be one, as we are one.... I ask not only on behalf of these, but also on behalf of those who will believe in me through their word, that they may all be one. As you, Father, are in me and I am in you, may they also be in us, so that the world may believe that you have sent me. The glory that you have given me I have given them, so that they may be one, as we are one. I in them and you in me, that they may become completely one, so that the world may know that you have sent me and have loved them even as you have loved me. [John 19: 11, 20-23]

Introduction

About 200 years ago the hymn writer James Montgomery said this of prayer:

Prayer is the soul's sincere desire, uttered and unexpressed; the motion of a hidden fire that trembles in the breast. Prayer is the burden of a sigh, the falling of a tear, the upward glancing of the eye when none but God is near. Prayer is the simplest form of speech that infant lips can try; prayer is the sublimest strains that reach the Majesty on high. O thou, by whom we come to God, the Life, the Truth, the way! The path of prayer yourself had trod; Lord teach us how to pray.

Teach us how to pray is, of course, reference to Luke 11, where after seeing Jesus praying the disciples asked that Jesus would teach them how to pray. In the form we call the Lord's Prayer he gave them guidance concerning the approach and the content of prayer. It was in giving them guidance, according to the account in Matthew 6, that he challenged them to make prayer more than a matter of just words.

The prayer life of Jesus is well attested in scripture; withdrawing with his disciples for prayer; withdrawing by himself to pray; praying in Gethsemane Garden when faced with the dreadful cross. He also underscored the critical nature of praying, saying that prayer was necessary to cast out demons. Jesus was a person of prayer and exhorts us to pray. Listen again to Montgomery:

Prayer is the contrite sinner's voice, returning from his ways; while angels in their songs rejoice and cry, Behold he prays! Prayer is the Christian's vital breath, the Christian's native air, his watchword at the gates of death: he enters heaven with prayer.

Montgomery may have been thinking of the thief on the cross who beseeched Jesus saying, "Jesus, remember me when you come into your kingdom." Jesus not only hears our prayer but he also prays for us. Let us consider, for example, his prayer for his disciple in John 17, often called the High Priestly prayer. The uniqueness of this is that in it we see the things that were in the heart of Jesus on the eve of his passion. Set as we are between his ascension and his coming again we might well consider the things in Jesus' heart, as indicated in the readings, John 17: 11 and 20-23. One cannot miss Jesus' concern for unity among the believers throughout these passages. The fact that the early church preserved this portion of scripture means that they also saw the relevance of it for their time. Further deliberations on it here will also show the relevance for our time.

Prioritising Unity

By beseeching the Father's protection on the eve of his death, Jesus reckoned that disunity could arise when he is absent from sight. The history of the Christian faith has shown this again and again to be the case. Ever since Jesus can be apprehended by faith alone, and not by sight, disunity has been a recurring issue among his disciples. Disputes among the early Christians led to the Orthodox East separating from the Catholic West. These divisions have been permanent since the early Middle Ages. Disputes in the late Middle Ages led to the emergence of the Protestant Community, which itself has seen disputes after disputes and division after division. Speaking about the Pentecostal/Charismatic community, one writer said that it has thrived on division as much as it has on opposition. Mind you, divisions are sometimes necessary for growth to take place. However, we see in the heart of Jesus not only concerns about division but also concerns about disunity, which is different. We should not imagine that the propensity to divide is only a feature of small communities. That threat is no less real even in small numbers because disunity among the disciples of Jesus does not result simply from numbers. In the heart of Jesus, was the awareness that disunity would be a threat after his departure and so he prayed for unity.

Jesus wanted the believers to make unity a priority because in doing so they would be modelling the divine life and imitating Christ. Unity is the Character of the Divine Life. Jesus prayed that his followers would be one even as he and the Father are one. For those who choose the way of Christ then, unity is not an option but an imperative. Jesus prayed that we would be protected from disunity so that the world would believe. Imitating Christ means we make unity a matter of prayer; we pray for each other and pray like Jesus that we would be one. An important antidote to disunity therefore is to imitate Christ.

Practising Unity

Of course, we also must practice and demonstrate unity. In this regard the writer in Ephesians 4:3, urged the saints to keep the unity of the spirit in the bond of peace because there is a relationship between unity and peace. Where there is disunity, disputes and conflicts are sure to arise. It is precisely because there are disputes and conflicts in the human community why the disciples of Jesus must strive to practice unity. Jesus said that the world would believe if his followers are united. Unity therefore is itself an instrument of witness in a divided world. Unity among believers is a hedge against the disintegration of families. The unity among believers is a hedge against the disintegration of communities. Disunity among Christians serves only to exacerbate that which is already present in the world. What is worse, however, disunity among the believers leads to hardening of people's heart and aggravates the unbelief that is real in the world.

The writer to the Ephesians points to how unity in the body of believers can be sustained: there is one body and one Spirit, just as you were called to the one hope of your calling; one Lord, one faith, one baptism, one God and Father of all. There is a sense then that we don't have to think of unity as if we are creating it. Jesus didn't ask that we create unity because unity is already given. The points is that disciples of Jesus must practice what they are – one in Christ. There are a number of things at the centre of disunity among Jesus' followers: lack of opportunity for the use of the gifts that have been given by the Spirit, doctrinal differences and the usurping or misuse of authority. Many communities of believers stifle the expressions of the gifts within it. When people feel they don't have opportunity to use their gifts they simple go elsewhere because there is no shortage of choice in what has become a free market of faith communities.

In many communities, as was clearly evident in the Middle Ages, authority ceased to be Christ-like and rather than imitating Christ, leaders imitated dictators. Some church leaders today, who trust their own judgement above the corporate judgement of the group, insist that the Church is not a democracy. With this point of view they refuse to discern the voice of the Lord as expressed in the opinion of the majority and suppress the gifts and calling that the Holy Spirit has given; gifts to equip the saints for the work of ministry and for the building up of the body of Christ. The practice of unity is sometimes difficult because so many of us find it hard to imitate Christ in his humility. The writer to the Philippians (2:3) challenged us to esteem others better than ourselves. This is something I have made my prayer that the Lord will help me not only to respect others and respect their account of the Lord's work in them, but that I would esteem them above myself. Jesus prayed for unity among the early disciples and among us who came to faith through their testimony. To prioritise unity in prayer is to imitate Christ, who is one with the Father.

Complete Unity

A final point is worth making. You will notice that Jesus was not only concerned that the believers would be one. He prayed also that they would be completely one (v.23). Completely one! It certainly isn't that the believers could be incompletely one! The word used here for "completely" carries with it the idea of perfection. There's also in it the idea of bringing something to the very end. The implications of this are enormous. First, the character of the unity cannot be one that is half-hearted. It cannot simply be that we tolerate each other. Jesus prayed that we would express a unity that is deep and profound, not one that is superficial and patronising. With the awareness of this concern deep in the heart of Jesus, you can appreciate his insistence on loving one another, which is a strong theme in the Gospel and Epistles of John. The unity must be deep, profound and complete.

There is another idea here though. It could be that for a period of time the unity expressed is deep and profound but somewhere along the way lethargy sets in and the believers, like Peter walking on the water, take their eyes off Jesus. It could be that fatigue sets in and the disunity in the world overtakes the church and so there is no difference between the church of the Lord Jesus and the human community. In this regard the prayer for complete unity, which carries the force of perpetual unity, becomes important. What we see in the heart of Jesus is that we must not be satisfied with unity for a time but we must be in prayer for peace and practice of unity at all times, to the very end.

"Completely one" then refers not only to the character of the community of believers here and now but also across time. Can we in our witness show our connection with believers past as well as present? In the ages to come we who are alive today will become the believers of the bygone times. How sad it would be that our posterity would imagine that we had nothing to do with the witness of the Christ! This is the principle and the ethic that must inform our attitude to our forebears. We respect unity in the body of Christ and recognising Jesus' concern for being completely one, we have regard for the believers who have gone before us, many of whom bore witness to Jesus to the end of their lives.

Conclusion

Concern for the community of believers was deep in the heart of Jesus and this became clear as he prayed for his disciples. He prayed that they would be one, as he was one with the Father. Our call is to imitate Christ. Unity is not an option but a must-be among believers. He prayed that we would be one so that the world may believe. This oneness is itself an instrument of witness in a divided world. We not only pray for unity but we must make it our practice.

CHAPTER 29

The Discomfort of Grace

*These last [workers] worked only one hour, and you have
made them equal to us who have borne the burden of
the day and the scorching heat. [Matt 20: 12]*

Introduction

The story about the landowner who went out to hire workers
for his vineyard is one of the parables in Matthew about
the kingdom of heaven. It seems this particular parable
was meant to explain the meaning of the saying, "the first being last
and the last being first," because it is lodged between two accounts of
that saying (19:30 & 20:16). The parables are drawn from everyday
happenings with which the hearers would have been naturally familiar.
For this reason, both the details of the story as well as the main point
of the story would have made connection with the experiences of the
hearers. The meaning of the saying, the last will be first and the first
last remains somewhat obscure. Early Christian commentators saw
the late afternoon workers as a reference to Christians, while the early
workers would be to the Jews. More recent commentators have tended
to identify the later workers with believers who come to the Lord at a
late stage of their life. It seems though that the point of the parable,
which was meant to communicate a value of the kingdom of heaven, is
more than a matter of chronology.

Equality & Grace

There is a detail in this parable that is particularly revealing. A closer reading of the passage yields something of the discomfort the graciousness of the landowner caused the early workers. The complaint of the early workers (20:12), in which we see a reversal in the parable, was that by giving them the same pay they were being treated as equal with the later workers. To their surprise, the later workers did not lose any points! Or, putting it another way, the longer hours of labour by the early workers did not earn them any extra points. They were not given the status of "most favoured workers." To their displeasure, it seems that the landowner did not value their labour above the rest. It appears that the longer hours of work did not affect the judgement the master placed on the merit of the work. The generosity to the later workers, as far as the early ones were concerned, was unjustifiable.

The concern of the early workers find much sympathy in our time, whether we consider the church, political parties, clubs, companies or non-government organisations. We honour people for long service and we equate long with meritorious. We also feel dissatisfied if a newcomer or, as the Irish like to say, a recent "blow-in," gets equal treatment, equal recognition and equal reward.

Probably the main lesson of this parable, though, is the graciousness of God, who welcomes us and treats us all in a manner that we do not deserve. God's grace has a levelling tendency. This is a problem in a world that thrives on inequity. When looked at from the perspective of some, the grace of God smacks of injustice and should be challenged, as the early workers sought to do.

Blind Kindness

Our attitude is a kind of corrective measure to the blind kindness of God. I call this the early workers syndrome. Think for a moment of the people whose place in the Kingdom of God we question and see whether it is not based on the early workers syndrome. This is a negative reaction to the kindness and grace of God. It is a blatant rejection of the idea that certain people can be called "one of us." Symptoms of this syndrome were expressed, for example, in the disciples' stern speaking to those who were bringing the children to Jesus (19:13). Jesus' request that the children should be allowed to come to him leads us to understand that the aim of the disciples was to block the way to Jesus. The truth is that the way we organise our church, our communities and our personal lives sometimes are like hurdles in the way of those who would come to know Jesus. The early worker syndrome is a wish to exercise a veto on access to the kingdom of God. The early workers believe they are gatekeepers to the company of the Saviour.

This syndrome is also evidenced in the insistence that worship must conform to a certain style and language and that the life of a true believer is evidenced by a specific set of religious rites and practices. In some places the insistence is on conformity to a certain notion of ministry and apostolic succession. In other places the insistence is on a specific form of baptism or the display of specific gifts of the Holy Spirit. Happily, we may have emerged from the period in which there was the insistence on dress and other cultural customs, the consequence of which was the demonising of certain aspects of foreign cultures that we do not like or cannot understand. So the early workers did not want to be treated equally with the rest. They believed that the duration of their labour made them a different calibre and raised them to a level that the later workers had not yet attained. The word of Jesus, which gleams through this parable, is that our place in God's kingdom is at God's invitation and offer and surprisingly, does not depend on us, *per se*. It is a sort of blind kindness. We must then be cautious about the spiritual integrity we question and those whom we declare to be not worthy of the place in God's kingdom. When they accept God's invitation they are treated equally alongside us, the existing workers.

Conclusion

Since access to the kingdom of God is typified in participation at the communion table we should close with a brief comment about sharing at the Lord's Table. One of challenges for churches that have not yet faced the "danger" of inter-communion is that they are obliged to accept the equality at the Lord's Table. The truth is that some of us find it difficult to show equality because it is more important that we show the difference that fosters inequality. This too is an indication of the syndrome of which we have been speaking. For us who are afflicted with this syndrome, the challenge we face is to consider others worthier than ourselves - or at least to consider them equally worthy.

Something More
Discipleship and Communion

Introduction

*I*t was in response to the request from the Greeks to see him that Jesus is said to have declared, 'The hour has come for the Son of Man to be glorified' (John 12:23). A question that arises immediately is why should such a request be indicative of this hour, ominously called the hour of glory? We can certainly coin the saying, 'Be careful when the Greeks ask for you.' In the schema of John's Gospel, it is not altogether surprising that Philip is the first port of call from these Greeks. Unlike the case in the Synoptics, Phillip plays a leading role here in John, asking the kind of questions we tend to associate with Peter. Moreover, he was from Bethsaida, which, we are told, was home to Greek immigrants. Nor is it altogether surprising that Philip in turn reported the matter to Andrew. Except for the absence of Peter, we find here the players who were present at the first call to discipleship in John 1. It would seem that there is an issue of discipleship at stake here for us to consider. The way in which the issue is presented suggests that the writer wanted his readers to see that there are at least two critical things that are associated with discipleship.

The Threat of Death

The juxtaposing of glory (v.23) with death (v. 24) suggests that the disciple, whose witness creates interest among the Greeks, must contemplate the reality of death in discipleship. I don't believe the writer was simply talking about the death to self, meaning the putting an end to preoccupation with one's own interests. He meant literal dying, where we no longer walk on the face of the earth. In another place (John 15), the writer uses the imagery of the branches on the vine to make the point about bearing fruit. It is in the bearing of fruit that the Father is glorified. In John 12 the hour of the Son's glory was one in which others were coming to seek him out.

The analogy leads us to contemplate what it means for churches and Christians to be bearing fruit in their communities. The branch will not bear fruit unless it remains, unless it persists, unless it is permanently connected to the vine. The extent to which we bear fruit is a function of our communion with God. It seems to be a pretty straightforward, logical assertion. Unless we remain in intimate communion with God, we will not bear fruit. If we are not in communion with God we might have activity, we might even be very busy but that does not amount to bearing fruit. The threat of disconnection from the community is as real as the threat of disconnection from the vine, which leads to barrenness and death. Indeed, that disconnection from the community may even be a sign that we are disconnected from the vine. For when we are out of touch with the hurt and pain and frustrations in the community, how can we claim to be in communion with God? If we are not responding to the threats to life and livelihood in the community, if we do not represent the "balm in Gilead", if we do not function as the means whereby wholeness and healing can come to our communities, then it may be that we are not in communion with God. This is death of a certain kind.

As the prophets of old knew, it was falsehood to attempt to speak when they did not hear from the Lord. If they did not hear from the Lord it was because they did not occupy a place in his presence, "where there is fullness of joy, where there are pleasures for evermore".

Reflecting on the beauty of being in the presence of God the Psalmist said, "How lovely is your dwelling place, O Lord of Hosts! My soul longs for the courts of the Lord; my heart and my flesh cries out to the living God. A day in your presence is better than a thousand elsewhere. I would rather be a doorkeeper in the house of the Lord than to dwell in the tents of wickedness." (Ps 84)

It could be that when we struggle to see visible fruit in the life of the church we are under the threat of barrenness and death. In order to grow there must be connection and communion. If there is to be sensitivity to the cries and pain of the youth then we must be connected to the community and in communion with God. The evangelistic achievements that we long to see are the natural outcome of our connectedness and our communion. The fruit we bear is what glorifies God but there can be no fruit if there is no connection. If there is no connection then there isn't any glory. "*Herein is my father glorified that you bear much fruit.*" (John 15:8)

Bearing Much Fruit

Notice though that for the disciple bearing fruit it not enough. The true disciple, who is keen to glorify God, is the one who bears **much** fruit. The word used for "much" in this context is particularly significant. It can also be translated *large, extensive, strong or profound*. The same word is used in John 15:2, where we are told that the branches that are bearing are pruned so that they bear **more fruit.** This is fascinating! God is glorified not simply in the bearing of fruit but in the fruit that comes after the pruning, the cleansing and the purging. Probably the best analogy for this is the production of a pearl. The pearl is produced by the oyster as it secretes fluid to rid itself of the pain and discomfort caused by a grain of sand under its shell. The beautiful thing we see as a pearl is the result of hard labour, which is caused by stress and discomfort. This is the idea that John conveys here. Do not be satisfied with bearing fruit but bear much fruit – the kind of fruit that conjures up the beauty of a pearl; the fruit that results from hardship and the pain of pruning.

Note also that those branches that are pruned are the bearing branches. Could this be the reason why the writer of 1st Peter challenges us to count it as pleasure when we pass through the trial? If you sense that you are being pruned by trial and hardship then give thanks that the Vinedresser recognises your potential and your capacity to bear much fruit. My wish is that I would recognise the pruning of the Master and to be patient as the Lord prepares me for greater production. When you are experiencing your pruning then say that the Lord is seeking to increase the efficiency and productivity of the branches, which are connected to the vine.

The analogy used so far would suggest that pruning must be seen as physical suffering and hardship. This is understandable because we recognise physical suffering and the hardship of loss – whether it is financial and emotional - quite readily. However, if we follow closely the text in John 15:3, we might come to see pruning in another way also. According to that text, the pruning, washing and cleansing take place through the word. This is not simply then a physical experience but also one in which the individual is challenged to reform his/her view of the world, as the word of God gives a new perspective. Given the times in which we live, when there is popular rejection of scripture, it might seem that we are overestimating the capacity of scripture, as God's word, to appeal to people. If people are not reading or not hearing God's word, how then can they be influenced or challenged by it? Moreover, if people read or hear the word of God but do not understand it, how will it be of value to them?

With these challenges, two important tasks are placed before the person of faith in these days. There is a homiletic task and there is a hermeneutic task. We say homiletic to mean the task of speaking from the stand point of the word of God and hermeneutic, meaning interpreting the word of God. This calls for innovative ways of both presenting and interpreting the word and we should not rule out the use of modern technology and unconventional marketing strategies. Both tasks are connected and it seems that pursuing them together is what will make for the bearing of much fruit. Bearing fruit is not enough because that which brings the glory is the bearing of **much** fruit; the kind of fruit that emerges from the crucible of hardship and suffering.

CHAPTER 30

Finding your Purpose

So we are ambassadors of Christ, since God is making his appeal through us; we entreat you on behalf of Christ, be reconciled to God. [2Cor 5:20]

Introduction

Recently I had a conversation with some young people who were grappling with the idea of their purpose in the world. With so many theories and ideas about how the world began and the point at which the human being came into the picture, it is not surprising that this question of purpose should preoccupy the minds of my young friends. As one fascinated by modern theories of how the planets were formed and the whole idea of the expansion of the universe, I was quite ready to join in the conversation. There's now the idea that another solar system is on a collision course with our Milky Way, a collision that will result in the formation of a new solar system. The only consolation is that this planetary event is not likely to happen for another few billion years. When we consider what past planetary events might have been and when we think what future events might be and the apparently inconsequential place of the earth in the larger scheme of things, we are right to contemplate what our purpose is.

Excellence and Arête

In reflecting on purpose 2Corinthians 5 might be a helpful place to begin. This passage makes the bold claim that we should see ourselves as ambassadors of Christ. We understand from modern usage that an ambassador is the official representative of the government of a particular country. At the very least, the ambassador must have accurate, up-to-date knowledge of the priorities and policies of the government he or she represents. In this respect it is also clear that different countries would have different requirements of individuals named to this position. However, apart from knowledge, what other qualities would be critical?

We are not sure what qualities and virtues the writer of the passage might have had in mind when he speaks of ambassadors. The New Testament scholar, Frederick Danker believes that based on an inscription found at Corinth, one of the qualities that an ambassador in the 1st century might have been expected to show was excellence, understood in a moral or ethical sense.[14]

The word in Greek that describes this virtue of excellence, of superior merit, especially as an athletic quality, was *arête* (Phil 4:8). So when Usain Bolt set the world record for the 100m in Beijing in 2008, he was displaying what the Greeks called arête. So too was Asafa Powell whose 9.91 seconds in the 100m was a record for some time. The same can be said of the Russian athlete who set a new world record for the pole vault in 2004 and the many athletes who have won the annual *tour de France*. Their performances expressed their *arête*. It described the physical prowess and high athletic achievement that was demonstrated in the games. Later, however, *arête* came to describe not just something physical but also referred to moral and ethical excellence.

The Corinthian inscription mentioned by Danker was written to Gallio, who was proconsul in Corinth around 52CE. The inscription provides an interesting backdrop to understanding some ideas in this chapter because it describes the qualities of the public official. We have the impression from the inscription that people who were in high political office were expected to have this moral/ethical excellence, arête. So when Paul in 2Corinthians used the term, **ambassadors of Christ**, he, like the people in Corinth, would have had in mind the excellence in virtue, the arête, which the ambassador was expected to exhibit.

Let's look at an inscription that was found in Corinth, which was written about Nero for virtue, his *arête*. Whereas Nero – Lord of the Cosmos, Supreme Imperator,… Father of the country, New Sun that brightens Hellas… is unique in the annals of time as Supreme Imperator has proved himself the friend of [the gods] and has granted us our liberty… and whereas this liberation is his gift to us, and has restored [to our country] its ancient autonomy and freedom, and has added to his great and unexpected gift release from taxation,… in view of all this, it is decreed by the magistrates, the council, and the people forthwith to consecrate the altar… and to inscribe it: To Zeus Liberator [Nero] forever.[15]

The persons who represented the state as ambassador, like the athlete in the Olympics, were therefore expected to demonstrate that excellence and superior merit in virtue, in morality and ethics. He was to be superior among his/her peers. As an outstanding athlete towers above peers in physical strength and prowess, so the ambassador was one who stood out because of excellence in knowledge, morality and ethical standards. The values and attitudes of the ambassador were the ideals that others were expected to emulate.

Finding your Arête

My observation was that one's *arête* is related to one's purpose and that a way to discover your purpose is to focus on those things in which you excel. *Arête* implies knowledge, and skill but also passion. It suggests that one is committed to a cause or that one has a particular ability, calling or sense of mission. Your *arête* might be determined by your family, community or country, for which you are an ambassador in an unofficial and general sense. It might be that you will strive to be the ideal of what your family, community and country ought to be at a particular moment in its history. Furthermore, it might be that by representing that ideal you will also be showing the ideal that a Christian ought to be at this time in our world. For it is true to say that our world is in many respects lacking in *arête*. It may not be "cool" in the eyes of your peers but you might find your purpose by focusing your arête on what it might mean to be an emissary or ambassador of Christ.

The specific task that Paul assigns to such ambassadors is that they were to see themselves as instruments of God's appeal. Consider then what is might mean to be ambassadors of Christ, as if God were making his appeal through us. The word that is translated appeal (παρακαλουντος - *parakalountos*) can also mean to **invite** and to **implore**. We are instruments of God's invitation and of God's imploring. In a practical sense, this suggests that part of our tasks as ambassadors of Christ would be to extend the invitation to others on behalf of God, as a way to help them find their purpose in the world. Many people testify that they have grown up in the Church and no one really extended to them the invitation to commit their lives to Christ. People often want to make the step towards a life of faith in Christ but do not know how. It helps and makes a difference when they receive a direct challenge and a personal invitation. This is particularly true for young people who tend to operate in clubs, cliques, packs and social circles. Unless we invite a new member in, it is virtually impossible for that person to push their way in because we also tend to act as gatekeepers for our little groups. When the circle is a group of Christians, it is no different; we include those we like and get along with and exclude others. The challenge that this ambassadorial role puts to us is to broaden our circles, cliques and packs for God's sake - on behalf of God. Some people will not readily come in at your invitation and so we should understand our ambassadorial role of making God's appeal also as imploring. This means we might have to strongly urge, entreat and plead. Bear in mind at all times that you are acting on Christ's behalf, which really means facilitating and encouraging the formation and development a relationship with the divine.

It is clear from all this that one's arête, that is, one's moral, ethical and spiritual excellence, must also be worthy of being emulated. One's *arête* must be appealing. It is a real let down when our friends and peers or people we admire, behave in an undesirable manner. There have been many examples of undesirable conduct among people in leading positions at local and national levels. The years are littered with people in the public eye who have performed or conducted themselves well below their expected *arête*. Their arête is public and well known. However, from the point of view of the Christian they are not appealing because it is below Christian expectation. They are not making an appeal for God because the quality of their arête is well below those who are ambassadors of Christ. What a difference it would make if, with all the many fans that celebrities have, they were making an appeal for God. Many high profile individuals in our time, become models for their fans but the appeal is not for Christ.

The call to be ambassadors for Christ, which can be seen as one's purpose in the world, is counter-culture and requires individuals with guts and backbone. The question, then, is whether the young people, who are seeking to fulfil their purpose in life, will respond to the invitation, the appeal, the imploring and the challenge to be ambassadors of Christ. If you want to find your purpose in life consider your arête. Let your moral, spiritual and ethical virtues, your skills and your passions guide you. Then consider how you might use your arête to represent the divine life, which was revealed in Christ.

CHAPTER 31

The Unusual in the Usual

*Moses was keeping the flock of his father-in-law Jethro, the
priest of Midian; he led his flock beyond the wilderness, and
came to Horeb, the mountain of God. There the angel of the
Lord appeared to him in a flame of fire out of a bush; he looked,
and the bush was blazing, yet it was not consumed. Then
Moses said, 'I must turn aside and look at this great sight, and
see why the bush is not burned up.' When the Lord saw that
he had turned aside to see, God called to him out of the bush,
'Moses, Moses!' and he said, 'Here I am.'* [Exodus 3:1-4]

Introduction

*G*etting the meaning and the message of a portion of the **Bible** is
truly a matter of enlightenment because there are several levels
of prejudices and biases through which we must plough each
time we read. We are hindered by our own, personal biases, which can
be most dangerous, especially when we don't realize that we have them.
Beyond that, we have the biases of those who translated the Bible into
English, which itself is not a static language. This fact accounts for the
existence of many different versions of the Bible in circulation today.
For my own part I have tended to use the Revised Standard Version,
mostly because of the ecumenical scholarly tradition that underlies
it. Beyond the level of translation though, we have the prejudices and

biases of those forebears in the faith that selected and preserved the original manuscripts. Further back we have the prejudices and biases of those forebears who, under the inspiration of the Holy Spirit, wrote the manuscripts. Still further back we have the biases and prejudices of the people of faith who preserved the original stories before they were written down. It is only after that we come to the experience of the individuals or incidents to which the text actually refers.

When we come to read the Bible we should therefore exercise due care as if going through a minefield. We must read with great care, some caution and with a little suspicion, because there are generations of explosive biases through which we tread. The title of this meditation is, "the unusual in the usual" because each time we read familiar passages, as the one above, we hope to get a new and hitherto unheard-of message. If that were not the case we would read it only once and throw it away. We read it again and again because we hope to find something else, something unusual; something we had not seen before.

Evangelistic Moment

The story in the biblical quotation above is about evangelistic moment. I call it evangelistic for three reasons. First because it involves an angel and the word angel and the word evangelistic have the same root meaning. The angel appears and announces a message. Secondly, it is also an evangelistic moment because in it there is a calling and an answering. In that sense it is a complete evangelistic moment because the answer comes immediately after the call. In our experience of evangelism it could seem to us that it is all calling, all announcing and no answer. The third reason is that it represents God as the evangelist. It is God who calls and to whom the response is made. The importance of this cannot be overstated because in our zeal or in our disobedience we sometimes get into people's way and we block their vision of God. Even Christians can make themselves hindrances to the perception and reception of the good news. It could be for this reason that many people are looking for God but not in the usual places of the religious traditions. Some of the religious traditions, some new and some old are so preoccupied with their own systems that they become ends in themselves. Indeed, leaders of religious traditions must be careful that they don't lead the faithful into idolatry, as they make the religious forms and content of greater importance than the Eternal to whom the religious tradition points.

So this story is about an evangelistic moment and by your reading it now it becomes such a moment for you. We are not only considering the story of the revelation made to Moses years ago. By looking at it now, it becomes one in which an invitation is being issued again. In other words, by revisiting the story, we make this moment also one in which God is also beckoning us. As we read, we are situating ourselves in the story because only in that sense can we understand it as an imperative. We are the ones to whom the call is being issued and are expected to respond. More than that however, in reading the story again we are learning what it means to encounter God.

Encounter

Note first of all the place of the encounter. The place in which Moses encountered God was in the normal course of his daily work. When Moses set out for work that morning he had no idea what was going to meet him. He may indeed have decided beforehand that he would lead the flock beyond the wilderness. As a shepherd it was not an unusual thing for him to be looking for greener pastures. The Psalmist says the shepherd makes the flock to lie down in green pastures and leads them beside still waters (Psalm 23). Moses was in the normal course of his daily chores but he was not satisfied with the first pastures he met and so he pushed on a little further beyond the wilderness. Many shepherds and their flock would have been attacked by either bandits or wild beasts as they went further towards the wilderness. By going further he would have gone into a place of fear and insecurity. Green pastures were beyond the wilderness but he could only get there if he pressed on. What he was about to experience was more than green pastures but he did not know that; he was simply being bold and was pressing on. The normal course of his duty that day landed him beyond the wilderness, beyond danger, beyond fears, beyond dry stream beds and beyond dry grass. He pressed on towards greener pastures. The reward for this perseverance was going to be much more than he could have imagined.

I do not know where you are presently in terms of your faith but I suggest that you press on. I do not know where you are in your fears and anxieties but you should press on. Press on beyond your wilderness for only in pressing on will you encounter greener pastures. Much more than that, your moment of encounter might well be beyond the wilderness, so press on. When you move forward looking for green pastures but not knowing who you will encounter, pressing on is an act of boldness. When you keep going, not knowing what you will find, pressing on is an act of faith.

Moses set out for a normal day's work but he was not satisfied to remain in the fields to which he was accustomed so he pressed on beyond the wilderness. Now let's see what he found and who he met.

Usual and Unusual Drama

In going further Moses arrives at Horeb, which is also called the mountain of God. It is here that God the evangelist makes a presentation to him. At the time the story was committed to writing, Horeb was already an important place in the piety of the people of God. It had also become a place of pilgrimage. However, Moses would not have known that it would have become so. Horeb became the place of significance partly because of Moses' experience and the presentation made to him. As before, the presentation involved those things in the normal experiences of Moses. The sudden occurrence of fire in the bushes on a mountain was a normal thing. Falling stones could ignite under high temperatures, in the same way forest fires are set off today. The burning bush itself was not enough to turn Moses' head. It was something unusual within the usual occurrence that caught his attention. We must return to that moment when he turns to see the unusual drama but let us stay with the burning bush a little longer.

An important and relevant observation to be made is that bushes are burning every day. This means that all around us presentations of the Holy are being made by God, who uses the regular elements of our life experiences. We encounter people at the usual places at work, on the bus or train, or as we walk to work or school. These regular, daily occurrences have within them opportunities to offer a word of encouragement, or rebuke. There are opportunities to share, help or give account of the hope that is in us. The problem is that often we miss those opportunities. This reflection may be seen as a way to sharpen our awareness so that we learn to look and to identify these "burning bushes". It was with the same intention of using the usual drama that Jesus made presentations in parables, which were based on things to which people were accustomed. He used these to call the attention of his hearers to important life lessons. With this awareness we can appreciate why the apostle Paul says, "Do not say to your heart, 'Who will ascend to heaven, that is to bring Christ down, or who will descend to the abyss that is to bring Christ up from the dead. But what does it say? The word is near you." (Romans 10:6) In other words, the presentations that create an evangelistic moment are not things foreign or strange. Rather, it is the dramatic presentation of the unusual within the usual that makes the moment so memorable and filled with expectation and potential.

Along the same lines the writer of Hebrews explains God's evangelistic intent in the presentation of Jesus by saying that since the children are flesh and blood, he himself likewise took part of the same. In Jesus God is making a dramatic, evangelistic presentation that in a similar way draws on the usual things to which we are accustomed, that is the human life. The question then is whether people will see the unusual or will it be for them the same, usual drama. Therefore when your bush is on fire, so to speak, you should look closer at it. In other words, pay more careful attention when something unusual is presented in the usual place. My fear is that rather than looking for the unusual in the usual we simply dismiss the moments. We panic and extinguish our burning bush. When you encounter someone familiar in a fit of rage, for example, or when someone familiar seems withdrawn, don't panic and "pour cold water" on the opportunity. When you encounter someone who makes you uncomfortable think whether that could be your "burning bush" moment. Moses was not quick to put out his burning bush but instead he moved towards the scene to take a closer look. In a sense this is what I'm inviting you to do. Take a closer look and think in a more focused way on the strange within the familiar. Like Moses, the places of the strange might be your usual daily routine. The unusual drama is set within a usual scene. This brings us to that moment when Moses turns to look.

The Invitation

According to the story, it is only when God saw that Moses turned to see the presentation that he issued the invitation. There was no invitation before Moses' investigation. He did not hear a voice until he took interest in the event. An important guide for all interactions, especially when we have something we might wish to share, is to notice the moment when the person shows interest. This could be in the form of questions or some non-verbal expression. This is a critical moment for an evangelistic presentation. The word of God is urging us to be mindful of timing. When God saw… then he called. God took advantage of a moment of interest. People in the sales business can well appreciate how important timing is to make the presentation or to close the deal. Probably the main difference between good and great sales persons is that the latter knows the time for the punch line.

Timing is no less important for people who are in the business of sharing faith. For leaders who are keen to introduce and implement change, timing is equally critical. Our prayer should be for the patience and the wisdom to choose the moments well to issue the invitation to those we encounter in our daily work. Our zeal for success should not frighten the hearer away. Timing is important. If there is someone whom the Lord has laid on your heart to help, support, rebuke or share faith, then, it is for you to look carefully for the opportunity. Look for the interests and the occasions of openness or moments of curiosity because these are the unusual within their usual activities. Look for those moments when you see the willingness to explore. People who feel that they carry a burden to share something, not least testimony of personal faith, must have patience and an open eye.

The curiosity to explore is what creates the atmosphere for the new assignment and prefaces the call to further service. As it was for Moses, so was it for Samuel, whose sharp ear allowed him to hear again and again the voice of the Lord calling in the temple. It was also in the temple that Isaiah had his epiphany (appearing) of the Lord high and lifted up, filling the temple. Saul had his epiphany on the road to Damascus and, as with countless people of faith, he came to a sense that he should undertake something new for God. The desire to see more, the curiosity to investigate the unusual within the usual is what creates the opportunity for new service. It is only in the moment of curiosity that the call of God is heard. We must therefore explore the questions and pursue those ideas that the usual situations of daily life throw at us. Pay attention to those questions that keep coming up again and again. Have regard for those discomforts and the uncomfortable situations that are presented again and again. Don't be afraid of the burning bushes but draw closer and take a more careful look.

Conclusion

The burning bush is an evangelistic moment. It might help to rummage through our experiences to see what opportunities within our usual day-to-day activities we've missed. This perusal of our experiences is important for in this respect we are seeking for our burning bush. Through the review of our experiences we check to see whether we have missed or are missing important opportunities. By way of analogy, when we review our experiences to see what we have missed it is as if we are seeking to re-position ourselves at Horeb. Bear in mind that Horeb is beyond the wilderness and beyond fears and anxieties. To experience Horeb we must press on beyond the wilderness. Horeb is the joyful experience of those who are not satisfied with confining themselves within unnecessary boundaries. When we press on to greener pastures and press on still a little further we come to the mountain of God. At Horeb God issues the call and makes the presentation by inserting something unusual with the usual experiences. God sets our bushes on fire so that our attention can be drawn. It is out of the "burning bush", out of those peculiar situations that God calls Moses! Moses! And he answered, "Here am I."

CHAPTER 32

What do you think of yourself?

So you also must consider yourselves dead to sin
and alive to God in Jesus Christ.
[Romans 6:11]

Introduction

Some time ago the USA Tele-evangelist TD Jakes gave a most interesting message entitled "Coming out Head First." Using the occasion of the New Year and linking it to the text from Rom 12:2, he weaved together a very inspiring address, which challenged his audience to see that, in a similar way to our human birth, our new birth through Christ must lead to a new way of thinking. We must come into the new situation head first. Our thinking must lead the way. The New Testament passage, *Rom 6:11*, reminds us that how we think of ourselves is important. Our thinking can be the difference between whether we are considered dead or alive: "*So you also must consider [think of] yourselves dead to sin and alive to God in Christ.*"

So for this reflection we will explore our "head space" and have us consider carefully what we are thinking about ourselves. Some people might find this surprising because we have become accustomed to suspecting thinkers and tend to associate the persons of faith with someone who does not think about what he or she believes. For some people, a person of faith is a fanatic who must not be taken seriously because they do not think for themselves. Furthermore, the lack of mental training sometimes means any excess demand to use our minds puts us to sleep. Some people come to church because they don't want to have to think. Some would say that people go to church because they have stopped thinking. The text for our reflection says, *"So you also must consider..."* This means to think for ourselves. I hope that by the end of this reflection you would have seen that how we think of ourselves is a matter of death and life.

Thinking

The points in the book of Romans at which Paul uses this classical Greek word λογίζεσθε [logidesthe], from which we get the word logic, seem to underline the significance of the word in explaining the Christian faith. The first place we meet the idea is in Rom 2:26, where Paul deliberates on *"thinking"* of circumcision. He says we are to think of it as nothing because its presence or absence will not affect how God thinks of us. We meet the idea again in Rom 4:11 where Paul's focus is on how to *think* of Abraham in terms of righteousness. We are to *think* of him as righteous prior to circumcision because God thought of him or considered him to be righteous because he believed God.

In our text in Rom 6:11 the question to which he is responding relates to our state of affairs as human beings. Given the reality of sin, on the one hand, and of the abounding grace of God on the other, how are we to understand ourselves? A number of important things arise from the answer that he gives to the question. The first arises from the expression *"you also must think"*. It seems we cannot avoid this consideration of ourselves. Our Lord Jesus thought of his purpose and was apparently aware of his impending death. The text says, *"You also must think."* We all operate with a view of whom and what we are in the world. Indeed, more often than not how we live explains how we think of ourselves. We cannot exist in a mental vacuum, where we have no understanding of who we are. The fact that some people are carefree and can't be bothered with these contemplations does not free them from the force of this imperative, "you also must think."

This is something we have to put before our children and other family members. Coming to a view of what we are in the world will determine how we live. This is the basis of the evangelistic ventures that we pursue. The point is that people will always give evidence of what they think of themselves, even if they do not do so consciously with words. We therefore do not have to be shy about questioning others about what they think about themselves. This is what happens when people are invited to think about God and about the claims that people make about Jesus. It is perfectly logical for people to be asked what they *think* about Christ. It is probably a myth to imagine that people delay the consideration of this question because as soon as we come to an awareness of ourselves and can formulate thoughts about the world, we begin to form a view about who we are. The existence of the Christian religion arises from the belief that faith in Jesus Christ offers a way to thinking about the world.

Although a different word is used in Rom 12:3, we have a similar idea about thinking where Paul writes, "*I say to everyone among you not to think of yourself more highly than you ought to think, but to think with sober judgement.*" There is a caution here to be sober in our thinking because people can suffer from grand delusions. We are to be cautious about what we imagine and to be realistic about whom we understand ourselves to be in the world. It is forcing us to consider the state of affairs in which we find ourselves. Rom 12:3 cautions us about opinions and ideas we form but Rom 6:1 offers to us a way of understanding what we are and can become. We live according to how we are to regard ourselves and so it is proper to ask, "Who or what are you in the world? No one is exempt from this consideration.

Dead to Sin

Bearing in mind that what we are concerned with is our condition, let's think about the expression "*dead to sin*," *which* leads us to think about sin. There are different ways in which the NT speaks about sin. For example, in 1Peter 2:22 sin is spoken of as an action that departs from the way of righteousness. Christ did not step out of this way and so he was considered to be without sin. Another way is found in John 15:24 (cf John 9:41) where we get the idea that sin is a condition into which we are born (John 9:34). A third way is found mainly in Paul's epistles, where sin is spoken of in personal terms. For example, in Rom 5:21 sin has the capacity to reign or have dominion. Similarly in Rom 7:17 & 20, Paul sees sin as something systemic and speaks of it as having power to act on its own. For this reason (as in Rom, 6:6) we can be slaves to sin or can be under its systemic power.

It is probably in the third sense that we are to understand sin in Rom 6:11 where it is contrasted with God. Sin is a systemic force that operates in opposition to God and leads primarily to the denial of God and refuses accountability to God. It has a power of its own and operates outside of our control. As a systemic principle, in which individuals are held, Paul says we are powerless to the principle of sin that dwells within. (Rom 7:22). It is pervasive and no one is excluded from the sway it holds. Given the reality of the presence and power of sin, the question then arises of how we are to regard ourselves in relation to it.

Some people simply dismiss this way of thinking, citing their right to think rationally. However, rational people can accept the reality of systems of powers outside of the individual's control. Similarly, national laws are enacted because rational people accept the need to have moral and ethical accountability. It would seem then that we cannot be free from accountability to others, unless we believe that we are ultimately accountable to ourselves alone. Thinking that we are ultimately accountable only to ourselves can be given different names but from the Christian, biblical point of view it is called, "being under the control of sin." It may be called other names but its reality cannot be denied.

The fact that some people might be unaware of systems of power does not render the systems unreal or unrealistic. It becomes then a question of awareness, knowledge and acceptance. Paul proposes that instead of dismissing the reality of sin we must regard it as part of how we think of ourselves. The subjection of the human being to sin means that the mind and body are under its influence. How are we to contend with this system of control? If we regard sin as an act by which individuals make themselves morally unclean, we can see the relevance of the symbolism of the blood of Jesus by which people are cleansed. When sin is seen as a systemic force, by which the human being is controlled, the symbolism of washing will need to give way to a symbolism of liberation. In the presence of the systemic force, by which we are controlled, Paul's advice is that first we need a new way of thinking of the situation. We should think of the body as being dead to sin because only in that way will we regard it as being unresponsive to the reality of sin. The advice then is to refrain from thinking of ourselves as needing to live with sin. Instead, we should think of ourselves as being dead to it.

The pervasive power of sin means that a strategy has to be developed to deal with it. The idea that the writer describes here is similar to what happens when intimate feelings we once had for someone is lost. Some people have had this misfortune and when the feelings of love and tenderness give way people describe it as, "I feel nothing for him or I feel nothing for her". The pre-existent love and desire no longer exist. Paul means something similar when he says consider yourself dead to sin. When the body considers itself dead to sin then it is not stimulated into action by it. There is no interest in sin because it no longer appeals or entices me.

What then is your state of affairs? Paul said I'm dead to sin and when I'm tempted I will say I'm dead to sin. When I feel pride and envy rising within me I will say, I'm dead to sin. When I feel angry and impatient I will say I'm dead to sin and will say the same when I'm drawn away by lust. When I feel disgust and hatred making their way into my mind or when I'm faced with the temptation to lie I will say I'm dead to sin. When I see my neighbour's property and envy begins to raise its head or when I'm tempted to overcharge my clients, I will say I'm dead to sin, When I'm faced with ethical and moral decisions and am tempted to compromise my convictions I will say, I'm dead to sin. When I think of people in hunger and destitution and realize how much I waste, I will say sin must not have dominion over me. When I think of those in prison, the sick, orphans and the homeless and when I consider how unresponsive I am to their plight and needs I will say, sin must not have dominion over me. When I think of my luxuries and my comforts I will say, sin must not have dominion over me. When I think of the death of Jesus Christ, that he died to sin, and when I think of the power of sin and its capacity to enslave me I will say, I'm dead to sin. So you also must say I'm dead to sin, for sin will exert its power to reign in you. In order that sin will not have the power over my mind and body I will consider myself dead, unresponsive and not enticed or interested in it.

Alive to Christ

What else do I think and how else might I consider myself? I will conduct myself as one with no interest and feeling for sin but I will also say I'm alive to God in Christ. Dealing with sin is a matter of death and life. We must die to sin and remain uninterested in it so that we might experience the joy and beauty of the new life in Christ. This is where our heads must be in the right place. You probably know people who have found a new reason for living, with a zest for life and who live with passion and intensity. For them every moment matters and they redeem the times. They seize opportunities and make the most of the day. They can't wait for the dawn of the next day to get up and hit the ground running. Many times people come to this approach to life because of some serious event, for example the death of a loved one. They might have had a near death experience that reminds them of the precious gift of life.

So the question for you today is whether you have a reason for living. Have you settled the question of why you are in this life? Paul puts it to us saying we have two choices: on one hand we can choose to be just dead. This is the default choice. If you do nothing about your life this is in effect the choice you make. It is a life of enslavement; a life of sorrow; a life of sadness. Paul describes it in Rom 7: 24 as living in a body of death. The good news is that we don't have to live that way because we can consider ourselves alive to God in Christ.

Although we think we are on top of the food chain in the world, we are equally as vulnerable as every other creature on the planet. We are not only vulnerable to diseases but if we are not careful we could even become food for other creatures. We are disposable creatures but we have a purpose and can be instruments for good. We can choose what kind of instruments we want to be and whose interest we will serve. Are you simply your children's instrument and is your life lived only to serve them? Are you your spouse's instrument and is your meaning in life simply to serve him or her? Is your purpose in life simply to serve your employer or your business? To what project are you committed and for which purpose will you die? These are relevant issues that are thrown up by the idea of being alive in Christ. It is all about those things for which we are prepared to live.

Paul advises that we should consider ourselves alive to God in Christ. To be alive to God is to be responsive, available and ready for his purpose. You will become an instrument of something or someone by choice or default. Being alive to God in Christ is to think of ourselves as instruments of God's will and ready to be pressed into divine service. There are many people who live in the myth of being accountable only to their egos because they perceive themselves to have money, power or influence. They have missed the caution that Paul gives in another place, for us to think about ourselves with sobriety. Quite unintentionally they are fooling themselves but the good news though is that we don't have to think in that way.

I also sympathise with those who do not know what to do with their lives and where they are headed in this life. The good news is that there is a solution to this dilemma; the solution begins with how we think of ourselves. We can consider ourselves available to God. When you have come to retirement and you do not know what to do, you can choose to live for God and for his purpose. When you have completed your exams and you are uncertain about what you are in the world, then say, "I'm alive and available to God in Christ". When you've lost your job and you feel a deep sense of uselessness, you can say, "I'm alive to God in Christ and available to him". When you have lost your loved one, whether your mother, your father, your child, your uncle or your aunt, or when you have lost someone precious to you and a sense of meaningless overtakes you, then say, "I'm alive to God in Christ and available". When you've accomplished all you hoped for in life and you do not know what next to do, then say, "I'm available to God". When you face the frustration of life and are tempted to end your own life, think of yourself as being alive to God and available.

I'm alive and so I have a purpose. I'm alive to God in Christ and so I'm an instrument of his will. I know what I am in the world - I'm dead to sin and alive to God in Christ.

A PRAYER
Lord, let your **light**, light of your face, shine on us!
Lord, let your light, light of your face, shine on us!
That we may be saved, That we may have life,
To find our way in the darkest night, Let your light shine on us.[16]

Something More
Why Church?

Introduction

*M*ost early Christians, especially the Gentiles, would have known the Old Testament in Greek and not Hebrew as some might think. That Greek version is called the Septuagint, from the Latin word for 70. The name comes from the tradition that 70 scholars undertook the translation from Hebrew to Greek about 200 years before the birth of Jesus. In a few places in the Septuagint, for example Deuteronomy 31:30, we find the word *ecclesia* which, when it appears in the New Testament, is translated church. For example Deuteronomy 31:30 reads, "Moses recited the words of this song, to the very end, in the hearing of the whole assembly of Israel." The word *ecclesia,* which is translated assembly, is the word of which I speak.

The question might be asked, how did ecclesia become church? The reason the word church appears in the English translation is due to the Scottish influence on the English language. Church actually comes from Kirk, from the Germanic word *kirche,* which is a translation from the Greek *kuriakos,* meaning the "Lord's;" that which belongs to the Lord. Therefore, what used to be called the Lord's assembly, or the Lord's house, was eventually abbreviated to the "Lord's," which in Scottish is *Kirk*, from which we get the English word Church. So the word Church, really means, the "Lord's" (from κυριακόν in 1Cor 11:20), which as you can see is an abbreviation of a longer term, the "Lord's Assembly."

The word ecclesia, which means those who are called out, does not necessarily refer to God's people. It might also refer to a political gathering and some of the Greek writers before Jesus even spoke of the assembly (*ecclesia*) of animals. When the apostle Paul used the word ecclesia, he did so with qualification: In 1Cor 1:2 and 2Cor 1:1, for example, he refers to the *ecclesia* of God. The church is the Lord's and we are the ecclesia, the called out, those who gather in the name and purpose of the Lord.

This brings to mind a text from Ephesians, in which the word ecclesia appears: *"so that through the ecclesia, the wisdom of God, in its rich variety, might be made known to the rulers and authorities in the heavenly places; this was in accordance with the eternal purpose that he has carried out in Christ Jesus our Lord."* [Eph 3:10] If then the ecclesia is the means by which the manifold wisdom of God is to be made known to the ruler and authorities, we can say the ecclesia is God's instrument. In the book of Ephesians, probably more than any other place in the New Testament, we have the clear statement of what the ecclesia is: It is God's instrument of manifold wisdom, God's instrument of mystery and God's instrument of mercy. Let's look a little closer at each of these.

Instrument of God's Manifold Wisdom

You might have heard the saying, "a lot of information but little wisdom." As I reflect on the church in the information age I find some truth in this expression. Recently we had online pictures taken of outer space which showed millions of galaxies. A galaxy is a system of planets that have at least one main planet at the centre, which in our case is the sun, with a series of other smaller planets orbiting the centre. There is no accurate sense of how many galaxies there are but earth is located in the one called the Milky Way. In previous eras, it was thought that this was the only Galaxy but as more powerful telescopes were developed, we came to see other Galaxies, running in the millions. We on earth live on one planet, in one of the many galaxies. When I consider the universe with its millions of galaxies and the apparent arbitrariness of our living on earth, I marvel at the wisdom of God. The more we come to know about our universe is the more we realize how much we do not know. For that reason it seems, the generations, ours being foremost among them, is preoccupied with the gain of knowledge. It is not unusual for the age in which we live to be called the information age. Yet, despite the information overload, we have a serious deficit of wisdom. Having information is one thing but grasping what to do with information is wisdom.

It is in relation to this deficit of wisdom we can place the ecclesia. Ephesians says the ecclesia of God is the means by which the manifold wisdom of God can be made known. I have an interest in knowing how these galaxies were created but I would be quite disappointed if after discovering that there wasn't a clue about the purpose for which they were formed. The issue of purpose is a more urgent question to me. The galaxies were there before the human being came into existence and in all likelihood will be there for some time after us. I take the position that if there is a universe, which there is, then, there is a Lord. This is a basic principle and so it is not only that I cannot prove it but also that I don't need to prove it. If you accept this we share a common faith. If you don't, we still live in the same world but we conceive it differently. The Lord of the universe, Ephesians assures us, not only created the universe, with all its galaxies, but more importantly is concerned to sustain a relationship with the creatures in his world. The question of how the universe came into being is important but the manifold wisdom of God relates to why and not only how it came into being.

The troubling question fuelling scientific theories have traditionally been about how the universe came to be and there have been a few attempts to simulate the origins. In recent years, however, more and more scientists are giving attention also to the why, as they try to grapple with the question of purpose. It is because of that purpose why we have the called out, the church. The ecclesia of God is the means by which the wisdom of God and the reason for the creation of the world is made known.

Instrument of God's Mystery

As the apostle reflected on his call to become a part of the ecclesia of God, he said grace was given to him so that he would declare the mystery, hidden for ages in God who created all things. He took it for granted that God created all things and was not preoccupied with the question of how he did it. The mystery, about which we speak, has the ecclesia as the mouth-piece that declares this mystery. The mystery of the universe is a concern for all peoples, who in Paul's time were referred to as Jews and Gentiles. The mystery is about God and how God considers the peoples of the world. The mystery, Ephesians says, had been hidden, which might explain why nations of the world have at times regarded each other as enemies. They did not know that they were designed to be one under the same Lord. Now, however, the mystery of Christ and God's plan for all nations has been made known. All nations of the world are now fellow-heirs and sharers of the same promise in Jesus Christ. The church is the instrument for communicating that mystery about God's intention for our relationship with him. God intends that the peoples of the world would be one people and come to see that they have a common heritage in and through Jesus Christ.

As surprising as it may sound, many people of the world do not know this and many who have heard about Jesus do not see him in that way. People are still piercing their souls with many sorrows and anxieties, trying to understand their purpose. The conflicts and crises in the world spring from ignorance of this mystery. People hate, despise or even kill each other because they don't know that they are meant to be one in Christ. We have to tell the authorities and rulers responsible for the fuelling conflicts this message. I don't want my government to be fighting and killing people in my name. That is why envy, malice and things that pertain to hatred, dissension and unkindness cannot be present in the ecclesia, which is instrument of God's mystery.

Note too that the ecclesia is not confined to one place, one community or one country. As we meet we must think of the ecclesia of God in other places because the ecclesia is one: down the road, up the road and across the road. We must be mindful of the ecclesia of God across country borders: Armenia and America, Barbados and Bolivia, Canada and Cameroon, Japan and Jamaica, and so on. Part of the mystery is that in every place God is calling the ecclesia into being. We have a common heritage in Jesus Christ so let us practice and be what God intends us to be.

Instrument of Mercy

Arising from the fact that the ecclesia is an instrument of God's mystery, we might also add that the ecclesia is an instrument of God's mercy. On account of the mystery Paul said, "*I bow my knees before the Father, from whom every family in earth takes its name... and I pray.*" The mystery of the ecclesia is also expressed in prayer to the God of Mercy. *I pray that you would be strengthened in your inner being; I pray that Christ would dwell in your hearts through faith; I pray that you may have power to comprehend the love of Christ; I pray that you may know the love of Christ which surpasses knowledge; I pray that you will be filled with the fullness of God* [Ephesians 3:14-19].

Let us not under estimate the power of prayer. We should also pray together and make a habit for praying for each other. We should pray not only for those in our families or others in our circles but also for others in the world. Prayer implies mercy and it is through prayer that we discern the courses of action. If the ecclesia is unclear about where it is to go, it could be that the ecclesia is not making time for prayer. Likewise, if the ecclesia is not clear about what it is to do, it could be that the ecclesia is not in touch with the God of mercy. How can the ecclesia be sensitive to the needs of the community and reach out in mercy if the ecclesia does not bow the knee to the God of mercy?

Bowing the knee is an act of reverence but also an act of reliance. Bowing the knee is an act of mercy for the ecclesia is God's instrument of mercy. To bow the knee is not just about words it is also about attitude of mercy towards the neighbour. How can I pray that the ecclesia would be compassionate and I do not show compassion, as a part of the ecclesia of God? It is through prayer that we come to experience and express the ecclesia as an instrument of God's mercy.

Conclusion

So we are the ecclesia of God, the called out: called out to declare the manifold wisdom of God. The ecclesia is called to make plain the mystery of God, which had been hidden but which has now been made plain through Jesus Christ our Lord.

APPENDIX 1

What did you expect to see?

Address given at the 250th Anniversary Service of the Moravian Church in Jamaica

As they [John's disciples] went away, Jesus began to speak to the crowds about John: 'what did you go out into the wilderness to look at: a reed shaken in the wind? [Matthew 11:7]

Introduction

*W*henever we have large gatherings, as in festivals or national anniversary celebrations, there is usually an air of expectancy. I can still recall the very first large evangelistic crusade meeting I attended in Mandeville, Jamaica during the 1970's. Word had gone out that people with all kinds of ailments were being cured through the healing ministry of Evangelist V.T. Williams. Never before had I seen so many people gathered in one place. The air was charged with expectation as thousands of onlookers came to witness something strange and miraculous. The stories of miracles, re-told of course with a fair amount of embellishment, generated even greater interest and the crowds kept growing larger and larger from night to night. People went with the expectation that something unusual would happen and they were not disappointed.

The size of that gathering in Mandeville was similar to the crowds that came out to see the late Ray Charles performing at a music festival in Bethlehem, Pennsylvania. Charles' reputation was phenomenal and so the crowds came with the hope of seeing one of the great singers of the 20th century performing live. This would have been the last time that many would see him performing live because he was already well advanced in years and died sometime later.

It seemed that the crowd in Matthew 11 had a similar sense of expectation as they went out to see Jesus about whom stories were circulating. As I read again the account, my eyes became fixed on the question that Jesus asked the crowd concerning John the Baptist. It was evident that there was something in the text beckoning me because I saw it as if for the first time, even though the text was quite familiar to me. My next task then was to discern the connection between the text and our time.

Expectations

With several hundreds of us gathered for this 250th anniversary of the Moravian Church in Jamaica there is a similar air of expectation. Some of you are worshipping with the Moravians in Jamaica for the first time and others are well used to doing so. However, no one here has been in a 250th anniversary celebration of the Moravian Church in Jamaica before. In fact there has been nothing like this and of course none of us present will participate in the celebration of the next 250 years. So it is as unique an occasion as one could have it. You can then understand that the air is filled with expectation. It is rather interesting but also welcoming that the text for today is based on this story about expectations. You have come to be a part of this special event but what do you expect to see.

According to Matthew, the question about their expectations was the third question that Jesus put to those listening to him. The first question was during the storm on the Sea of Galilee, which may symbolise the storms of life. After being unceremoniously awakened, Jesus asked his disciples, "Why are you so fearful?" The Jamaican dialect would put it, "*How unu so fraid?*" According to Matthew that was not going to be the last time that fears would characterise the attitude of the disciples. We can identify with them because fear is usually the first emotion that arises when we are faced with a threatening situation. When our sense of security is threatened, even our faith may be put on hold. In his book, *Fear Itself: The Origin and Nature of the Powerful Emotions That Shapes our Lives and Our World,* Pulitzer-nominated author Rush Dozier Jr, said,

Fear is the quintessential human emotion. Fear of disease, fear of injury, fear of poverty, and a thousand other fears mould the most mundane aspects of our existence: what we eat, how we drive, where we work. Yet fear is also behind the highest natures and the grandest tides of world history. By facing and overcoming our fears, we mature and fulfil our deepest human potential. Fear can start wars or end them. Fear can make us embrace or deny God.[17]

Knowing this, it might not surprise us that the question, "why are you so fearful" is the first that Jesus put to the disciples. It was important that they faced their fears as a matter of first importance. The second question, which is similar to the first, can be found in Matthew 9, where blind men came to Jesus. Jesus asked them, "Do you believe I am able to do this?" This question is also about the character of disciples' faith in Jesus. The attitude of people to the witness of Jesus remains an issue today and whether or not people have faith in God is a basis on which the world is divided – some people simply do not have faith in God.

However, the third question is our main interest – "What did you expect to see?" The interest arises from the fact that we are forced to consider two kinds of expectations facing Jesus' disciples. One is the outward expectations of others and the other is the inward expectation the disciple has, based on how he/she understands the demands of the gospel. In coming to preach in the same place where John ministered, Jesus realised that the outward expectations of the crowd and the internal demands did not coincide. One had to do with responding to people's interests while the other had to do with non-negotiable imperatives. The dilemma for the disciple comes from this kind of conflict. Put another way, it is a dilemma for the person of faith when those issues that are fundamental to our convictions are of little of no interest to the hearers.

The imprisonment of John marked a turning point in his own ministry as it marked the end of an era. John saw it and was already looking beyond himself to the one who would succeed him in bringing the witness of the Kingdom of God. One of the difficulties that leaders in the churches face is that they sometimes fail to see when the curtains are falling on their era. It is hard to see when it is time to prepare for the new dispensation, the transition to new leadership and the handing over to a new team. The inability to manage leadership change has not only led to the downfall of many honourable institutions but has also led to great instability in countries and lost opportunities in industry. Our prayer must be that the Lord would help us to see when the new moment has come, so that we help to give it flight and not kill the opportunity. So John saw that a new moment was emerging and sought to test this by asking Jesus to comment. We must ask ourselves today whether we are at a turning point in the history of the church; whether the curtains are falling on our time and whether these celebrations might mark the emergence of a new dispensation. In seeking to clarify their expectations, Jesus wanted to point out to his hearers that some things are likely to change in terms of the witness of the kingdom of God. The realisation of the need to change is the issue being put to us today.

Courage & Commitment

While some emphases in our work remain relevant, there are some things that may have to change. For example, we must remain committed to a vibrant evangelistic witness and continue calling people to make a commitment of their lives to Jesus Christ, as the way of salvation. We must also remain committed to education, urban and rural development. However, we must be different in terms of our courage– not the kind that is used to pursue war but the kind needed to pursue peace. Mark Twain is believed to have said, "It is curious that physical courage should be so common in the world and moral courage so rare." The courage of which I speak is one that enables us to engage current attitudes in our world, which is bent on frustrating justice and peace. Having seen how unjust, immoral and unethical actions can lead to irretrievable changes in peoples' lives, I have come to appreciate the need to be courageous in insisting on just and reasonable actions.

The time in which we live requires a more courageous engagement in the world. This was implied in the question Jesus put to those who came to hear him. What were you expecting to see? If you came here to see a reed shaken in the wind or some weakling, you have come to the wrong place because John was no weakling. If you came to see some "posh" person, with a lot of style but no substance, you came to the wrong place because the witness you are seeing here is a rugged man of God who's concerned about God's kingdom. He is not dressed for dinner in a hotel or in the palace. Being sensitive to his context, the man is in the wilderness and he is dressed for work! He is not out of touch with the demands of his situation.

We live in a violent society, in which the things that make for peace and the strategies for resolving disputes without death must be taught. We face a serious situation of urban crime, which arises from the lack of opportunities for personal advancement, especially among young men. We face a desperate situation of rural poverty, which is exacerbated by development projects that are focused mainly in the urban areas. We face a critical situation with HIV/Aids, which many congregations are still treating as something that has nothing to do with them. A prophetic witness in our time means that the church cannot be oblivious to these realities. In a recent meeting of ministers, the Rev Rupert Clarke cautioned the group that "It cannot be business as usual."

When a church pauses to celebrate 250 years of witness, it is not a stroke on the back about achievements. Doreen Spence said celebrating 250 years is first and foremost a moment of thanksgiving but also represents a new situation that calls for courage to face the realities of our time. Our forebears stand out because they looked at the realities of their times and were not afraid to address them. The generations to come will judge us irresponsible if we overlook the demands of our day. When I consider the situation of the church in Asia Minor (present day Turkey), it reminds me that a church can go out of existence. Any church which fails to respond to the challenges of its time can become irrelevant and will be relegated to the scrap heap of history. The first thing that must be different, then, is the courage with which we face the realities of our time.

Community

The second thing that must be different is how we think of community. To Jesus' amazement, the community that called John a devil for his life of fasting called Jesus a glutton because he ate and drank. The fact is that time had elapsed and the outlook of the community had changed. What does this imply for us? It implies that the church must be prepared to re-think its relationship with the community. This will be a difficult and painstaking task when the church has operated in same the way for many years. For example, the church has focused its ministry over the 250 years on the idea of rural community development and primary education, as a way to create a sustainable society. In so doing, it has concentrated its energies in a narrow geographical area to develop monuments of achievements. It has introduced to Jamaica primary education, the Irish potato and rural water supply. Notwithstanding the notable achievements, the demand for relevance has not been diminished and there is need to look carefully at the present and structure an appropriate response. A new moment has come and a new set of realities must be faced and overcome.

We live today in a globalised world in which people do not think of space and community in the same way. People no longer think of communities as actual geographical spaces but rather as "virtual communities". These are communities without boundaries in which space is compressed in such a way that people disregard lines of community demarcation. There is no such thing anymore as a Christian community, which underlined our approach to evangelism. Churches used to grow by following members as they move into new areas and constructed communities around them. For a time that was fine but the approach to evangelism cannot be built on following people as they move because people are moving rapidly and are also forming communities not based on geographical locations. People are everywhere and the witness we bring has to be in every place.

This new understanding of community affects the attitude of the younger generation to the traditions and history of the church. If the younger generation seems uninterested in the burial grounds, outstanding personalities, or the monuments of a previous era, it is not because they don't love the church. They are living at a time when space, time and identity do not depend on these things. This new understanding of community must drive the work we do in each congregation, in each school and in each college. Bear in mind that what you do in your school or congregation can be broadcast from the rooftops anywhere. We have to think continuously of the world at large as we act locally in each place. The Provinces of the Unity might have to limit the weight that is put on our geographical boundaries and allow for free movement of personnel and resources between these areas. The emergence of free trade areas in the Americas, Europe and Asia illustrates the need to review the traditional attitudes to borders, for the purpose of expanding influence and optimising growth potential. The churches that have not made borders in their evangelistic drive are making an impact well beyond the shores in which they were initiated. This is true for many of African Instituted Churches, which have grown beyond the narrow confines of their homeland and in a very short period have expanded their work in the metropolitan areas of Europe and America.

It was this idea of a borderless parish that supported the expansion of Christian witness out of Europe into the regions of the South. The reverse is taking place and churches initiated in the South are also rapidly expanding in the North. In his book, *The Next Christendom: The Coming of Global Christianity*, Philip Jenkins argues that the labours of European missionary movement have not only borne fruit but in the process have also catalysed the shift of the centre of gravity of Christianity from North to South. More people are joining the church in Africa, Latin America, and the Pacific than anywhere else. On account of the growth in those continents, Christianity is growing faster than at any other time in 2000 years. The shift of the centre of gravity has given credence to the view that, "being church in the third millennium will be largely defined and influenced by developments within Third World Christianity."[18] These figures are supported by the World Christian Encyclopedia 2001, which estimated that in European and North America taken together, 6000 members a day are leaving the church. On the other side in Africa alone it is estimated that on average 8.5 million were being added to the church (about 23,000 per day).

Conclusion

The challenge we have is to discern the new moment that is arising in which the message of Jesus must take root. John saw that the curtain was falling on the era of his ministry and looked to Jesus as the one who would bring in a new dispensation. Jesus came realising that the moment of his ministry called for strategies that were different from John's, even though the crowd had different expectations. Jesus, however, was focussed on the imperatives of the gospel that the new situation threw up. So what did you come expecting? It is not business as usual. We need new eyes for seeing and new courage for acting because we are now operating with a new concept of community in a globalised world.

APPENDIX II

A Word for Church Authorities

Introduction

*T*his reflection is dedicated to the memory of the late Rev Canute McDaniel, who invited me to make a presentation at a meeting of clergy and their spouses, for which the core theme of this reflection were formulated.

The 2nd and 3rd Epistles of John were chosen for reflection because of their relevance to the church and family life. They reflect a tension in the Christian community, which is not unlike the tension and the internal struggles in the church today. The effectiveness of the Church and the stability of families depend on the extent to which they can resolve their internal tensions. I believe that the text can help us both to discern these internal tensions and to clarify whether there is any truth to the claim that the dynamics of life in our homes and other interpersonal struggles bear resemblance to the internal tension in the Church as a whole.

For the study of the Epistles of John I am indebted to Raymond Brown, particularly his book, *The Community of the Beloved Disciples: The Lives, Loves, and Hates of an Individual Church in New Testament Times,* New York: Paulist Press, (1979). I became aware of this reconstruction of the community that developed around the Beloved Disciple (John 21:20), when I was researching the tradition of Phillip the Evangelist, as part of my graduate studies. Brown tells us that the

Gospel of John was addressed to outsiders but that the epistles reflect the internal struggles of the community. From this he argues, against other NT scholars, that the epistles were written after the gospel, though the Epistles are quoted by early writers a few decades before the Gospel. Polycarp makes allusion to these epistles in chapter 7 of his Epistle: "to deny that Jesus Christ has come in the flesh is to be the Antichrist. To contradict the evidence of the cross is to be of the devil." [*Early Christian Writings,* translated by Maxwell Staniforth et el., (1968).[19] I am also indebted to the commentary, J L Houlden, *Johannine Epistles,* London: Adam & Charles Black, (1973).

The ideas formulated here are about orthodoxy [right teaching], something that has focused the attention of leaders of the church from earliest times. It is worthy of attention for two reasons. The first, on one hand, is that the post-modern world in which we live is one where there is increasing difficulty to have set notions of right and wrong. More and more people are asserting their own right to determine for themselves what is right, without reference to any particular authority. Secondly, on the other hand, we have evidence of people yearning for clarity about what is right and what is wrong. Some sociologists believe that the search for clarity about norms and boundaries, in an increasingly plural world, accounts for the numerical growth in those religious bodies that have clear demarcations of boundaries.

Tensions Then and Now

For the purpose of illustration let us consider the Moravian Church in Jamaica. The decade 1955-1965 roughly represent the period in which the local administrative leadership in the Moravian Church in Jamaica was consolidated. The subsequent two decades, 1965-1985, was the period in which youth work was organized and stabilised. The achievements of that period have not been surpassed. 1985-1995 was the decade of loss and not the lost decade as some might think. In that period we lost the services of no less than 10 clergy, one being the Robert W. M. Cuthbert who was killed while serving as president of the Provincial Elders' Conference (PEC). Most of these losses were by resignation or where ministers were forced to leave due to unresolved differences with the administration. In the period since 1995 to present, a young cadre of ministers, who are having significant influence on the character of the Church, has emerged. I believe the current period evidences the need for liturgical renewal, missionary expansion and financial viability. I say this first because with the full indigenization of the leadership, the church will have less difficulty harnessing the benefits of the Pentecostal renewal of Christianity, which is sweeping across the globe. That renewal is primarily expressed in the way the churches worship. Missionary expansion will be seen as necessary because with the progressive decline over the last few decades, serious expansion determined to secure growth will be necessary to save the church from extinction. Coupled with this must be efforts to secure financial viability, which will have a similar objective.

So what does the recitation of all these have to do with tensions? Well, it is evident that the internal disputes the Moravian Church has experienced in past decades relate to these facts. There were internal tensions as the transition was being made to indigenous leadership, hence the need for stability in the succeeding period. The tension which gave rise to the loss of clergy was followed by a period of recruitment of young clergy. These new recruits were less passionate about the liturgical past of the church and wanted a more expressive form of worship, which the Pentecostal renewal provided. The period of new youthful entrants to ministry coincided with financial pressure on the church's budget as numbers progressively declined. While there is a common sense of what needs to be accomplished, there are differences of opinion about strategies and hence the tensions about which we can speak today.

Authority, Tradition and Truth

The sense of dispute is clear when we read this second epistle of John, although we are hearing only one side of the polemic. This makes it difficult to reconstruct the issues about which there were disagreements. A closer reading suggests that the disputes were doctrinal and political, for which reason it might offer some guidance for dealing with similar disputes today. To get a good grasp of the situation we must first get clarification on the authorship of the letter, which was written by the Elder [Ο πρεσβυτερος, ho presbuteros]. Senior ministers are called presbyters or priests, both coming from the same word. Although it literally means the older person, the word has been used as designation of an official status. This elder says nothing more about himself because he does not need to. Clearly his reputation required no qualification for as elder he is a bastion of the tradition. The Elder was evidently involved in establishing the criteria for orthodoxy. We know this because of his concern for the truth, an issue we must come to later. The reference is to the position rather than the person. The elder is a reliable rock in the sea of competing currents of doctrine.

The elder addresses the "elect lady" [εκλεκτη κυρια] but NT scholarship is divided whether the emphasis should be on elect or lady. We find reference to the elect 1Pet 1:1 but Electa is said to be a proper name for a woman. Is it the lady Eklekte or is it the elect of the Lord? The generality of the addressee has led to suspicion about the authenticity of the letter. Some people suggest that it is just a copy of the first epistle and that it adds nothing new that hasn't already been covered in John. However, from v. 4 & v. 13 we can conclude that the term "elect lady" is reference to the community of believers who, according to v.10, were meeting in houses, as is the case today.

One of the lessons we have learnt from dealing with tensions in the church is that the questions are not the same in each generation. Therefore, we cannot dismiss the questions that the present generation is raising. We can illustrate the difference using the words of greetings that we find in the epistles. For example, the epistle of 2John has, "Grace, mercy, and peace will be with us from God the Father and from Jesus Christ, the Father's Son, in truth and love (v.3). There is no reference here to the Holy Spirit, which suggests that the Trinitarian understanding of the Holy Spirit, as one with the Father and the Son, had not yet been fully developed. In subsequent years and certainly today it would be expected that in a greeting like this reference would be made to the Holy Spirit. During the time of the Reformation there was much concern about the role of Jesus, the Son in the life of the believer. Today, through the influence of the Pentecostal renewal, the role of the Holy Spirit is much more emphasised. There was no concern for the role of the Holy Spirit in the second epistle of John, which was seeking to resolve issues relating to authority, tradition and truth.

Oversight and Truth

These issues of authority, tradition and truth are introduced in the problem related to the ministry of oversight, which developed to protect the faith from falsehood. The expression "I was overjoyed to find" (v.4) suggests that a visit had been made by the elder and we see that a further visit was being planned for the near future (v.12). This is the practice of oversight in its infancy and we will find it in a much more developed form in the letter of Ignatius of Antioch. His writings provide the apostolic justification for the way in which the ministry of oversight has developed in the historic churches.

An issue related to oversight and doctrine seem to be behind the expression "walking in the truth," (v.4), which in this context refers to continuity with the received traditions of the faith. From the reading of the 1st Epistle (1:7) we get the impression that there was a group of people who denied the reality of Jesus' life and death. There is consensus in the NT research that this is a reference to the Gnostics, a group known for is separation of matters relating to the flesh and those relating to the spirit. Their outlook led to the depreciation of the material world, a fondness for esoteric, speculative religion and spiritual elitism. This Gnostic outlook subsists in those who today believe that Christians should have involvement in politics and social issues.

We want to discover though why there was such a concern for walking in the truth. In a world when ideas of truth and falsehood are hard to determine, this is an important issue. Tensions between the generations, whether in the church or society at large, relate the different values and different perceptions of what is truth. The clash of worldviews can be seen in the younger generation pressing the older to understand why things have to be done in a certain way. The rejection of the authorities in which earlier generations trusted is a hallmark of our time and fuels some of the tension we experience. We find in the text a reference to accepted and trusted authority: "it was commanded by the Father" [v.4]. This is similar to saying we accept what the medical practitioner or technician has to say because we respect their authority. Another basis for deciding what is true and acceptable has to do with tradition: "[it is] from the beginning" [απ αρχης] [v.6]. The writer is making an appeal here to the long held opinions that have never been questioned. In this sense truth is seen as a convention and those who fail to see it that way, the writer says, do not have God [v.9].

The respected authority and tradition are important bases for deciding truth. Some might then say that considering today's world, the writer has excluded an important basis, which is the perspective of the individual. However, the role of the individual is not excluded, as some might have imagined but is captured in the expression, "Be on your guard." [βεπλετε εαυτς], which might also be translated "look out!" Each individual has a responsibility to guard truth but always within the context of the tradition and accepted authority. There is a challenge to guard the accomplishments, which means not wasting the opportunities created by the labours of previous generations or squandering the heritage passed on from our predecessors.

Dealing with Dissent

Could it be that the present generation of Christians, by the way we have handled tension and conflicts, have made a mockery of the heritage we received? This is a relevant question when we consider what has been done with dissenters. From the days of burning at the stake, through imprisonment to today's practice of exclusion, the Christian community has had problems with dissenters. Those who practice exclusion and excommunication find justification in the expression, "Do not receive" [v10-11]. The picture we sometimes have of the early church, as a golden era of unity in the faith, does not accord with passages like these. It is evident that in the early Christian community there were also difficulties in resolving differences. However, it might be that the practices of exclusion and excommunication and "burning" at the stake, have run their course. Our challenge is to deal with dissenters as insiders, who, like our children, may opt for a different faith and a different set of values than what they learned from us.

Managing Disputes

We find some help for dealing with dissenters in the 3rd epistle of John where it is possible to reconstruct some aspects of the tension in the community of the Beloved Disciple. The problem of Gnosticism, which is reflected in this epistle, became a widespread theological movement in the early church, which would be analogous to the New Age movement in our day. The Gnostics, who were themselves in the search of truth, claimed that they had access to truth through special insight, because of the germ of immortality that was in them. Members had a special revelation that gave them access to the truth. They did not need the tradition of the church, which preserved the testimony concerning Jesus, and through which the interpretation of scripture was preserved. In other words, Gnosticism represented a way to by-pass tradition and accepted authority, which were the ways in which truth was determined.

The concern for by-passing the tradition of authority was the concern the Elder had for Diotrephes who, according to the Elder, liked to put himself first. In a pejorative sense, it means this person was power hungry. Although the expression for, loves to put himself first" [φιλοπρωτευων] appears in Plutarch and other classical writers, the editors of the Greek Lexicon have found its usage only in ecclesiastical settings. This makes it unique to the religious community. According to v. 9, it was not the first time that the elder was writing to the congregation in which Gaius worshipped. However, the leader and power broker in that congregation, Diotrephes, treated the letter and the emissary of the Elder in the same manner in which the Elder advised that people like Diotrephes should be treated. He expelled them from the church and would not allow others who were sympathetic to the position of the Elder to have any say. The leadership of the congregation was now in the hands of persons who did not acknowledge the authority of the Elder. The Elder suggested that it would be quite a scene when he arrived because he planned to expose Diotrephes (v. 10) and counteract the false charges he was making. The exact nature of those charges we are not told but the Elder would say much more face to face. (v. 13) The Elder had now to deal with a firebrand "cleric" who was having local influence and could not be easily dismissed.

Trust & Mediation

Diotrephes represents a stage in the church where a congregation, like a teenager seeking independence, wishes to emancipate itself from dependence on those individuals and groups to whom it owed its earliest formulation of the faith. In our efforts to understand the dispute a number of questions come to mind: was the Elder stifling the creativity and zeal of the local leader in an effort to maintain control? Does the Elder represent one who gives a conservative interpretation to the tradition, which required new formulation and expression in new situations? How is the minister (Church authority) to deal with a church leader who undermines his authority?

Apart from Gaius, who is on the side of the Elder, the letter also mentions Demetrius, about whom everyone testifies favourably. This assessment of him is in contrast to the assessment made of Diotrephes. Demetrius also enjoys the support of the Elder, who believes he is walking in the truth. The fact that he is mentioned by name means that he, like Gaius, is probably a leader in the local church, or is destined to become one. Demetrius is a respected ministerial candidate who is grounded in the tradition. We do not know of whom the Elder speaks when he says, "everyone." Could this mean that Demetrius had a good relationship with Diotrephes' party also? If he did, he would be a good brother [αδελφους - adelphous] to mediate in the dispute.

In several verses (2, 5, 10, and 15) reference is also made to the brethren (AV) or friends (NRSV). They are the church workers. The letter paints a picture of the work that church members were doing in those days. They were (a) a source of joy to the Elder, who they visited (v. 3): (b) they testified of Gaius and of his love for truth & the Church (v. 3, 6): (c) they received hospitality from Gaius to whom they were strangers (v. 5): (d) they were workers for Christ who would not accept (financial) support from non-believers v. 7; (e) they were deserving of the church's support because they were co-workers for the truth (v. 8): (e) they were overlooked and not recognised by Diotrephes (v. 10): (f) they sent greetings (v. 15) and (g) they were to receive personal mention (v. 15):

We get the picture that the dispute was at many levels and had many sides and players, which means that a resolution to such a dispute would not come easy. The tone in which the Elder speaks suggests that he wanted a categorical and immediate resolution to the problem. While we cannot be sure about what happened to that community following that dispute, we can surmise that the dispute was not resolved and that the less powerful were put out of the congregation. When there's not a culture of dialogue the only outcome is that we have winners and losers where the losers leave with bitterness to seek an opportunity for payback. The truth is that the church has advanced and grown through internal tension and disputes. Therefore creating a culture of dispute resolution in which each party tries to put themselves in the place of the other will not only help to save egos but also lives.

Appendix III

A Time for Innovation

The Moravian Church through the Years

The Moravian Church in Jamaica, which was established in 1754, represents a continuation of the Caribbean Moravian mission, which commenced in 1732. Prior to its mission in the Caribbean, the Moravians established work in the Continental and British Provinces. The work in Jamaica was then under the supervision of the Supreme Executive Board in Britain. The local executive board at the time consisted of Rev. Edwin E. Reinke, the President, Rev. George H. Hanna, the treasurer and Johnan P. Pulkrabek, the secretary. The period between 1754 and 1884 can be called the period of establishment because of the efforts made to secure a foothold on the island. Probably the most significant and certainly the legacy of this period, is the large parcels of land that were acquired for the establishment of the work. The Moravian Church in Jamaica and Vesting Law was formally incorporated by an act of the Parliament in 1884. Vesting law was the legal expression that gave the church the right to own property. Some of the larger portions of land listed at the time of incorporation include 469 acres at Lititz, 341 acres at Nazareth and 95 acres at Beaufort near Darliston. There were altogether 68 different parcels of land, most of which is still in the possession of the church today. At the time of incorporation, the Church had a training college for ministers at Fairfield, the teachers' college at Bethlehem, along with several primary education institutions.

The subsequent period between 1884 and 1894 has been described as the period of **expansion**.[20] During this time, Moravian mission emanated from 14 centres in the parishes of St. James, Westmoreland, St. Elizabeth and Manchester. The congregations of this period were: Beaufort, Bethabara, Bethany, Bethlehem, New Carmel, New Eden, Fairfield, Fulneck, Irwin Hill, Lititz, Mispah, Nazareth, Salem and Springfield. It was not until 1891 that work in Kingston was initiated. Since then, other congregations have been established in Richmond Park, Harbour View, Molynes Road and Portmore. Of particular note were the settlements, which were attempted or established between 1834 and 1861. The parcel in Beaufort, near Darliston, was purchased in 1833 and Lititz, near Nain in St. Elizabeth, in 1834, Nazareth at Maidstone in Manchester in 1840 and Salem, near Beeston Spring, in Westmoreland in 1860. Of these settlements, Nazareth was the most successful. The character of the work in that community today owes much to the community initiatives of the 1840's.

The fact that some 40 schools were established on the 68 parcels of land is a testimony to the emphasis that the Moravian Church placed on education in the period of expansion. The programmes of community development, which were centred at New Eden, near Bogue in St. Elizabeth, from as early as 1769 and Fairfield in Manchester from 1824, are the early precursors of the community outreach projects in which Unitas of Jamaica is involved today.

The period between 1894 and 1954 can be described as the time of **consolidation**. It was during this period that the first Provincial Synod was held (1899). Prior to this the Provincial meetings were referred to as conferences. Maybe the most critical factor facing the Province then was the matter of financial sustainability. The period also saw an intensification of attempts to develop an indigenous clergy and local ecumenical ventures. When the 150th anniversary was observed in 1904, less than twenty-five percent of the clergy was Jamaican but that would change in the ensuing period.

The years since 1954, the modern period, is one in which there has been a **transition** to a local clergy leadership. In terms of Presidents of the Provincial Elders' Conference, the first native President, Rev. Walter O'Meally was elected in 1951, having graduated from the Moravian College *at Fairfield in 1899. O'Meally was succeeded in that office by Bishop S. U. Hastings. The late Dr. R. W. M Cuthbert succeeded Hastings and Bishop Robert Foster, recently deceased, succeeded Br. Cuthbert. Rev. Stanley Clarke was president between 1997 and 2003. Rev. Dr. Livingstone Thompson served 2003-2005 and Dr Paul Gardner 2005 to the present. In addition to Hastings, Foster and Clarke who is currently serving as Bishop, the Rt Rev Neville Neil also served as bishop. Today the clergy is virtually one hundred percent Jamaican, with a few pastors from other provinces in southern hemisphere. The Moravian Church in Jamaica is now comprised of some 60 congregations, 27 educational institutions. The ordained ministers and lay pastors serve in Jamaican and Grand Cayman. Earlier work in Cuba was handed over to one of the American Provinces. According to recent censuses people who regard themselves as belonging to the Moravian community (as distinct from the Moravian Church) in Jamaica number about 30,000 persons.*

Towards the Future

*The future might be called **innovation** because it is not easy to predict the direction in which the Moravian Church in Jamaica will go. However, there are important trends that are likely to determine its character in the coming years. One issue is the conveyor-belt like trend in which trained and ordained clergy migrate to Provinces in the northern hemisphere, particularly North America. In the last twenty years about 10 trained and ordained clergy have moved to take up pastoral duties in the Moravian Church in the USA, Northern Province. In one sense this should not be surprising because it is a part of the broader societal migration to the metropolitan areas, primarily for economic and professional reasons. Another trend is the growing number of female clergy, which itself is part of the broader trend of females moving into vocations that historically were biased to males. This will help to ensure the sustainability of church leadership since no theological or doctrinal position in the church excludes women form administrative or pastoral office. Another trend is the increasing incidence of dual vocation among pastors, who hold other employment while continuing in full-time* *pastoral employment. This is largely a financial issue as the church is not in a position to remunerate pastors at a level to dissuade them from seeking additional income. This is not new but is reminiscent of the start of the work in Jamaica, when missionaries had to work to sustain themselves. Here also the trend is similar to what is happening in the Pentecostal Churches, which have had this feature of their ministry from the outset. It is of course curious that this Pentecostal-like dual vocation is happening at the same time that the church is becoming more akin to the Pentecostal form in its worship style. In this Pentecostal drift, the Moravian Church in Jamaica is responding to unassailable ecclesiological and economic pressures, as a strategy for relevance and survival.*

A critical bastion of Moravian tradition that is likely to change is the attitude to training for the ordained ministry. Signs of this are already emerging as churches are opting for students to have a shorter period in residential pastoral training. I suspect that this will be driven by economic pressure rather than a serious discussion on polity. The economic realities in Jamaica, coupled with a need for innovation will make the ecumenical project at the United Theological College of the West Indies unviable if fundamental changes are not made. The reduction in the number of years of training for the ordained, as a cost-push factor, is a quite likely development. This could be a precursor to the total elimination of residential theological training, which has already occurred for many denominations in other countries. The challenge then is the re-imagination of theological formation.

These trends in the Moravian Church in Jamaica suggest that sustaining the Moravian witness will require attention to leadership formation, polity drift and economic innovation. Ventures in these areas must reckon with the societal Northern drift and opportunities being thrown up by changes in communication technology. The future is as challenging as it is exciting.

End Notes

[1] At the end of the Communion Service in the Church at Bethelsdorf, Germany, on August 13, 1727, the residents of Herrnhut became united in the Renewed Brethren's Church. From this sense of unity in the Holy Spirit, there began a period of missionary activity, which brought the witness of the gospel by the Moravians to every continent. See J Taylor Hamilton & Kenneth G. Hamilton, *History of the Moravian Church: The Renewed Unitas Fratrum, 1722-1957*, Bethlehem, PA, Interprovincial Board of Christian Education, 1967, 23-33.

[2] This is speaking analogically because though I believe God is revealed to us in Jesus, the Word made flesh, God is Spirit and not human being. This is the point of the much misunderstood idea of the Trinity, which affirms faith in God who is not separate from but yet not confined to human form. From a philosophical point of view my conviction about the Ultimate Being arises from the undeniable fact that there are beings in the world, of which I am one. Moreover, unlike some people, I'm not prepared to make the human being ultimate being because that would make me Ultimate, which I know I am not.

[3] http://w w w.theribbon.com/poetry/notgrowingold.asp [accessed 25.06.2014]

[4] Missionary meetings were the premier evangelistic events. They were designed to be major conventions that would have overseas evangelistic work as their focus. Hastings and MacLeavy in the book, Seedtime and Harvest note that what became known as the Moravian Missionary Society of Jamaica (MMSJ) was formerly known as the Africa Association, an organization developed to support of missionary work in Africa. (S. U. Hastings & B. L. MacLeavy, Seedtime and Harvest: A Brief History of the Moravian Church in Jamaica, 1754- 1979, Bridgetown. Cedar Press, 1979, 90.) At both provincial and congregation conventions money was collected to support different project of the Moravian Unity, especially in Rajpur India, Tibet and Ramallah in Palestine. The MMSJ was incorporated into the Missions department of the Church.

[5] Words from Not An Easy Road, a song by Buju Banton, Jamaica Reggae Artist.

[6] From Bob Marley's song, Should we be Love.

[7] Maureen Warner-Lewis, Archibald Monteith: Igbo, Jamaican, Moravian. Kingston: University of the West Indies Press, 2007, p. 15

8   David Bosch, Transforming Mission: Paradigm Shifts in the Theology of Mission, (Maryknoll, NY: Orbis Books, 1995), 255

9   Zinzendorf, Twenty-One Discourses, VII, 96-97

10 Livingstone Thompson, A Protestant Theology of Religious Pluralism, Oxford: Peter Lang, 2009, 258.

11 Song by E. Edwin Young [http://www.hymnary.org/text/i_wonder_have_i_given_my_best_to_jesus?sort=text-refrainFirstLine. Accessed 25.06.2014].

12 *The Cost of Discipleship*, 99.

13 Portions of this address were included in the September 25, 2004 funeral for Ian Smith, the third child of Dotty Smith and the late H. Ashton-Smith to have died. Previously, two of their children, a son and a daughter were killed in a car accident in Manchester. They were buried together at the Zorn Moravian Church, Manchester Jamaica. Rev H. Ashton Smith died before Ian and was buried at the same location. Mrs Smith still has the company of their other two children, Hal and Dianne.

14 Frederick. W. Danker, Augsburg Commentary on the New Testament: II Corinthians (Minneapolis: Augsburg, 1989) 14.

15 Frederick. W. Danker, Augsburg Commentary on the New Testament: II Corinthians, 22.

16 From the sound track, "Our Utmost for his highest"; Lyrics by Michael B. Smith. [http://w w w.metrolyrics.com/shine-on-us-lyrics-phillips-craig-and-dean.html. Accessed 25.07.2014].

17 Rush W. Dozier, Jr., Fear Itself: The Origin and Nature of the Powerful Emotion that Shapes Our Lives and Our World. New York, NY: St Martins Press, 1998, 3.

18 Jehu Hanciles, "African Christianity, Globalization, and Mission" in Ogbu Kalu, ed., Interpreting Contemporary Christianity: Global Processes and Local Identities. Grand Rapids, Michigan: Erdmann, 2008, 77.

19 Polycarp makes allusion to the Epistle in chapter 7 of his Epistle: "to deny that Jesus Christ has come in the flesh is to be the Antichrist. To contradict the evidence of the cross is to be of the devil." See Early Christian Writings, translated by Maxwell Staniforth et el., 1968.

20 S. U Hastings & B. L. MacLeavy, Seedtime and Harvest: A Brief History of the Moravian Church in Jamaica, 1754-1979, Bridgetown, Cedar Press, 1979.

Lightning Source UK Ltd.
Milton Keynes UK
UKOW02f0356091114

241326UK00001B/12/P